CARE
&
REPAIR OF
FURNITURE

CARE
&
REPAIR OF
FURNITURE

ALBERT JACKSON & DAVID DAY

CARE AND REPAIR OF FURNITURE

was created exclusively for HarperCollins Publishers by Jackson Day Jennings Ltd.

Conceived, edited and designed by
Jackson Day Jennings Ltd trading as Inklink.

Text
Albert Jackson
David Day

Editorial director
Albert Jackson

Executive art director
Simon Jennings

Design and art direction
Alan Marshall

Editor
Ian Kearey

Illustrations editor
David Day

Illustrators
Robin Harris
David Day

Additional illustrations
Shirley Curzon

Studio photography
Paul Chave

Proofreader
Mary Morton

Indexer
Mary Morton

For HarperCollins
Editorial Director
Polly Powell
Production Manager
Bridget Scanlon

First published in 1994
by HarperCollins Publishers, London

Text set in Bembo and Caslon Openface
by Inklink, London

Color origination by
Colourscan, Singapore

Printed and bound by
Arnoldo Mondadori Editore, Italy

Copyright © 1994
HarperCollins Publishers

ISBN 1-56158-096-1

Library of Congress CIP Data
Jackson, Albert, 1943-
Care & repair of furniture/
Albert Jackson & David Day.
    p.   cm.
"A Fine woodworking book"
--T.p. verso
Includes index.
ISBN 1-56158-096-1
1. Furniture--Repairing.
2. Furniture Finishing.
3. Furniture--Conservation and restoration.
I. Day, David, 1944-
II. Title
III. Title: Care and repair of furniture.
TT199.J332 1994
684.1'044--dc20   94-31332
                              CIP

Taunton
BOOKS & VIDEOS
for fellow enthusiasts

The Taunton Press
63 South Main Street
Box 5506
Newtown, CT 06470-5506

Consultants
The authors are grateful to the following consultants for their contributions and assistance.

Roddy McVittie
General consultant

Richard Ricardo
Upholstery

Barbara Clarke
Chair caning

The authors and publishers wish to thank the following individuals and organizations for their help in the preparation of the book.

Berrycraft
Heathfield, Sussex
Connolly Leather Ltd
London, SW19
Rodney Cooper
Farningham, Kent
R. T. Coppin & Sons
London, E15
D. L. Forster Ltd
Great Dunmow, Essex
Franklins
Colchester, Essex
KJF Furnishings
London, SE10
Kwik Strip (UK) Ltd
Winscombe, Avon
Lamont Antiques Ltd
London, SE10
Pirelli Ltd
Burton on Trent, Staffordshire
H. Webber & Sons Ltd
Ripley, Surrey

The authors are indebted to the companies and individuals listed below who generously loaned furniture or samples of their materials and products for reference and photography.

Electric soldering iron
Cooper Tools (GB) Ltd
Washington, Tyne & Wear

Finishing materials and equipment
Foxell & James Ltd
London EC1
Liberon Waxes Ltd
New Romney, Kent
John Myland Ltd
London, SE27
Rustins Ltd
London, NW2

Furniture
Simon Jennings
Ian Kearey
Alan Marshall
Roddy McVittie
High Halden, Kent

General props
Shirley Curzon
Robin Harris

Spray guns
Clarke International Ltd
London, E5
Graco UK Ltd
Wolverhampton, West Midlands

Stencilling equipment
The Stencil Store Co Ltd
Chorleywood, Hertfordshire

Upholstery tools and materials
Bonners of Welling Ltd
Welling, Kent
A. J. Kingham
London, SE9
Richard Ricardo
Banbury, Oxfordshire
H. Webber & Sons Ltd
Ripley, Surrey

Veneers
The Art Veneer Co Ltd
Mildenhall, Suffolk

The authors wish to thank the following companies for allowing the use of their premises for location photography.

Antique Warehouse
London, SE8
Roddy McVittie
High Halden, Kent
Strip & Restore
London, SE18
Robert Whitfield Antiques
London, SE10

Picture sources and photographers

Paul Chave
Pages 10, 11, 12
**David George/
Barnsley House GDF**
Cirencester, Gloucestershire
Page 95
Alan Marshall
Page 21
The Stencil Store Co Ltd
Chorleywood, Hertfordshire
Page 38

CONTENTS

CONTENTS

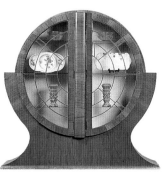

INTRODUCTION

THERE IS A GREAT DEAL OF ARGUMENT, even within professional circles, about how to restore old furniture. Some authorities contend that one should keep repairs to the absolute minimum, retaining as much of the furniture as possible in its present condition, so that future generations can see immediately what has been renovated. Other restorers try to return the piece to its original pristine condition, within obvious limitations. These arguments are largely academic for amateur restorers who merely want to mend relatively inexpensive old furniture that they can use and enjoy; the kind of furniture you pick up at an open-air market or local auction. If you are lucky enough to have inherited a rare or valuable piece, it would pay you to have it restored by a specialist, after discussing with him or her the merits of one school of thought over another.

So how much experience do you need to repair old furniture? Although you need to be reasonably competent with woodworking tools before you can tackle some of the more advanced repairs included in this book, that doesn't mean you have to be an expert. Anyone who has maintained their own home for a few years should have acquired enough experience of working with all manner of tools and materials to get started, and even a complete beginner can clean up and wax a dowdy finish. After all, we are talking about mending old furniture, not making it from scratch. And you don't need a workshop filled with specialized equipment. Many people happily restore furniture on a folding bench in the garage; some even manage on the kitchen table.

Traditionalists like to use the same sorts of materials that were used to construct old furniture, even if that means making them from basic ingredients. In this book, we take the view that it is preferable to use materials that are easily obtained and which will make the task of restoration as easy as possible, regardless of whether they were available to the original furniture makers. If you live in or near a reasonably large town, you should be able to buy most of these materials locally, and there are a number of mail-order companies who advertise in craft magazines, offering to supply modern and traditional materials.

But is it worth going to all the trouble to repair a chest of drawers or an old chair when you can buy brand-new furniture for a similar price? This is a fair question, and one that is difficult to answer objectively. The appeal of old furniture has much more to do with the quality of materials and the appreciation of shape and proportion than it has to do with economics. Everyone loves a bargain, but a restorer is just as likely to be driven by the prospect of saving an heirloom from the scrapheap. And if there is nothing more to be gained than the satisfaction of living with characterful furniture that you have brought back to life, isn't that justification enough?

BUYING OLD FURNITURE

KNOWING WHAT IS A FAIR PRICE FOR A PIECE OF OLD FURNITURE comes with experience. It varies widely from place to place and, perhaps more importantly for the restorer, condition affects the price considerably. It is also essential to keep your eye on the market – in a few months, you may find that prices have changed out of all recognition. Come back after a year or two, and furniture that was once plentiful may have all but disappeared, and styles that were ignored have become highly collectable.

Browsing the Market

There's no better way to learn about buying old furniture than regular browsing. You quickly get a feel for what type of furniture appeals to you and where you can find it in the kind of condition that is ideal for restoration. It pays dividends to take your time, noting and comparing prices until you can approach a sale with the confidence gained from first-hand experience.

ANTIQUE SHOPS

As an amateur furniture restorer, you are unlikely to be in a position to renovate genuine antiques. But most antique shops worthy of the name stock a variety of furniture, from the truly rare item to pieces that are expensive only because they have already passed through a restorer's hands, and that in itself is to your advantage. You can get some idea of how much you may save by repairing furniture yourself, and it is revealing to discover what can be achieved by someone who makes a living from restoring furniture. The work of an expert may be difficult to spot, but if you ask, an honest dealer will always be willing to point out recent restoration. In any case, a dealer knows what he or she can hope to make for a particular item, and may have been unable to pay a restorer to do what would have been required for a completely invisible repair. Consequently, you will come across perfectly adequate repairs which are not obvious at a glance, but which you can detect under closer scrutiny. Knowing what even professionals have to resort to gives you confidence in your own work.

JUNK SHOPS

Backstreet shops that specialize in the cheaper end of the house-clearance trade can be fruitful hunting grounds for the amateur restorer. However, don't expect to discover an unrecognized gem; the dealers in these shops are experts in their own field, and will have already hived off the better-quality pieces to an auction. Despite this, you will have the opportunity to sift through furniture of varying quality with an eye to finding items in need of repair or restoration, and at a realistic price.

Be prepared to bargain if you feel the furniture is overpriced – a five-to-ten per cent reduction is hardly ever refused, unless the dealer paid too much for the piece in the first place. You can hardly expect a dealer to drop the price if you want to pay by credit card, as banks make a charge for providing the service. Most dealers will accept a cheque backed up by a guarantee card, but as with so many other secondhand purchases, offering cash is preferable if you want to come away with a restorable bargain!

WAREHOUSES In cities or large towns, there are almost sure to be warehouses where old furniture is stored ready for bulk shipment to other parts of the country or abroad. The operators are usually willing to sell individual pieces, but since the furniture is never marked with the price, it can be a little frustrating searching one of these vast buildings for someone who can advise you. However, they can be fascinating places in which to browse, particularly as they invariably comprise several floors crammed with furniture. There is no guarantee that you will find

broken or dilapidated furniture in a bulk-shipment warehouse, because the nature of this type of business usually relies on a fast turnaround, and restoration takes time. On the other hand, with so much furniture to choose from, you are likely to find something unusual.

MARKETS It is well worth frequenting open-air markets. There is often a lot of furniture to choose from, and competition, coupled with low overheads, tends to generate keen pricing. The informal nature of a marketplace produces a relaxed atmosphere in which you can converse freely to stallholders who, once they get to know what you are looking for, will often reserve items which they think may interest you. There is very little pressure to buy at a market, and you can examine items of furniture at your leisure.

AUCTIONS Auctions are perhaps most people's favourite source of furniture. You are at least on a par with dealers, having an equal chance to pick up a genuine bargain. In fact you are at an advantage because you are not looking to make a profit and can usually outbid a dealer, who must guard against paying more than the market can stand. Almost anything can turn up at an auction, from high-class antiques to modern reproductions, with everything else in between. Moreover, bidding for something that really interests you can be an exciting experience, one which perhaps you should prepare for with some care.

    Try to visit the salesroom on the day before the auction itself. If you wait until the morning of the sale, you may not have time to inspect all the lots that interest you, and may end up buying something that is not quite what you had hoped for. Pick up a catalogue which will give a brief description of each lot, plus an estimate and sometimes a reserve price, which is the lowest the auctioneer can accept for each lot. You will not find a detailed description of the condition of furniture to be auctioned – you are expected to discover any defects for yourself, so feel free to examine every potential purchase thoroughly before you make up your mind to bid for it.

    Read the 'Conditions of Sale' carefully. They are probably printed on the back of the catalogue, and may be displayed in the salesroom. Check who is to pay the auctioneer's commission on any purchase: is it the vendor, the purchaser, or both of you? You will also have to add a percentage to any successful bids, to cover value-added tax.

On the day of the sale, make sure you know which lots you intend bidding for and how much you are prepared to pay for each one – and then stick to your decision! It is all too easy to get caught up in the heat of the moment and pay more than is reasonable.

In addition, don't be too hasty to open the bidding. The auctioneer will suggest a figure, but watch how the shrewd dealers wait for him to reduce it to the lowest possible price before they make a bid. When you want to enter the bidding, all you have to do is signal clearly your willingness to pay the price being suggested by the auctioneer with a nod of your head or by raising your hand – an experienced auctioneer knows the difference between a genuine bid and an involuntary movement of a catalogue. You may not always know who you are bidding against, especially as the auctioneer may be acting on behalf of a customer who is unable to attend the sale. However, provided you stick to your own reserve price, you can't go wrong.

PRIVATE SALE

At first sight, buying privately from a newspaper advertisement or at a house sale would appear to be the restorer's best option, but it pays to be well-informed beforehand. First, everyone thinks they have a valuable antique for sale, and it can be difficult to disillusion them if you can't back the contrary view with facts. Second, private vendors can take offence at any suggestion that their treasured piece is less than perfect, so be prepared for some haggling. You are also unlikely to have any chance of returning an item you have bought should you discover subsequently that it is damaged, so insist on inspecting the piece closely, despite any assurances from the vendor. A cautious seller may not be happy to accept a cheque, so either return to pick up your furniture after the cheque has cleared or make sure you bring cash with you.

TRANSPORTING FURNITURE

The thrill of the chase can temporarily dispel more pragmatic considerations – you wouldn't be the first person to buy a settee or wardrobe that refused to go through the door or up the stairs. Carry a tape measure with you when looking at old furniture, and try to ascertain before purchasing whether larger pieces can be dismantled easily for transportation.

You can usually arrange to have a piece delivered, in which case it should be covered for accidental damage by the carrier's insurance, but if you intend to transport it yourself, take sensible precautions, especially with larger items. So many pieces have survived unscathed for a century or more, only to be damaged on the way home from an auction or when moving house.

Dragging a heavy cabinet across the floor, for example, can dislodge a foot or split the plinth. And if a door suddenly swings open while you are carrying a cupboard, there is every chance that the hinge screws will be ripped out. Try to hire a trolley when transporting large items, and always lock cupboard doors or bind a length of upholstery webbing around the carcase to keep them closed. If you use string or rope, protect corners from abrasion with corrugated cardboard. Lighten the load by removing drawers, and carry them separately. Protect finished surfaces with blankets, and don't place heavy objects with sharp corners on upholstery, even for a short journey.

CHECKING THE CONDITION

The way a piece of furniture is used, and sometimes abused, determines the type of damage or wear you can expect to find. Naturally, this is also affected by the way the piece is constructed, and on the introductory pages to each chapter in this book there are tips on what to look for when buying various types of chair, table and cabinet. In addition there are some general points worth noting when visiting salesrooms, shops and markets. Until you become familiar with the different categories, you might find it helpful to carry a check list as a reminder.

Testing the strength of the joints

CHAIRS Regardless of its age or style, the average dining chair will have been put to hard use. Not only will it have been subjected to the strain of countless diners shifting their weight onto the back legs as they sit back after a meal, it will almost certainly have been used as a makeshift stepladder to reach a high bookshelf or fanlight. A well-made chair is immensely strong for its weight, but concentrating loads onto one or two legs puts undue strain on the joints, especially those between the seat rails and the back legs. Before you buy any dining chair, always inspect these joints for signs of weakness. With one hand on the back rest, tilt the chair onto its back legs, then press down on the front edge of the seat with the other hand. Any movement between the rails and back legs denotes slack joints. Loose joints can be reglued relatively easily, but if you can detect excessive slackness, it is possible that the joints have broken or have been consumed by woodworm.

TABLES Place the palm of your hand on a table top and attempt to slide it from side to side. A strong rigid underframe will resist any movement, but one with slack joints or missing stretcher rails will have a tendency to rack back and forth. Tables with any form of mechanical joint or moving component are prone to wear, so be prepared to put them through their paces before you decide to buy.

CABINETS In a similar way, look for signs of wear along the running surfaces and moving parts of cupboards and chests of drawers. And it is always worth trying to rack a cabinet from side to side to make sure the back panel and rails are fixed securely.

Woodworm will attack any piece of furniture, but cabinets are particularly susceptible, since they tend to stand immobile for much of their lives. It is essential that you check for indications of recent infestation inside a cabinet, and look carefully at the back panel and drawers.

FINISH The condition of a surface finish is invariably self-evident, but there is hardly ever the need to reject a piece simply because it needs repolishing. With a little practice, just about anyone can strip and refinish a piece of furniture, and that includes French polishing, if you are prepared to put in sufficient time to master the technique. And this assumes one needs to go that far; in many cases, there are little more than minor blemishes to take care of before cleaning up the finish and applying a surface dressing.

Is it what it seems?

To a collector, aiming to buy representative examples of specific styles and periods, authenticity and condition are of prime importance, but this book is intended primarily for people who simply want to furnish their homes with attractive old furniture at a reasonable cost. Many of us clutter up our homes with a mixture of styles in a variety of conditions, that somehow seem to coexist harmoniously. Nevertheless, we all like to know what we are buying.

No one bothers to fake run-of-the-mill furniture. If nothing else, the cost of the materials would be prohibitive. But this does not mean there aren't a lot of modern reproductions mixed in with older pieces. Furniture makers have always reproduced the styles of earlier periods: some Victorians, for example, were attracted to Regency-style furniture, and large amounts of pseudo-Jacobean and Queen Anne furniture were constructed for 1920s and 1930s consumers. These items are now sought-after in their own right, and go for fairly high prices. Contemporary reproductions are equally acceptable, if you know what you are buying, but to avoid any possible disappointment, look out for the telltale signs of modern factory production.

A modern finish is usually brighter and more even than an original, with a somewhat 'plastic-like' appearance. It is likely to be extremely tough and durable, but lacks the mellow qualities of an antique finish. And unless there has been some attempt at 'factory distressing', there won't be any of the familiar blemishes or worn patches that one associates with old polished surfaces.

Modern fittings are patently obvious. No old furniture would have been constructed using plated cross-head screws, and if a back panel has been fixed with staples, you can be sure the piece left the factory comparatively recently.

The majority of Victorian and Edwardian furniture was assembled by hand, and the makers took a pride in their hand-cut dovetails. These joints invariably feature relatively wide tails separated by extremely narrow triangular pins. A machine-made dovetail joint has equal-size pins and tails.

There is a thriving market in reproduction country-style furniture. Straightforward copies are relatively easy to spot, since the colour of the new wood and finish betray their age. What are perhaps more difficult to detect are tables, cupboards and dressers made from salvaged floorboards and joists. If the timber is well chosen, the general appearance can be fairly convincing. Even so, the mouldings are sometimes a little too crisp, compared to old country furniture, and you may even be able to detect the odd rectangular hole left by a cut floor nail. Also check the inside of cupboards and the underside of table tops to see whether there are pale stripes left on the timber, which will prove that at one time they were laid across floor joists.

Quite often, old furniture is cannibalized to make reproductions. You can find a recently-made kitchen table, for example, with genuine old turned legs. Unless the colour has been expertly matched, the amalgamation of different woods tends to give the game away. Another clue is the overall proportion of the piece; it is not uncommon to see an inordinately chunky occasional table sporting cut-down dining-table legs.

REPRODUCTIONS AND REBUILDS

Hand-cut dovetails on a late-nineteenth-century drawer

A machine-cut gate leg; not all 'old' furniture was handmade

Coffee table with cut-down legs

RESTORING AND REPLACING FINISHES

PROVIDED IT HAS BEEN CARED FOR, furniture ages gracefully, developing a subtle patina that is difficult to reproduce artificially and yet is easy to destroy by needless stripping and refinishing. Few restorers would argue against judicious cleaning to remove perhaps a hundred years' worth of dirt, and most would probably remove unsightly stains. The real bone of contention is stripping furniture to bare wood, for ham-fisted treatment at that stage can do irreparable damage. However, you have little option but to refinish a fire- or water-damaged piece, and to remove a totally inappropriate finish. There are no hard and fast rules to follow except that, when it comes to refinishing old furniture, it pays to do as little as possible and to proceed with caution.

CLEANING AND REVIVING THE FINISH

An old table or chest of drawers that has been sitting at the back of a workshop or garage will obviously need cleaning, but if you look closely at almost any oldish piece of furniture you will find that it has lost much of its colour and lustre, and dirt and grease have gathered in the nooks and crannies.

FINISH REVIVER

WHITE SPIRIT MIXED WITH LINSEED OIL

BURNISHING CREAM

Cleaning a clear finish

The aim is to remove the surface layer of old wax and grime, leaving the underlying finish intact. Provided you are not too heavy-handed, this is fairly straightforward.

1 Rubbing with the grain

To remove old wax, dampen a coarse-cloth pad with cleaning fluid and rub in the direction of the grain. The wax will gradually soften to a sludge that must be wiped from the surface with a clean cloth or paper towel before it coagulates.

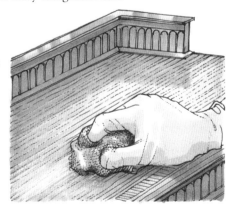

2 Rubbing into mouldings

You may have to use 000-grade wire wool to lift thick layers of wax, especially from recesses or mouldings. Dip it in the fluid and rub the surface as before, but not too vigorously. Finally clean the surface using a soft cloth and white spirit.

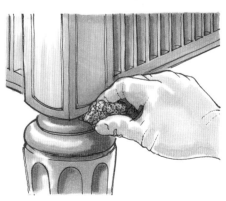

You can wash painted furniture with warm water containing a little mild detergent, but take care not to soak it. There are a number of proprietary fluids for cleaning clear finishes, but you can make your own by mixing 4 parts white spirit with 1 part linseed oil.

Reviving a dull finish

Initial cleaning always improves the appearance of old furniture, but don't be surprised if the finish itself still looks somewhat lifeless. This is due in part to natural ageing, but also to the fact that abrading the surface with wire wool will have matted it. All that is required in most cases is to buff the finish with a mild abrasive. Burnishing creams and liquid abrasives are sold as proprietary revivers; liquid metal polish or car-paint cleaner work just as well.

Buffing the finish

Pour some reviver onto a soft-cloth pad and buff the dull finish quite vigorously until it shines. Complete the renovation with a single thin coating of wax polish.

Rebuilding a protective coat

Sometimes the original protective coat of finish has worn so thin that it pays to rebuild it. You cannot always be sure what finish to use, but if in doubt, you can safely apply wax over any previous polish or varnish. However, you can make some simple tests to identify the finish before proceeding to refinish the furniture as described later in this chapter.

Identifying the finish

Initial cleaning will have removed any wax polish, and you may have to apply fresh wax to the bare wood.

To test for French polish, wrap a cloth dampened with methylated spirit around your finger and rub the finish in an inconspicuous area. If the cloth becomes grey you are merely removing surface dirt, but brown staining means you are actually dissolving French polish.

You can carry out a similar test for cellulose lacquer, using cellulose thinners.

It is impossible to redissolve most modern varnishes, except perhaps for some acrylic varnishes which may be affected by strong solvents and cellulose thinners.

Dissolve French polish with methylated spirit

REPAIRING THE FINISH

Most of us are content to live with minor blemishes – the scuffs, scratches and stains caused by everyday wear and tear on our furniture. Indeed, without them an old piece of furniture looks somehow devoid of character, almost a fake. But occasionally someone will spill alcohol onto a polished table or accidentally drag a bunch of keys across a hall stand, leaving a blemish that is unacceptable, and we are faced with the prospect of repairing, or at least disguising, the damaged finish.

WAX STICKS

Disguising scratches

If a scratch is not deep enough to have damaged the wood itself, you should be able to disguise it with a proprietary liquid retoucher, to burnish it out of the finish, or to fill it flush with wax or shellac. It is not always possible to make an invisible repair, but the damage will be far less conspicuous.

Retouching
Coloured, blended-wax liquid retouchers will not eliminate scratches, but can hide them, provided that the wood is not scratched. Apply retoucher liberally to the scratch, leave to dry for at least an hour, remove any excess and buff with a soft cloth.

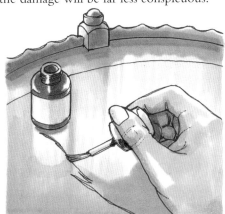

Burnishing out
Hairline scratches can usually be burnished out, using a finish reviver (see right). Do not attempt to burnish out a deep scratch, as this will wear down the body of polish locally and produce a pale patch that looks worse than the original scratch.

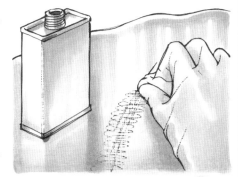

Using a wax stick
Small wood-coloured wax sticks are ideal for hiding deeper scratches. Rub the edge of a stick across the scratch until it is full, wipe off the surplus and buff with a soft cloth. Gently scrape off small lumps of wax with a piece of flexible plastic. Use a thin coat of wax polish or French polish to unify the surface colour.

Filling with shellac or varnish

Use a compatible finish to fill deep scratches in French polish or a modern varnish. Use varnish straight from the can, but pour a little shellac into a shallow dish and allow it to thicken slightly. It pays to use a white French polish on paler woods, as a filled scratch can look darker than the surrounding finish.

Filling flush
Using a small artist's paintbrush, trickle finish into the scratch. Leave it to set and, if necessary, refill the scratch until the finish stands proud of the surface. When it has hardened, carefully scrape down the filling, using a very sharp blade, and sand it flush with fine silicon-carbide paper. Finally buff the surface with a finish reviver.

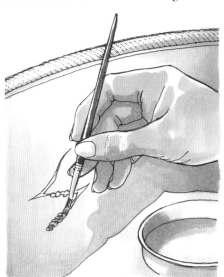

Removing white rings

Water and alcohol will readily etch French polish, leaving pale cloudy stains on a finished surface. This appears most frequently in the form of white rings, where a wet glass or flower vase has been left in contact with the polish for some time. Similar stains can result from placing a cup of hot liquid on a French-polished table.

Using a finish reviver
Fortunately, most of these blemishes do not penetrate too deeply into the polish, and it is usually possible to burnish them out with a mild-abrasive reviver on a soft cloth. You may have to build up the body of polish locally to disguise a pale patch worn in the finish.

STRIPPING THE FINISH

Stripping paint or varnish with a power sander or scraper is not a practical option. The dust created could be harmful, and it is difficult to remove the finish without destroying the patina of the wood at the same time. Heat can be used to soften the finish, but it is best to stick to an electric hot-air stripper to avoid scorching the work or, worse still, starting a fire. Even so, hot-air stripping is only suitable for larger items of built-in furniture, and would never be recommended for delicate items made from fine woods. It is far better to opt for a chemical stripper that will soften the finish so that it can be scraped harmlessly from the wood. It is a messy job that must be undertaken with care, but it is neither difficult nor dangerous provided you observe the manufacturer's health and safety recommendations.

Using solvents

It is possible to soften an old wax finish with white spirit, and methylated spirit will reactivate French polish, but it can take so long to complete the work that using these solvents is only practicable if you plan to strip a small area such as a damaged side rail or door panel.

Proprietary strippers

There are a number of commercially prepared chemical strippers that are suitable for use on furniture. You can buy them from any DIY or hardware store.

General-purpose strippers

These strippers are formulated to remove practically any finish you are likely to find on furniture, including water-based paints and varnishes. They normally contain chemicals that will burn your skin, and even the fumes they exude can be very unpleasant. However, you can work quite safely, provided the workshop is adequately ventilated or you strip the furniture outside. Always wear protective gloves and goggles; a face mask or respirator is also recommended when using some chemical strippers – check the instructions supplied with the stripper. Wear old clothing or a protective apron, and cover the floor with polythene sheets or newspaper.

Varnish removers

Some modern varnishes are notoriously difficult to remove. Although a good general-purpose stripper should cope with them, you can buy strippers that are made specifically for softening polyurethane varnishes and traditional copal varnish. Once again, strict safety precautions will apply.

Liquid and gel strippers

Most chemical strippers are available in a gel-like consistency that will cling to vertical surfaces, but some manufacturers also offer a liquid version designed for deeper penetration of wood carvings and mouldings.

Spirit or water-washable

All strippers have to be washed from the wood at the end of the job. As water will raise the grain, make sure you choose a stripper that is washable with white spirit or methylated spirit.

Safe strippers

If the thought of working with such potent chemicals causes you concern, you can opt to use one of the so-called 'safe' strippers. The fumes are harmless and there is no need to wear gloves, but these strippers react comparatively slowly with old finishes.

METHYLATED SPIRIT

WIRE WOOL

PROTECTIVE GLOVES

SCRAPING TOOLS

GENERAL-PURPOSE PAINT STRIPPER

FACE MASK

GOGGLES

Removing finishes with chemical stripper

Before you begin work, ask your local authority if there are any special arrangements for disposing of solvents and hazardous waste. Use an old brush to apply chemical stripper – even one clogged with dried paint will soon become pliable.

1 Applying the stripper

Paint on a liberal coat of stripper, stippling it into corners, mouldings and carvings. Leave to soften for about 10 to 15 minutes (check the instructions), then try scraping a small area to see if the paint or varnish has softened right through to the wood. If not, apply a second coat of stripper, stippling the blistered finish back onto the surface.

2 Scraping off

After another 5 to 10 minutes, use a paint scraper to lift the softened finish from flat surfaces. Scrape with the grain to avoid scarring the wood, taking care not to damage the surface with the corners of the blade. Deposit the waste onto thick layers of newspaper, ready for wrapping and disposal.

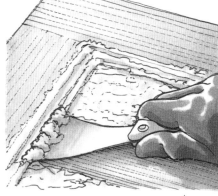

3 Cleaning mouldings and carving

Sharpen a piece of wood to scrape thick paint stripper out of mouldings and crevices, and clean thoroughly with balls of fine wire wool – turn the wool inside out if it becomes clogged with paint or varnish. Use pieces of sacking to clean oak, as metal particles may stain the wood.

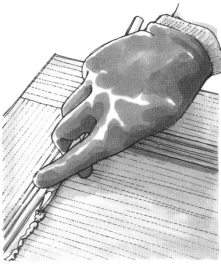

4 Washing the surface

Having removed most of the old finish, clean the residue out of the pores by rubbing in the direction of the grain with balls of fine wire wool dipped in fresh stripper. Finally wash the surface with white spirit (or possibly meths), using a cloth pad. Leave the wood to dry before preparing the surface for refinishing.

INDUSTRIAL STRIPPING

It may be tempting to save time by having furniture stripped professionally, but some industrial processes can do irreparable harm. Those that involve immersion in hot caustic soda and subsequent hosing with water invariably weaken joints, lift veneers and cause thin panels to split. The chemicals may stain the wood, and you can forget about preserving patina.

It is possible to have solid-wood furniture stripped in a cold-chemical dip without such drastic results, leaving you with only moderately raised grain to deal with. However, there are possible health risks associated with cold-chemical dipping which may eventually lead to fewer companies operating with the necessary solvents.

A few companies remove finishes by dipping furniture for a few minutes in a bath of warm alkali. The process is safe for man-made boards, including plywood, but you should seek the operator's guarantee before allowing old veneered furniture to be stripped, particularly if it has been painted.

Old furniture is scrubbed by hand in a tank of cold chemicals

PREPARING THE SURFACE

When you have stripped an old finish, it will be necessary to prepare the bare wood for refinishing. If possible, preserve the patina of old wood by doing nothing more than lightly sanding raised grain. You will also need to prepare and finish new components that you have substituted for damaged or missing parts. Don't be fooled into thinking that a wood dye or a layer of varnish will disguise a poorly prepared surface – in fact, a clear finish tends to draw attention to raised grain, scratches and dents. It is important to repair the worst blemishes before sanding the surface with progressively finer grades of abrasive paper.

Abrasives are also used to rub down hardened finishes between coats as you build a protective body of polish or varnish.

Filling blemishes

The materials used to fill cracks and small holes are made in a range of typical wood colours. However, as they do not absorb dyes and finishes quite like the surrounding wood, some restorers prefer to sand the wood first and apply one sealer coat of finish before trying to match the colour of the filler. Others prefer to fill first, having already tested a sample on another similar piece of wood or on an inconspicuous part of the furniture, and having applied the requisite finish to see how it reacts with the filler.

SANDING SEALER

STOPPER

WAX FILLING STICKS

SHELLAC STICKS

ELECTRIC SOLDERING IRON

FILLING KNIFE

Stopper

Stopper is a ready-mixed paste with a consistency similar to putty. It is probably the best filler for use with paint, although it can be used under most finishes.

When using a clear finish, choose a stopper that is similar to the colour of the wood, then adjust a small batch by gradually adding a compatible wood dye until you achieve an exact match. A less-than-perfect result can later be disguised with very light applications of artist's oil colours.

Ensure the surface is clean and dry, then use a filling knife to press stopper into the crack or hole. When it has set hard, sand lightly until flush with the wood.

Filling with wax

Coloured-wax filling sticks are ideal for filling woodworm holes and hairline cracks before applying wax polish or shellac. Cut off a small piece of wax and knead it between your fingers until it is soft enough to press into the holes with a blade. As the wax hardens, scrape it flush with a piece of flexible plastic and burnish the repair with the back of a piece of sandpaper.

Melting solid shellac sticks

Use a soldering iron to melt some solidified shellac into a hole and, while it is still soft, press it flat with a chisel dipped in water. Once the shellac has hardened, pare it flush with the wood, using a sharp chisel, before sanding it smooth with fine abrasive paper.

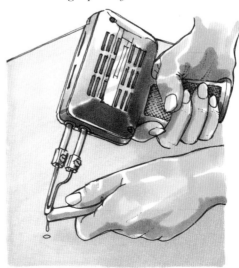

Removing scratches and burns

A burn left by a carelessly placed cigarette or a scratch across the grain can often be sanded out with abrasive paper. However, it is quicker to remove deeper blemishes with a cabinet scraper. As scraping is almost certainly going to cut below the level of the patina, you may have to blend in the small scraped patch with wood dye.

Using a scraper
Scrape diagonally across the grain of the wood from opposing directions, then finish by scraping parallel with the grain.

Raising dents

A heavy object dropped onto a wooden surface will crush the grain, leaving a depression that can usually be repaired without recourse to a filler. Applying water or steam to the dent makes the wood swell, lifting the crushed grain until the surface is flush again.

1 Applying water
Use a pointed paintbrush to drop hot water onto the dent, then allow the wood to absorb the moisture. Once the wood appears to be dry, apply more water until the dent disappears. Should this treatment prove unsuccessful, try using steam.

2 Using steam
Lay a damp cloth over the dent and place the tip of a heated soldering iron directly on top. The steam generated should cause the grain to swell. Once the surface is flush, sand the whole area smooth with a fine abrasive paper.

Types of sandpaper

Although not strictly accurate, sandpaper is a convenient generic term for all the types of abrasive paper used to smooth wood and finishes. Particles of abrasive material or 'grit' are glued to a paper or sometimes cloth backing, which can be wrapped around a block of wood or cork. When sanding small areas it is sometimes more convenient to simply fold the paper and use your fingertips alone to apply pressure .

Aluminium-oxide paper
This abrasive, usually brown or pale grey in colour, is generally considered the best paper for sanding hardwoods.

Garnet paper
Reddish-brown garnet paper is suitable for use on any type of wood, but it is usually recommended when sanding softwoods.

Silicon-carbide paper
Known as wet-and-dry sandpaper, black silicon-carbide is used with water as a lubricant to smooth paints and varnishes between coats. There is also a grey silicon-carbide paper that employs a zinc-oxide powder as a dry lubricant. This is ideal for rubbing down French polish.

GARNET PAPERS

ALUMINIUM–OXIDE PAPER

WET–AND–DRY PAPER

READY–LUBRICATED SILICON–CARBIDE PAPER

Grades of sandpaper

Abrasive papers are graded according to the size of the grit used. They are generally available as coarse, medium and fine grades for sanding wood, and very fine for rubbing down finishes. These grades are subdivided by number – the higher the number, the finer the grit. In addition, there are open-coat abrasives that are less likely to clog when sanding resinous softwoods or paintwork, and closed-coat abrasives with densely packed particles for fast sanding. Never use a coarser grade than necessary, and always work progressively through to the finer grades.

Sanding by hand

Unless you are making a new table top or replacing a complete side panel, there is little use for power sanders in furniture restoration. Most of the time you will be sanding surfaces that have been stripped and need nothing more than a light sanding to smooth the grain, or you will be preparing relatively small replacements that do not warrant power sanding anyway.

1 Sanding a flat surface

Tear a strip from a sheet of sandpaper to wrap around a cork sanding block or a convenient block of softwood. Sand in the direction of the grain, and keep the block flat on the work to avoid inadvertently rounding the edges of the workpiece. As the work progresses, wipe the wood dust from the surface and tap the edge of the paper on the bench to clear dust from the grit.

2 Sanding with shaped wood

One way of sanding simple mouldings is to wrap sandpaper around a previously shaped block of wood or a dowel. When the work feels smooth to the touch, wipe all surfaces with a damp cloth. Allow the wood to dry, then sand lightly with a fine-grade paper to remove the raised fibres of the grain.

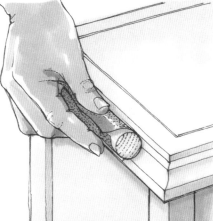

3 Sanding with folded sandpaper

Another technique is to fold the paper into a narrow strip and sand the moulding, using your fingertips. Sand out the corners and tight crevices with the sharply folded edge of the strip. Wipe and sand the wood as described above.

Filling the grain

Species such as mahogany, rosewood, oak and ash have large open pores that spoil the appearance of a glossy finish unless they are treated with a grain filler beforehand. A number of proprietary grain fillers are transparent and intended for use with any timber, but the majority available are wood-coloured pastes. If you are planning to fill previously stained timber, first seal in the colour with one or two coats of transparent French polish or sanding sealer. There is no need to grain-fill softwoods or close-grain hardwoods like birch or maple.

Using grain filler

Dip a pad of coarse-weave hessian into the grain filler and rub it onto the wood fairly vigorously, using circular strokes. Remove excess filler from the surface by rubbing across the grain with a clean pad of hessian, and use a pointed dowel to clean out any residue of grain filler from mouldings or carving. Leave to dry overnight, and then sand the surface lightly in the direction of the grain.

Sanding sealer

Although it is not essential to the finish, it is possible to produce a silky-smooth surface on close-grain wood such as yellow cedar, birch, spruce and maple, by spraying or brushing on a sanding sealer.

Sealing the wood

Always check before starting work that the varnish you intend to use as a finish will set satisfactorily over sanding sealer. Sand the work perfectly smooth and wipe off all wood dust before applying the sealer.

Allow the sealer to dry before carefully rubbing it down with very fine sandpaper, then add a second coat and allow this to dry. Finally rub the surface down with 0000-grade wire wool and apply your chosen finish.

MODIFYING THE COLOUR OF WOOD

TWO-PART
BLEACH

OXALIC-ACID
CRYSTALS

LIMING
WAX

It will sometimes be necessary to modify the colour of the wood before you refinish a piece of furniture. You may want to eradicate an isolated stain, for example, or to enrich the colour of wood that has been bleached by strong sunlight. Occasionally you will have to blend in a new component with wood dye, though it may be simpler to bleach both the old and new woods so that you can stain them all the same colour.

Removing isolated stains

Oxalic acid is the traditional wood bleach. Available in crystalline form from specialist restoration suppliers or from your local pharmacist, it is the ideal bleach for removing small stains. Store and mix oxalic acid in glass or plastic containers only, never metal ones.

1 Making an oxalic-acid solution

Half-fill a glass jar with warm water and gradually add acid crystals to the water, stirring them gently until they dissolve (never pour water onto acid crystals). Continue to add crystals with a dry spatula, stirring them until you have made a saturated solution – that is, when no more crystals will dissolve. Let the solution stand for about 10 minutes.

2 Applying the bleach

Paint the solution evenly onto the stained area, using a white-fibre or nylon brush – bleach will destroy ordinary bristle paintbrushes. Let the wood dry and add more bleach if the stain persists. Once the stain disappears, neutralize the acid by swabbing the surface with water. Let the wood dry out and, while wearing a face mask, lightly sand the raised grain.

Bleaching out the colour

To change the colour of a piece of wood, use a strong two-part bleach. This is normally sold as a proprietary kit containing both constituents in separate, clearly labelled containers. Since not all woods bleach well, it is worth testing a small sample beforehand.

1 Using two-part bleach

Brush the first solution evenly onto the surface to be bleached. Try not to splash adjacent surfaces, and do not let the bleach solution run. After about 20 minutes, during which time the wood may go darker in colour, apply the second solution, using another brush.

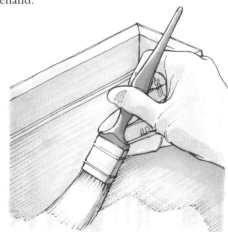

2 Neutralizing the bleach

Leave the bleach to work for up to four hours. As soon as the required colour is achieved, wash the wood thoroughly with a weak acetic-acid solution (one pint of water to a teaspoon of white vinegar). Let the wood dry and sand it smooth.

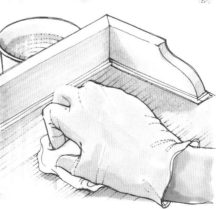

USING WOOD BLEACHES SAFELY

Because we use bleaches every day as cleaning agents in our homes, we tend to regard them as harmless and should guard against becoming careless with them. Wood bleaches are hazardous, and must be stored where children cannot reach them. Wear protective gloves and goggles, and an apron or overalls. Ventilate your workspace or work outside, in which case have a bucket of water handy, so that you can wash your skin immediately if you get splashed with bleach.

Liming wood

Liming produces a distinctive effect, which is traditionally associated with oak furniture. The finish is created by filling the deep pores in open-grain timbers with a special wax paste. Even when dry, the white liming wax contrasts with the darker wood, emphasizing the grain pattern. To prepare an item of furniture for liming, sand the wood smooth and remove any traces of grease by wiping the surface with a cloth dipped in white spirit.

Accentuate grain with liming wax

1 Opening the grain

Using a clean wire brush, scrub the wood in the direction of the grain only, to clean out the pores. Check your progress quite regularly by glancing across the wood into the light, ensuring that there is a fairly even distribution of open pores. If required, apply wood dye and seal the surface with a coat of transparent shellac.

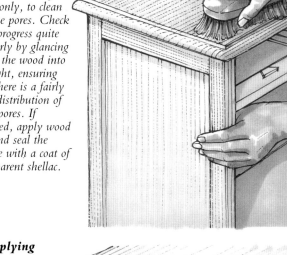

2 Applying liming wax

Dip a hessian pad into the liming wax and rub it into the grain with circular overlapping strokes, until the surface is evenly covered. Wipe across the grain with clean hessian, leaving wax in the pores. After about 10 minutes, remove excess wax from the surface by gently burnishing along the grain with a dry cotton cloth. The next day, apply a standard wax polish.

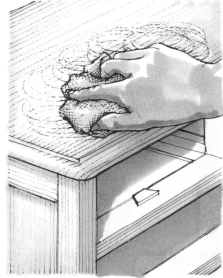

Staining with wood dye

Unlike paints and varnishes, which are surface finishes and do not actually change the colour of the wood itself, wood dyes soak right into the timber. The colour is permanent, even after stripping the surface finish, unless you apply bleach. Wood dyes are used to enrich a dull-looking batch of wood or to modify the colour of new wood so that it blends with an old piece of furniture.

Types of wood dye

Traditionally, wood dyes were supplied in the form of dry powdered pigments which were mixed to the required strength by the restorer. Similar powdered pigment dyes are still available from specialist suppliers, but since only experience can teach you to mix specific colours, most amateur restorers prefer to use ready-mixed dyes, which are nowadays made in an extensive range of realistically wood-like colours. You can mix compatible dyes to achieve colours not offered in the manufacturer's range, and it is also possible to reduce the strength of colour by adding the appropriate thinner (see opposite).

FUMING WOOD

You can chemically alter the colour of woods that contain tannic acid by exposing them to ammonia fumes. Oak reacts well to fuming, turning a rich golden-brown. You can also fume walnut, chestnut and mahogany. A strong ammonia solution, known as '.880' or 'eight-eighty', is available from a pharmacist, or you could use ordinary household ammonia, though this takes considerably longer to have an effect. Remove any exposed metal fittings that could stain the work before you fume it.

Always wear safety goggles and a respirator when you are handling strong ammonia solution.

Building a fume tent

To make a fume tent, build a rough framework that will surround the workpiece, and drape black-plastic sheeting over it. Erect the structure outside, and place the workpiece inside the tent along with several shallow dishes containing ammonia solution. Seal the tent all round with adhesive tape, and leave the workpiece inside for about 24 hours for the desired result.

READY-MIXED
WOOD DYE

PROTECTIVE
GLOVES

PAINT
PAD

STAINED
VARNISH

DRY PIGMENTS

Applying wood dye

Before you apply your chosen wood dye to a piece of furniture, always test it for colour and strength on a sample of similar, if not identical, wood. Paint on two or three overlapping coats, then check the final appearance by covering the test sample with your intended finish.

If possible, set up the work so that you are staining a horizontal surface, even if that means turning the workpiece as you proceed. To prevent runs showing, always stain the underside of a panel first.

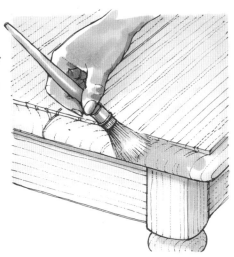

1 Preparing the surface

The wood must be clean, free from grease and sanded smooth in the direction of the grain. Any cross-grain scratches will show after staining.

To prevent end grain absorbing too much dark solvent-based dye, seal it with a mixture of equal parts white spirit and linseed oil 24 hours before you stain the wood.

2 Staining the wood

Use a paintbrush or a broad paint pad to apply a generous coat of dye to the wood, blending wet edges and spreading the dye along the grain as much as possible.

When using a water-based product, immediately mop up any excess dye with an absorbent rag, distributing the colour evenly.

3 Colouring turned details

Use a soft-cloth pad to rub dye onto turned legs and rails. Wearing protective gloves, dip the rag into the dye, squeeze it out and rub it onto the wood.

It is easy to use the same method if you have to stain vertical surfaces.

Water-based dyes

Water-based dyes are popular because they dry slowly, giving an inexperienced restorer plenty of time to achieve an even distribution of colour. You can modify the result by applying additional coats or, if the dye is too dark, by swabbing the freshly stained wood with a damp cloth to remove some of the colour.

Once dry, a water-based dye is unaffected by subsequent finishes. Its one drawback is a tendency to raise the grain, but this can be minimized by raising the grain first with water and sanding it smooth before staining.

Spirit-based dyes

Spirit-based dyes are sometimes employed by hard-pressed professionals because they dry quickly. However, this can be a setback for many amateurs, who find it impossible to swab or brush on the dye without leaving

obvious overlap marks. For this reason, even experts often choose to spray spirit-based wood dyes.

Since both are thinned with methylated spirit, spirit-based dyes can be used to tint French polishes. Applying French polish over a spirit-based dye may disturb the colour.

Solvent-based dyes

Most dyes stocked by local DIY outlets are solvent-based (sometimes called oil-based), which means that they can be thinned with white spirit. They should not be confused with the true spirit-based dyes described above. Even though they dry relatively quickly, solvent-based dyes are easy to apply.

If you want to apply a polyurethane varnish or wax polish, seal the stained wood first with a shellac sanding sealer. Solvent-based dyes are only available ready-mixed.

Stained varnish

To avoid having to strip discoloured or dowdy varnish, you can overlay it with a coat of stained varnish. Available in the usual wood shades, stained polyurethane varnish is hard-wearing, but is best protected with a coat of clear varnish.

FRENCH POLISH

In the Victorian era, French polish was used more than any other finish to impart a high gloss to furniture made from mahogany and other fashionable woods of the day. Consequently, as a restorer you will almost certainly have to deal with the prospect of refinishing with French polish at some time or other. Unfortunately, the sheer quality of a French-polished surface and the mystique that has surrounded the technique for generations have tended to make it a daunting process for the amateur. Traditional French-polishing does take practice to master, but the actual methods of applying the polish are relatively straightforward. The key to a successful finish is not to rush the work, but to build up a translucent film with a number of thin coats applied over several days.

Preparing for polishing

As with any finishing process, it is essential that French-polishing is carried out in a dust-free environment with good lighting. Ideally, one would always have a separate room for applying finishes rather than having to work in the main workshop, but this is a luxury most amateur restorers cannot afford. A more realistic approach is to keep the shop as clean as possible and to make sure you vacuum the workbench before you begin polishing, remembering to allow plenty of time for any fine dust to settle.

Keep the room warm and dry – damp conditions may cause milky 'blooming' to develop as the polish dries. However, do not use a fan heater to warm the workshop, as this will disturb the dust again. Portable gas heaters release a great deal of moisture into the air, so they are not suitable either.

Prepare the surface of the wood thoroughly and apply wood dyes prior to polishing.

Although they are not essential, disposable gloves will keep your hands clean and protect your skin from solvents.

STANDARD BUTTON POLISH

WHITE POLISH

GARNET POLISH

TRANSPARENT POLISH

METHYLATED SPIRIT

AIRTIGHT JAR FOR RUBBER

BRUSHING FRENCH POLISH

DISPOSABLE GLOVES

Rubbing polish with wire wool dipped in wax produces a subtle sheen

Types of French polish

All French polishes are made by dissolving shellac in methylated spirit, but there are several varieties to choose from. Standard French polish is perfectly adequate for most jobs, but dark red-brown garnet polish is sometimes preferred for restoring old mahogany furniture. Use milky 'white' French polish or even transparent polish for finishing pale-coloured woods. Most DIY shops stock French polishes, or you can obtain them from specialist suppliers.

Making a rubber
French polish is applied with a 'rubber' – a pad of upholsterer's wadding or cotton wool wrapped in a 225 to 300mm (9 to 12in) square of white cotton.

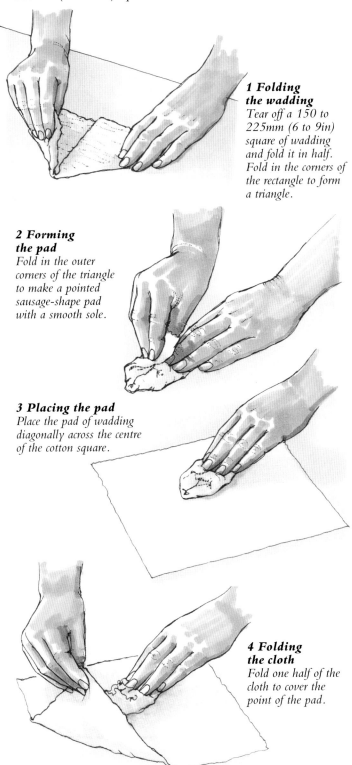

1 Folding the wadding
Tear off a 150 to 225mm (6 to 9in) square of wadding and fold it in half. Fold in the corners of the rectangle to form a triangle.

2 Forming the pad
Fold in the outer corners of the triangle to make a pointed sausage-shape pad with a smooth sole.

3 Placing the pad
Place the pad of wadding diagonally across the centre of the cotton square.

4 Folding the cloth
Fold one half of the cloth to cover the point of the pad.

5 Wrapping the pad
Wrap all the triangular corners of the cloth over the centre in turn to form a neat package.

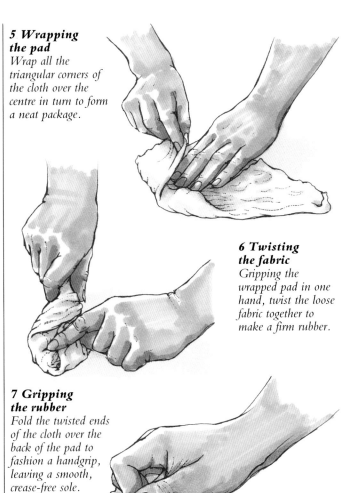

6 Twisting the fabric
Gripping the wrapped pad in one hand, twist the loose fabric together to make a firm rubber.

7 Gripping the rubber
Fold the twisted ends of the cloth over the back of the pad to fashion a handgrip, leaving a smooth, crease-free sole.

Charging the rubber
At the beginning of the job, and each time the rubber begins to run dry, you should pour polish onto the wadding. Never dip the rubber into French polish, and do not pour it directly onto the sole.

Wetting the pad
Unfold the cloth and pour on enough polish to wet the pad without actually saturating the wadding. Refold the rubber and press it against a piece of scrap wood to squeeze out surplus polish. Smear a drop of linseed oil onto the sole with your fingertip; this will lubricate the rubber.

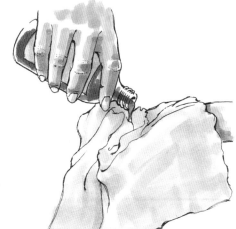

Applying the polish

Polish is distributed by stroking the rubber across the wood. You need very little pressure with a freshly charged rubber, but as the work progresses, press harder to encourage the polish to flow. Sweep the rubber smoothly on and off the surface; never let the rubber come to rest while in contact with the work, or the sole will stick to the shellac. Recharge the rubber occasionally as it becomes dry, and add another drop of linseed oil if the sole begins to drag on the surface of the wood. Whenever it is not in use, store your rubber in a clean, airtight screw-top jar to prevent it going hard. Begin by sealing the wood with slightly thinned polish on a pad of wadding, using overlapping parallel strokes.

1 Filling the grain with polish

The first few applications of full-strength polish are sufficient to fill close-grain wood. Make overlapping circular strokes with a rubber until you have covered an entire panel to the edges.

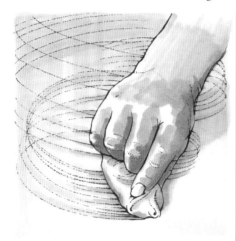

2 Distributing the polish evenly

Polish the same area again, this time using figure-of-eight strokes – this combination of different strokes will distribute the French polish evenly. Again, make sure you work right up to the edges of the panel.

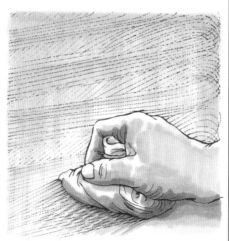

3 Finishing with parallel strokes

Finally go over the panel once more, now using straight and overlapping parallel strokes. Leave this first combination of strokes to dry for about half an hour, and then repeat the whole process three or four times.

4 Rubbing out blemishes

Leave the polish to dry overnight, then lightly sand out any blemishes or dust particles that have become embedded in the surface. Use very fine ready-lubricated silicon-carbide paper, rubbing along the grain only, and wipe off the dust with a clean duster.

5 Bodying up

Give the wood another four or five coats of polish, with half-hour breaks between applications, then leave it to harden once more. Gradually build up a protective body of polish over three to four days, until you are satisfied with the overall colour and appearance.

6 Spiriting off

Any linseed-oil streaks should be removed by 'spiriting off'. Dampen the pad with a few drops of meths. Sweep the rubber on and off the surface using straight strokes, adding meths if the rubber begins to drag. Repeat the process every two or three minutes until streaking disappears, occasionally changing the cloth to help remove the oil.

Gloss or satin finish

After spiriting off, leave the surface to harden for half an hour and buff it to a high gloss with a dry duster. Put the work aside for about a week until the polish has completely finished the hardening process.

1 Burnishing

If you are dissatisfied with the shine of the fully hardened polish you can buff it, using a proprietary burnishing cream or finish reviver.

2 Flattening

Some restorers prefer a slightly flattened finish to a high gloss. Cut back the surface slightly with 0000-grade wire wool dipped in wax polish. Rub lightly along the grain until the polish is matted evenly, then wipe over with a duster.

French-polishing carved wood

It is not practicable to polish carved work with a rubber. Instead, use a squirrel-hair brush to paint slightly thinned shellac onto carving, not too thickly in case it runs. If you cannot buy a special brush, make do with a soft paintbrush. When the polish has hardened, spirit off the high points with a rubber and burnish with a duster. Do not rub too hard, or you will wear through the polish.

Paint carving with thinned polish

Brushing French polish

The furniture industry invariably employed traditional French-polishing methods, but other trades would sometimes resort to a simpler method of applying shellac – brushing it onto the work. Special brushing French polish contains a retarding agent that gives you enough time to paint it onto the wood; if you tried this with standard French polish, the surface would be covered with brush marks.

1 Building a protective coat

Apply the first coat with a paintbrush, allow it to dry for about 20 minutes, then rub down with silicon-carbide paper. Repeat the process twice more.

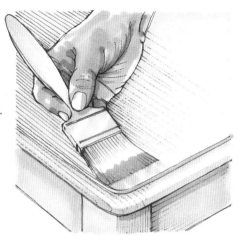

2 Rubbing with wire wool

Apply soft wax polish to the now-hardened shellac with a 0000-grade wire-wool pad. Rub fairly gently along the grain, making sure you cover the whole surface evenly.

3 Finishing with a soft duster

Finally bring the polish to a shine by burnishing with a soft, clean duster.

WAX POLISH

Wax polish, one of the oldest wood finishes, can be used as a dressing over shellac or varnish, or can be employed as a finish in its own right. It is not particularly hard-wearing, but wax is easily renewed with additional coats of polish when necessary. It is popular, not only for its subtle sheen, but also for its ease of application; even a beginner can achieve successful results using wax polish.

Applying cream polish
Prepare the wood and seal it with a coat of transparent French polish or sanding sealer, rubbing down lightly with very fine ready-lubricated silicon-carbide paper.

ANTIQUE WAX POLISH

CREAM POLISH

PASTE POLISH

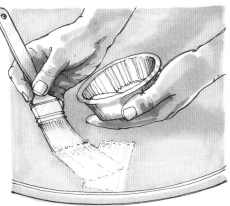

1 Applying the polish
Pour some cream polish into a shallow container and paint it liberally onto the wood with a paint-brush. Leave the wax to harden for about an hour.

2 Building up the finish
Apply the second coat with a soft-cloth pad, covering the surface with circular strokes and finishing parallel with the grain. Allow the wax to harden, and add a third coat if required.

3 Burnishing the wax polish
Leave for an hour or two, then use a clean, soft duster to buff the surface vigorously in the direction of the grain, until the wax shines to your satisfaction.

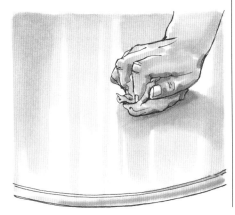

Using paste polish
Prepare and seal the bare wood as described for applying cream polish (see left).

1 Applying the first coat
Wipe a cloth pad across the polish to pick up a generous measure of wax, and apply it, using overlapping circular strokes to cover the surface evenly. Finish this stage by rubbing with the grain.

2 Using wire wool
After 15 to 20 minutes, apply more polish, using a ball of 0000-grade wire wool, but this time rubbing in the direction of the grain only. Gradually build a protective coat of polish, allowing the wax to harden between applications. Finally burnish with a duster.

WOOD-
FINISHING OIL

Types of wax polish

Wax polish is made in a range of colours, from white to yellow, with which you can create a beautiful mellow finish that does not alter the colour of the wood to any great extent. A range of dark-brown 'antique' polishes is available, to maintain the patina of old furniture and to hide fine scratches.

It is not necessary to fill grain before applying a wax polish, but it is worth sealing it with shellac to prevent dirt from being absorbed and discolouring the wood.

Cream polish
Polishes with the consistency of thin cream can be brushed onto the wood, gradually building a protective coat of wax.

Paste polish
Thick paste polishes, sold in flat tins or foil containers, are applied with a cloth pad or fine wire wool. They make an ideal dressing over another finish or for renewing wax polish.

Silicone polishes
It is best to avoid polishes that contain silicones. They can be buffed easily to a relatively high gloss, but they are incompatible with most finishes, including other wax polishes.

Types of oil
Linseed oil is available if you want an authentic oiled finish for an old piece of furniture, but it dries so slowly that dust inevitably becomes imbedded in the tacky surface. Modern, fast-drying oils are superior for almost all purposes.

Tung oil
Tung oil, perhaps the most durable of oil finishes, can take up to 24 hours to dry, but any dust particles that stick to the surface can be rubbed out with fine silicon-carbide paper between applications of the oil.

Danish and teak oils
These finishes, based on tung oil, contain synthetic resins to make them hard-wearing. Depending on humidity and ambient temperature, teak and Danish oils will dry within six hours.

Edible oils
Special 'salad-bowl' oils are available for finishing chopping boards and other wooden items used to prepare and serve food. However, you can also use olive oil or some similar non-toxic oil.

SPONTANEOUS COMBUSTION
Oil gives off heat as it dries, and oil-soaked fabric has been known to burst into flames. Leave oily rags in a bucket of water overnight before disposing of them.

OIL FINISHES

Most people associate an oil finish with relatively modern furniture made from teak or similar hardwoods, yet linseed oil has been in use as a wood finish for centuries. Present-day oil finishes are so easy to apply that success is practically guaranteed, even if you have no previous experience in finishing wood. Should the finish lose its vitality with age, it can be revived with a coat of fresh oil, provided the surface has not been waxed in the meantime.

Oil can be used on any wood, but its soft lustre seems particularly apt for stripped pine, which turns a rich amber colour when oiled. The finish can be marred by heat or water; however, all but the worst stains disappear naturally within a short time.

Oiling wood
Use the following methods to apply any oil finish; you may need to thin tung oil slightly with white spirit before it will brush on successfully.

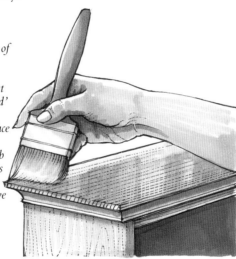

1 Sealing the surface
Apply the first coat of oil liberally with a fairly wide paint-brush, to ensure that the surface is 'wetted' evenly. Before it dries, wipe the surface with a soft cloth to distribute and absorb excess oil. Six hours later, brush on a second coat and leave to dry overnight.

2 Creating the sheen
Apply another coat of oil with a soft cloth pad, and burnish the surface with a duster. For a silky-smooth satin finish, let the oil dry completely and burnish lightly along the grain with a ball of 0000-grade wire wool.

PAINT, VARNISH AND LACQUER

Paints, varnishes and lacquers are similar finishes, in that they lie on the surface of the wood, forming a protective film. Traditionally, furniture makers used clear finishes to enhance the pattern of the grain, while opaque paints were primarily employed to disguise inferior materials. Softwood once fell into this latter category and, apart from kitchen tables and chairs, which were often ritually scrubbed once a week, most pine furniture such as dressers and chests of drawers would have been painted. In contrast, today's furniture restorers tend to prefer the appearance of clear-finished softwood.

WATER-BASED
ACRYLIC VARNISH

ONE-COAT
PAINT

SOLVENT-BASED
VARNISH

SHELLAC
KNOTTING

SOLVENT-BASED
UNDERCOAT

Paint

Ordinary household paint is perfectly acceptable for finishing furniture. With most solvent-based paints it is necessary to apply a primer to seal the wood, followed by a heavily pigmented undercoat. The final coat of paint, which can be matt, semi-matt (also known as satin or eggshell) or glossy, will provide the required surface colouring. There are also one-coat paints that do not require undercoating.

Water-based acrylic paints dry so quickly that you can finish a piece of furniture in a single day, but these paints must be applied in a dry atmosphere, as any damp or humidity can prevent them drying properly.

Choosing a finish

A modern hard-wearing varnish is a perfectly practical alternative to paint, but having stripped a piece with the intention of using a clear finish, the results may lead you to consider repainting. For example, the original makers would not have used the best-quality softwood for painted work; even knotty pine was considered second-rate. The stripping process may also reveal open joints or ugly splits that were once disguised with filler.

Clear varnishes

Solvent-based varnishes are little more than paints without the solid coloured pigments. These extremely tough wood finishes are waterproof and heat-resistant, making them ideal for utilitarian furniture that must put up with everyday wear and tear. Made from synthetic resins such as polyurethane, clear varnishes have a gloss, semi-matt (eggshell) or matt finish.

Some varnishes have to be mixed with a catalyst before they can be used. These two-part varnishes exude fairly unpleasant fumes, and they are not as convenient to use as a standard, ready-to-apply varnish.

Water-based acrylic varnishes are practically odourless, but make sure you dampen the wood and sand down before varnishing, to prevent raised grain spoiling the finish.

Cellulose lacquer

Much of the furniture manufactured during the 1920s and 1930s was sprayed with cellulose lacquer, a fast-drying, almost water-clear finish. If you do not have access to spray equipment, you can use a brushing version of cellulose lacquer (see opposite).

SAFETY WITH SOLVENTS

Wood finishing is not a particularly hazardous activity, but it pays to always take sensible precautions when using solvent-based varnishes and paints.

● Ventilate the workshop when using finishes, and wear a respirator if you have any respiratory problems.

● Store solvent-based materials where children cannot reach them. If you need to decant paints, varnishes or thinners, label the new containers clearly and don't store them where they could be mistaken for drink or foodstuffs.

● If a child appears to have swallowed finishes or thinners, don't induce him or her to vomit, but seek urgent medical advice.

● If you get solvents or finishes in your eyes, flush them with running water, and if symptoms persist, consult a doctor at once.

● If possible, store flammable materials outside the house in a shed or garage. Don't smoke, either when using solvent-based materials or in a workshop where they are drying on wood.

● Don't clean paint or varnish from your skin with thinners. Instead, wear a barrier cream and use a proprietary skin cleanser or warm soapy water.

● Never pour solvents down the drain. Ask your local authority for advice on careful disposal.

Applying finishes with a brush

Applying finishes with a paintbrush is not demanding; a degree of care and patience is all you need to achieve first-class results. Natural hog bristle is generally considered to make the best brushes, but you can make do with well-made synthetic-bristle brushes. You'll need a couple of general-purpose paintbrushes, say 25 and 50mm (1 and 2in) wide, plus a 100mm (4in) brush for large flat surfaces.

Applying varnish

Having prepared the wood, apply a sealer coat of varnish thinned by 10 to 20 per cent with white spirit. Either brush on the sealer coat or rub it into the grain with a soft-cloth pad.

Loading the brush
Dip only the tip of the brush into the varnish, and flex the bristles against the inside of the container to remove excess finish. Don't scrape the brush across the lip of the container; this creates air bubbles that may become trapped in the setting varnish.

Varnishing a flat surface
Brush the varnish onto a flat surface, spreading it evenly in all directions before 'laying off' with light strokes along the grain. Blend in the wet edges as you go, to prevent brushmarks spoiling the finish. Apply at least two coats of varnish.

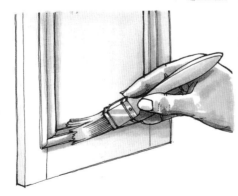

Varnishing mouldings
Brushing across a moulding invariably makes a teardrop of varnish run from the bristles of a loaded brush. Always brush along mouldings, working outwards from a corner.

Modifying the finish

Matt varnish dries with a finely textured surface. For a similar finish that is also smooth to the touch, rub down a gloss varnish with 0000-grade wire wool. Produce a soft sheen by dipping the wire wool in wax polish and buffing the surface afterwards with a soft duster.

Brushing cellulose lacquer

Since cellulose lacquer dries so rapidly, you must brush relatively quickly to avoid leaving brushmarks or ridges in the finish. Apply two or three coats, rubbing down between with very fine silicon-carbide paper.

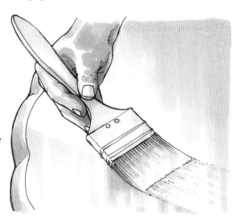

Brushing on the lacquer
Use a soft cloth to apply a sealer coat of lacquer thinned by 50 per cent. Brush on further coats of full-strength lacquer, holding the bristles at a shallow angle to the work and laying on with long, straight overlapping strokes – don't brush out like varnish or paint.

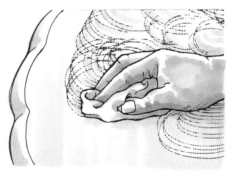

Burnishing the final coat
If the final finish is less than perfect, rub down the last coat of cellulose lacquer with very fine silicon-carbide paper and polish the surface with a finish reviver or burnishing cream.

Applying paint

Apply conventional solvent-based paint as if it were varnish, spreading the finish and laying off with a brush. Don't brush out thixotropic (non-drip) one-coat paint or acrylic water-based paints, but lay these finishes on with more-or-less parallel strokes, allowing the brushmarks to flow naturally.

To remove hardened paint runs or imbedded particles of dust, dip a strip of wet-and-dry paper in water and sand the surface smooth. Wipe off the slurry with a cloth and repaint.

Using knotting
Live knots in new softwood can exude resin that will 'bleed' through paintwork, staining the finish. Seal knots with two coats of shellac-based knotting, available from DIY stores.

Spraying finishes

No one would dispute that spraying paints, varnishes and lacquers produces a superb finish, but unless you intend to take up furniture restoration in a serious way it is probably not worth the necessary investment in time and money to equip yourself for spraying wood finishes. Although it is possible to hire spray guns and other equipment, you still need to erect a safe spray booth unless you are prepared to work outdoors.

Spraying equipment and facilities

A spray gun atomizes the finish, producing a fine 'mist' of paint, varnish or lacquer that is deposited onto the surface of the work. Consequently, it is possible to produce a more evenly distributed coating than is possible by painting on the same finish with a brush.

Spray guns
Squeezing the trigger of a spray gun opens a valve that allows compressed air to flow through the gun. There it is mixed with paint, varnish or lacquer drawn from a reservoir in the form of a gravity-feed cup mounted on top of the gun or a canister carried below, from which the finish is siphoned by the flow of air. The atomized finish emerges from a small hole in the centre of a nozzle known as the air cap. You can adjust the spray pattern from a narrow cone to a wide fan, depending on whether you are coating slender components, such as the legs of a chair, or a large flat area like a table top.

Compressor
Air is pressurized by a compressor and fed to the spray gun through a flexible hose. You will find that an electric compressor that simply plugs into the mains is the most convenient type. Check with the supplier that the compressor you are considering is safe to use within a spray booth; if not, you will have to install it outside, with a connection for the hose passing through the booth wall.

Protective equipment
Always wear goggles and a respirator when spraying, even when you are working outside.

Spray booth
In order to spray safely indoors, you should construct a simple enclosed booth from hardboard panels nailed to a lightweight softwood framework. Line the inside with replaceable sheets of paper to absorb the overspray.

Mount an extractor fan in the rear of the booth to remove solvent fumes, and cover the fan inlet with a gauze filter to trap airborne particles.

Stand a turntable for the workpiece in front of the extractor fan. Your cheapest option is to build your own, using a disc of chipboard mounted onto a discarded swivel-chair base.

The atmosphere inside a spray booth can be highly flammable, and you should install special explosion-proof lamps controlled from outside.

Thinning the finish for spraying
Although it is possible to buy cellulose lacquer, for example, in a consistency that is already ideal for spraying, most paints and varnishes are too thick and must be diluted with the appropriate thinners.

Testing the viscosity
Professional sprayers use a special funnel called a viscosity cup to check that a finish is just right for spraying, but you can also follow a simple rule of thumb. Thin a batch of the required finish according to the manufacturer's recommendations, then stir it with a stick. Lift the stick from the finish and observe how the liquid runs from the tip. If it runs smoothly and continuously, it is ready for spraying, but if it flows spasmodically, add a little more thinner. Always test the viscosity of a finish by spraying a scrap board before you try it on an actual workpiece.

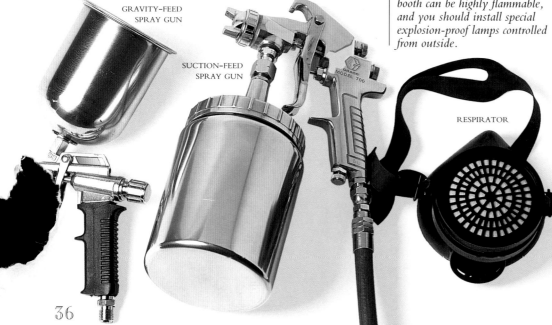

GRAVITY-FEED SPRAY GUN

SUCTION-FEED SPRAY GUN

RESPIRATOR

Spraying techniques

Spraying wood finishes can be very satisfying, once you have mastered the basics of achieving an even coverage. Most of the disappointing results achieved by beginners stem from applying too much or too little finish to the surface.

Spraying a panel

To spray a vertically mounted panel, adjust the gun to produce a vertical, fan-shaped spray pattern.

1 Making a straight pass
With the gun aimed to one side of the panel, squeeze the trigger, then make one continuous pass across the work. Don't release the trigger until the spray pattern clears the opposite side of the panel.

Flex your wrist so that the gun is pointing directly at the work throughout the pass, and keep the nozzle about 200mm (8in) from the surface. Don't swing the gun in an arc, even if it seems easier, as you won't coat the panel evenly.

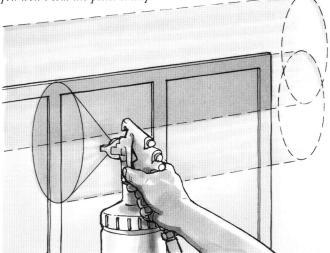

2 Overlapping passes
Make a return pass in the opposite direction so that the spray pattern overlaps the first pass by about 50 per cent. Make similar overlapping passes until you have coated the entire panel.

Spraying a table top

It is probably best to remove a table from its underframe and lay it horizontal on your turntable. Spray the underside first, and when that is dry, turn the top over.

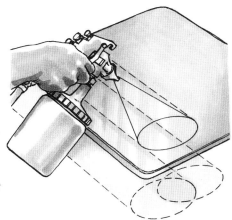

Coating the surface evenly
Spray the edges first, and then make overlapping passes to coat the table top, holding the gun at 45 degrees to the surface. It is best to work away from your body; and take care not to accidentally strike the work with the paint canister that is mounted below some styles of gun.

Finishing legs and rails

If you are finishing a chair or table underframe, always spray the inside of the rails and legs first.

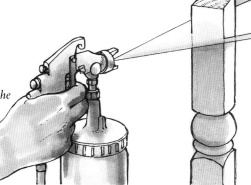

Spraying square legs
When spraying a square leg, you can cover two surfaces simultaneously by aiming the gun at the corner of the leg.

Spraying inside a cupboard

Finish the interior of a cupboard before you spray the outside.

Planning a sequence
Choose a convenient sequence that deals with each panel in turn. For example, start with the top panel, then spray down one side and across the back panel. Treat the remaining side panel next, and finish by spraying the bottom one.

STENCILLING

Stencilling is a centuries-old method of decorating walls and floors, as well as items of furniture. Border patterns are to be found on table tops, for example, and central motifs are used to embellish door panels, drawer fronts and chair backs. You can either cut your own stencils to restore existing worn paintwork, or buy ready-made stencils to paint cheap items in a folk-art style.

Stencils

Craft shops offer a wide selection of stencils with traditional patterns and motifs cut from oiled card or transparent acetate. Blank sheets of the same materials are available if you want to design your own stencils, or you can buy printed stencils that you can cut out yourself. Multicoloured patterns are made using two or more matching stencils.

Stencil brushes

Use special brushes with square-cut fillings of short bristles to stipple paint onto the surface. You may need a range of brushes, depending on the scale of the stencil, and it pays to use one brush for each colour.

Stencilling coordinates disparate styles of furniture

CUTTING MAT

STENCIL PAINTS

ARTISTS' ACRYLIC PAINTS

CRAFT KNIFE

PLASTIC STENCILS

STENCIL BRUSHES

Revive a damaged table by stencilling a painted border

Paints

Just about any paint can be used for stencilling but, apart from specialist stencil paints, perhaps the best are tubes of acrylic artists' paints. They are available in small quantities in a wide range of colours and, more importantly, they dry quickly.

It is a good idea to choose a limited range of muted colours rather than bright garish ones, and applying them in graded tones will create the appearance of aged, handcrafted work. Mix paints to a creamy consistency.

You can stencil directly onto unfinished wood sealed with thinned matt varnish or sanding sealer. Alternatively, you can apply a base coat of water-based household acrylic paint or conventional solvent-based paint, using one with a matt or semi-matt (eggshell) finish.

If you decide to stencil onto an already-painted surface, it is important to clean the paintwork first by washing it down with sugar soap, to remove traces of grease. Allow the paint to dry thoroughly before stencilling.

Making stencils

To recreate a pattern, use a pencil to trace the original and transfer the design to a sheet of stencil material. When using transparent acetate, trace from the drawing, using a fine felt–tip pen charged with compatible ink. To copy onto oiled card, lay your pencil tracing face-down on the stencil and draw over the linework to transfer the pattern to the card. Make sure the stencil has a generous border all round the design. You can use similar methods to make a stencil from your own design.

Cutting the stencil

Lay the stencil on a plastic cutting mat, or use a new sheet of card. Cutting on toughened glass keeps stencil edges crisp, but the glass blunts knife blades rapidly.

Use a craft knife or scalpel, turning the stencil rather than twisting the blade to follow the lines.

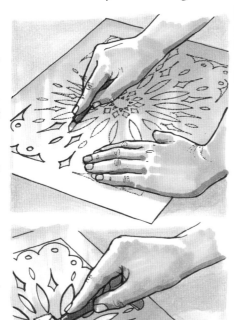

Repairing a bridge

Detailed stencils are reinforced by leaving narrow strips of paper to bridge the gaps. If you sever a bridge or crack an acetate stencil, repair it with self-adhesive tape on both sides, trimming the tape flush with the cut edges.

Registering stencils

To apply each colour of a multicoloured pattern, make a series of separate stencils.

When using oiled-card stencils, punch holes through all of them in the same place so that you can draw registration marks on the wood or back-ground with a soft pencil. Erase these marks when the painting is complete.

Acetate stencils are transparent – register them by tracing selected shapes in ink on the plastic.

Stencilling with a brush

Secure the stencil to the workpiece with masking tape; the stencil must be held completely flat along its length, or the paint will creep under the cut edges.

1 Applying the colour

Dip just the tip of the stencilling brush in a saucer of paint and blot the brush on a paper towel until the bristles are almost dry. Stipple paint around the edges of each cutout shape, and then fill in the middle. Gradually build up the colour, grading the tone as required; the paint will always look darker when the stencil is removed.

2 Lifting the stencil

Holding one edge of the stencil firmly on the work, peel back the opposite edge to check your progress. When you have finished applying one colour, remove the stencil and wipe it clean with a damp rag. Don't overlay stencilling until the paint is dry, but you can transfer the stencil to another part of the workpiece.

3 Protecting stencilling

Leave the paintwork to dry overnight, then apply two protective coats of matt or eggshell varnish.

GILDING

Repairing items gilded with real gold leaf is not recommended for the amateur. Not only does it require considerable time and practice to become proficient, but the materials are costly and you need a number of specialized tools. In the long run, it makes economic and practical sense to employ a professional gilder.

However, many so-called gilded items are merely covered with a brass alloy or some form of gold paint or varnish. Base-metal leaf is about a quarter of the price of gold, and handling it is not as demanding. There are also a number of products with which you can retouch inexpensive picture frames and mirrors.

CLEAR LACQUER
FINISHING LIQUID
READY-MADE GESSO
GILT CREAM
FILLING WAX
WAX CRAYONS
FONTENAY BASE
GILT VARNISH
METAL LEAF

Retouching dilapidated frames

It is not always advisable to refinish an old frame just because it is showing signs of wear. Even cheap frames improve in appearance once their original shiny finish has mellowed and the dark base colour shows through on the high points. These are qualities worth preserving, though you might want to disguise scratches, and patch holes or chipped mouldings.

Gilt wax sticks are ideal fillers, and softer wax crayons are marketed in sets comprising a range of gold colours and tones for touching in scratched frames.

Hiding scratches
Rub the crayon across the scratch until the red or white base colour is obliterated, then gently scrape the wax off the surface with flexible plastic . Try mixing colours to make a close match. If this does not quite work, smear the filled scratch with a little gilt cream on your fingertip.

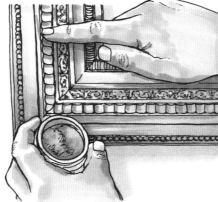

Filling holes
To patch a hole or rebuild chipped moulding, cut a pea-size piece of filling wax and put it on a radiator to soften. You can also knead two waxes together to achieve a good match. Press the soft wax into the hole and smooth it level with a penknife or your thumbnail. Finish with gilt cream.

Refinishing gold-coloured frames

While rummaging through junk shops or market stalls, look out for old picture frames that can be given a new lease of life, using a combination of gilt finishes. They may have been originally gilded but overpainted later, to fit in with modern taste. Use the same materials if you want to 'gild' a new frame.

Preparation is important for any finish, but gilding looks particularly cheap unless it is applied to an immaculately prepared surface. Rub down and fill the grain, or smooth a painted frame with wet-and-dry paper.

1 Applying Fontenay base
Fontenay base both seals and provides the traditional dark-red undercoat. Paint it onto the surface and leave to dry hard, then rub down lightly with 0000-grade wire wool or very fine silicon-carbide paper. A second coat may be required for the right depth of colour.

2 Applying gilt cream
Gilt cream is a soft waxy paste in a range of gold colours. Rub it onto the surface with your fingertip or a soft cloth, using circular strokes to spread the paste evenly. Finish with straight parallel strokes. Use an old toothbrush to rub cream into carvings and mouldings.

3 Burnishing and protecting

Leave gilt cream to harden for at least 12 hours, then burnish the surface with a soft cloth. Only rub hard if you intend to show the red base on the high points. If you don't like the result, apply more cream. Gilt cream provides a permanent finish, similar to wax polish; protect it by painting on special gilt-finishing liquid, which will give an extra-glossy finish.

Using gilt varnish

Gold-coloured varnish will gild a frame quickly. It may not be as satisfactory as using a gilt cream, but it's ideal for picking out separate slip mouldings or small sections of the frame itself. For a rich finish, apply gilt cream over a coat of gilt varnish.

Applying the varnish

Prepare the surface and paint it with Fontenay base. Use a soft paintbrush to apply gilt varnish, taking care not to leave a streaky finish. Use a pointed artists' brush to varnish small sections.

Ageing a gilt finish

If a new gilt finish looks a little too 'raw' for your taste, give it a worn appearance by rubbing the high points vigorously with a soft cloth until the red undercoat begins to show through. If necessary, use 0000-grade wire wool, but abrade very gently.

Rubbing with dark wax polish

To 'age' a new gilt finish, rub on dark, 'antique' wax polish with your fingertip. Burnish with a soft cloth to remove wax from the high points and leave a dark-coloured residue in deeper crevices and mouldings. Apply coloured wax over gilt cream, then coat with gilt-finishing liquid.

Gilding with metal leaf

Metal leaf, or common leaf, is an inexpensive substitute for genuine gold leaf. It is an alloy of base metals available as very thin 100mm (4in) squares, bound in books of 25 sheets. It is somewhat easier to apply than gold leaf, but must be protected with a varnish or 'glaze' to prevent discoloration.

Metal leaf has been employed for centuries for work where the price of gold was prohibitive, so recreating a gilt frame with base metal is perfectly acceptable in terms of authentic restoration.

Preparing a wood surface

Make sure you eliminate any blemishes and sand a wooden frame as smooth as possible. Wipe it with white spirit to remove any traces of grease before you apply a traditional gesso undercoat. Professional restorers often make their own, but a ready-made synthetic gesso is ideal for metal leaf. It is available as a dark red paste for gold-coloured leaf, but there is also a white gesso for silver leaf. Gesso can also be used as a glue to repair old pieces of broken gesso.

1 Applying the gesso

Warm ready-made gesso in a bain-marie or glue pot until it is liquid enough to be brushed onto the surface. Don't let excess paste collect in carved areas or mouldings. Let the gesso dry overnight, then rub down lightly with fine wet-and-dry paper. You should apply four or five coats to achieve a smooth surface ready for gilding.

2 Sealing gesso

Use a rubber to seal the surface with an application of shellac mixed half-and-half with methylated spirit. If necessary, you can erase any blemishes after the sealant is completely dry, by rubbing them very gently with fine, 0000-grade wire wool dipped in soapy water. Thoroughly dry the surface with a soft cloth.

Sizing the surface

Apply a coat of proprietary quick size, which serves as an adhesive for the metal leaf. As the leaf must be applied at just the right moment, it pays to divide a large item into easily manageable sections in such a way that joins will not show.

1 Painting with size

Brush on an even coat of size, laying off lightly with parallel strokes. Paint up to all edges, and make sure that there are no runs or similar blemishes in the size.

2 Testing the size

It is important that the size is firm but has just enough adhesion to hold the leaf in place. Work in accordance with the manufacturer's recommendations, but also check by gently touching the surface with your knuckles. It is ready for gilding when the surface feels very slightly tacky but does not show the marks where your knuckles touched.

Gilding with metal leaf

Before you handle metal leaf, dust your hands with talcum powder to prevent the leaf disintegrating in your fingers.

1 Preparing metal leaf

Prepare a book of metal leaf by removing its outer covers and by cutting off the spine with scissors. With its tissue backing intact, cut each individual leaf into suitable squares or rectangles to fit the workpiece.

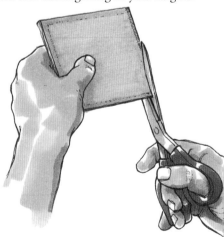

2 Applying metal leaf

Using both hands, carefully pick up each strip of cut leaf and lay it face down on the sized surface. Rub it down firmly with your fingertips before peeling off the tissue backing.

3 Joining pieces of leaf

Apply the next strip of leaf in the same way, overlapping the piece you have just laid by about 3mm (⅛in). Apply a third overlapping strip and so on, until you have covered at least one sized section. Size adjacent sections in turn and apply metal leaf until the entire workpiece is gilded.

4 Patching with skewings

Remove overlapping sections of leaf and blend the joins by brushing them with an oxhair brush. Brush only in the direction of the overlaps, placing a piece of card beneath the workpiece to collect the scrap leaf, or skewings. Pick up skewings on the tip of the bristles and brush them onto any tiny areas of exposed base.

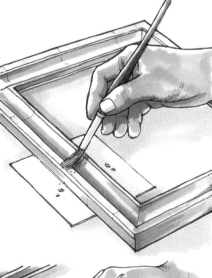

5 Burnishing metal leaf

The following day, burnish the leaf gently with cotton wool until the metal shines softly. To prevent tarnishing, coat the gilded surface lightly with a clear metal lacquer.

CLEANING AND FINISHING METAL

There are relatively few pieces of furniture made from metal. You may be lucky enough to pick up a cast-iron garden seat or table, though they are likely to be expensive items these days, and there are similar pieces constructed from wrought iron. Apart from the tubular-steel furniture designed in the 1920s and 30s, you are unlikely to come across any interior furniture made from metal. However, a knowledge of how to clean and polish different metals will prove invaluable when you are faced with the restoration of painted or rusty door handles, strap hinges, castors and other hardware.

Stripping painted metal

You can have large items dipped or even sandblasted without any of the potential disasters that might befall wooden furniture. If you want to do the work yourself, try using one of the proprietary chemical paint removers, though stripping an ornate piece of furniture is liable to be time-consuming. However, there is no point in trying to use a hot-air gun – the metal merely serves to dissipate the heat.

1 Stripping small metal items

Remove overpainted door handles, escutcheons and other hardware, and place them in a shallow foil dish. Pour a fluid chemical stripper over the metal and use a small paintbrush to stipple the paint remover onto the hardware until every surface is covered.

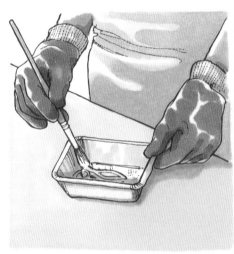

2 Cleaning off softened paint

Wearing protective gloves, wipe off the softened paint with balls of 0000-grade wire wool – don't use a coarse grade in case the hardware has been plated with a soft metal. Apply more stripper if there are traces of paint adhering, then when the metal is perfectly clean, wash it in hot water and dry gently with paper towels.

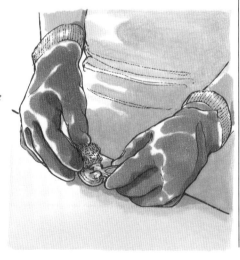

Cleaning tarnished brass

When left exposed to the air, brass turns a dull-brown colour. The layer of oxidation is usually very thin and can be removed easily with a proprietary metal polish, but it sometimes helps to wash heavily tarnished brass with a natural acid.

Cleaning brass

Cut a lemon in half and sprinkle it with salt. Rub the metal with the salted flesh of the fruit until the tarnishing softens.

An alternative method is to mix a tablespoon of vinegar with one of salt in half a pint (280ml) of hot water. Dip 0000-grade wire wool in this solution, and rub to remove the corrosion.

Polishing brass

Having cleaned brass hardware with a natural acid, burnish it with a long-term polish. If you want to protect brass from further corrosion, paint each item with a clear lacquer that is specially formulated for metal.

Painting iron furniture

Steel and iron door furniture or drawer handles can be left unprotected indoors, provided the atmosphere is dry. If hinges begin to show shines of corrosion, wipe them occasionally with an oily rag or smear them lightly with petroleum jelly.

Protecting iron furniture

Iron garden furniture needs to be protected from the elements, or it will rust in a very short time. Coat the bare metal with a rust-inhibitive primer followed by a good solvent-based undercoat and paint.

CHAIRS AND BENCHES

CHAIRS HAVE FASCINATED DESIGNERS and makers for centuries, and continue to do so today. Perhaps more than any other piece of furniture, a chair tests the skills of its creator, for it must closely relate to the human form to be comfortable, be constructed to resist the considerable forces placed upon it in use, and be visually interesting and attractive.

Generations of furniture makers have produced a vast number of pieces that present a seemingly endless choice for the restorer. Some were successful solutions, others not, but each has a place in the history of chair-making, and examples that have survived the ravages of time deserve to be preserved.

CHAIR CONSTRUCTION

For all their diversity of style, chairs are for the most part principally made of wood, and broadly use one of three methods of construction: frame construction, stick construction and bentwood.

The development of cast iron in the nineteenth century and bent steel in the twentieth century gave designers the opportunity to develop alternative methods of construction, but the older, 'traditional' techniques based on wood still prevail. Typical examples of chair designs are illustrated here, and show the methods of construction and the problems you are likely to encounter.

FRAME CHAIRS

The typical frame chair has seat rails jointed into the front and rear legs. Mortise-and-tenon joints are most common, but dowel joints may also be found, particularly in machine-made reproduction chairs.

The strength of the chair is dictated by the size of the joints and, to some extent, by the section and shape of the component. In order to counter the considerable strain exerted on the seat frame, the rails are usually set on edge, to give a longer vertical shoulder against the lever action of the legs. In some cases, the seat rails are joined together to make a flat

SPLAT-BACK FRAME CHAIR

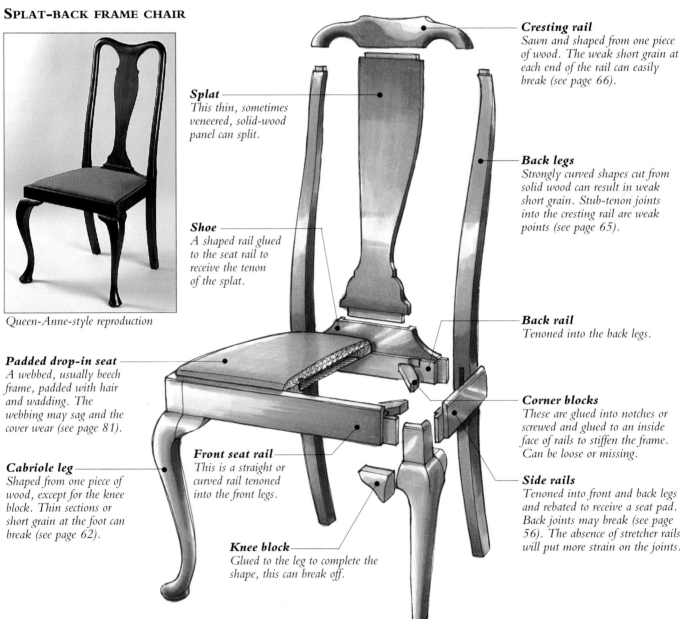

Queen-Anne-style reproduction

Splat
This thin, sometimes veneered, solid-wood panel can split.

Shoe
A shaped rail glued to the seat rail to receive the tenon of the splat.

Padded drop-in seat
A webbed, usually beech frame, padded with hair and wadding. The webbing may sag and the cover wear (see page 81).

Cabriole leg
Shaped from one piece of wood, except for the knee block. Thin sections or short grain at the foot can break (see page 62).

Front seat rail
This is a straight or curved rail tenoned into the front legs.

Knee block
Glued to the leg to complete the shape, this can break off.

Cresting rail
Sawn and shaped from one piece of wood. The weak short grain at each end of the rail can easily break (see page 66).

Back legs
Strongly curved shapes cut from solid wood can result in weak short grain. Stub-tenon joints into the cresting rail are weak points (see page 65).

Back rail
Tenoned into the back legs.

Corner blocks
These are glued into notches or screwed and glued to an inside face of rails to stiffen the frame. Can be loose or missing.

Side rails
Tenoned into front and back legs and rebated to receive a seat pad. Back joints may break (see page 56). The absence of stretcher rails will put more strain on the joints.

frame, thus creating a lighter-looking chair. The seat is usually caned or upholstered with a shallow seat pad. These chairs are not very strong and are most often reserved for occasional use, for instance in a bedroom.

Stretcher rails set at a low level between the legs help to resist the racking forces applied to the chair.

Frame chairs which feature strongly curved lines and carved features are likely to be more difficult to repair than simple and unornamented chairs. They will require large sections of wood from which to cut the shaped part.

BALLOON-BACK FRAME CHAIR

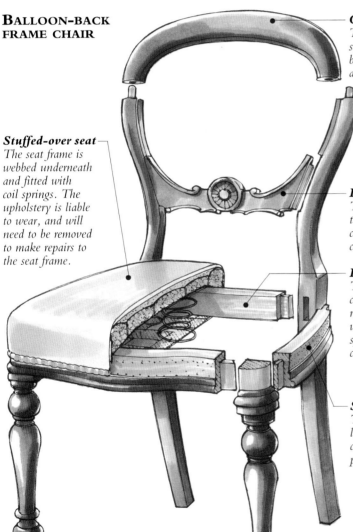

Stuffed-over seat
The seat frame is webbed underneath and fitted with coil springs. The upholstery is liable to wear, and will need to be removed to make repairs to the seat frame.

Turned legs
Shaped on a lathe, these are weak where the wood is reduced in diameter. Brass socket castors are sometimes fitted, and these can break.

Design variations
Typical examples of frame chairs.
1 Chippendale style with padded upholstered seat.
2 Victorian double-C balloon-back with caned seat.
3 Straight-backed 1930s dining chair with drop-in seat.

Cresting rail
This is sawn from one piece of solid wood and doweled to the back legs. The short weak grain at the ends may break.

Back rail
Tenoned into the back of the legs, this may be carved as shown or curved in a similar way to the cresting rail to form a hoop shape.

Back seat rail
Tenoned into the back legs and covered with upholstery, the seat rails are prone to infestation by wood-boring insects. They also split due to nail holes from re-covering work.

Side seat rails
Tenoned into the back and front legs. The rails may be completely covered or made to show a polished beading.

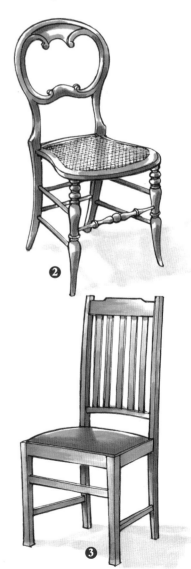

STICK CHAIRS

Stick chairs, also known as Windsor chairs, can be identified by their unique construction, which uses turned spindles and 'sticks' jointed into a solid wooden seat. Made in rural areas, these distinctly country chairs took on many localized forms. They became an important influence in North America, where a number of different styles developed.

The legs were usually turned spindles, but some featured simple cabriole-style front legs. It was the style of the back, however, that determined one type from another; examples were known as wheel-back, comb-back, fan-back, hoop-back and bow-back. Typical English versions used beech for the legs and spindles, elm for the seat and ash or yew for the bows. Some chairs were made from mahogany. In America maple, birch or beech were used for the legs, ash or hickory for the sticks, pine or poplar for the seat and ash, oak or beech for the bows. Chairs were sometimes painted red, black, yellow and green, a feature popular in America.

Ladder-back chairs, so-called from the use of the horizontal slats that form the back, are similarly constructed, but have straight, turned legs and rails, and caned or rush seats.

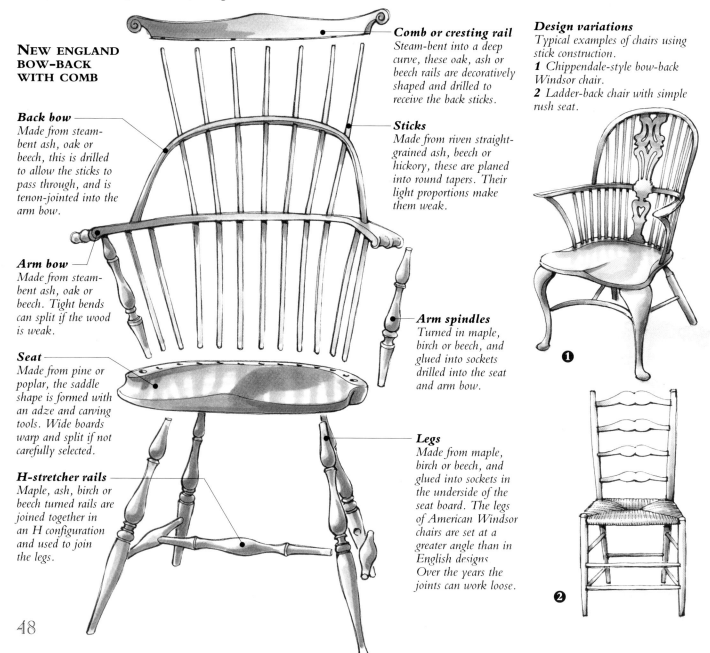

NEW ENGLAND BOW-BACK WITH COMB

Back bow
Made from steam-bent ash, oak or beech, this is drilled to allow the sticks to pass through, and is tenon-jointed into the arm bow.

Arm bow
Made from steam-bent ash, oak or beech. Tight bends can split if the wood is weak.

Seat
Made from pine or poplar, the saddle shape is formed with an adze and carving tools. Wide boards warp and split if not carefully selected.

H-stretcher rails
Maple, ash, birch or beech turned rails are joined together in an H configuration and used to join the legs.

Comb or cresting rail
Steam-bent into a deep curve, these oak, ash or beech rails are decoratively shaped and drilled to receive the back sticks.

Sticks
Made from riven straight-grained ash, beech or hickory, these are planed into round tapers. Their light proportions make them weak.

Arm spindles
Turned in maple, birch or beech, and glued into sockets drilled into the seat and arm bow.

Legs
Made from maple, birch or beech, and glued into sockets in the underside of the seat board. The legs of American Windsor chairs are set at a greater angle than in English designs Over the years the joints can work loose.

Design variations
Typical examples of chairs using stick construction.
1 Chippendale-style bow-back Windsor chair.
2 Ladder-back chair with simple rush seat.

❶

❷

BENTWOOD CHAIRS

The classic bentwood chairs that graced the cafés of the world in the late nineteenth century were the creation of Michael Thonet. Made from steam-bent, turned rods of beech, they were the first truly mass-produced chairs. With their sinuous curved forms and light construction, they were cheaper to produce than traditional jointed-frame chairs and avoided the short-grain problems associated with shaped solid wood.

The frames were made up from separate bentwood units, usually screwed and bolted together to form a strong, if slightly flexible, chair. The seats were either caned or fitted with decoratively pressed plywood panels or upholstered pads. They were perhaps the first 'knock-down' chairs, as they were often shipped in parts for assembly by the purchaser.

The manufacturing system was soon adapted to produce a wide range of furniture, which included side chairs, armchairs, settees and rocking chairs, as well as tables and hat stands. Some designs are produced today, but you can still find old bentwood chairs at bargain prices. If the main sections are beyond repair, it should be possible to salvage 'spare parts' from another, damaged chair.

THONET BENTWOOD CHAIR

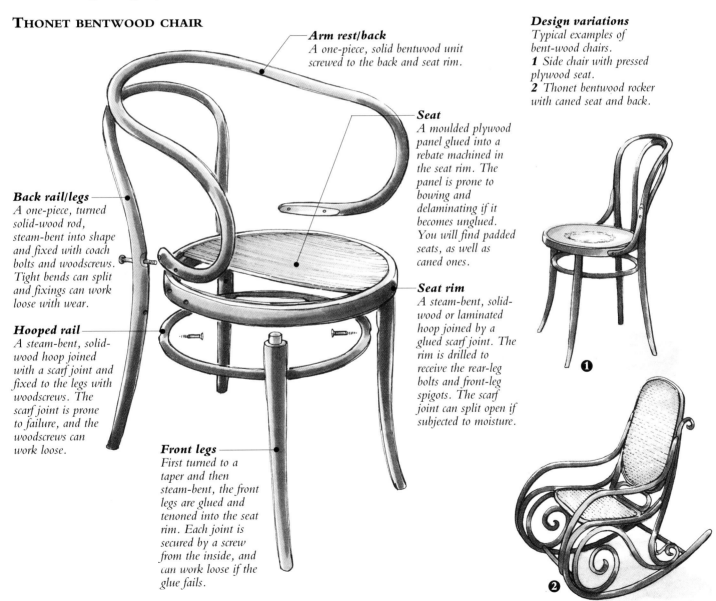

Arm rest/back
A one-piece, solid bentwood unit screwed to the back and seat rim.

Back rail/legs
A one-piece, turned solid-wood rod, steam-bent into shape and fixed with coach bolts and woodscrews. Tight bends can split and fixings can work loose with wear.

Hooped rail
A steam-bent, solid-wood hoop joined with a scarf joint and fixed to the legs with woodscrews. The scarf joint is prone to failure, and the woodscrews can work loose.

Front legs
First turned to a taper and then steam-bent, the front legs are glued and tenoned into the seat rim. Each joint is secured by a screw from the inside, and can work loose if the glue fails.

Seat
A moulded plywood panel glued into a rebate machined in the seat rim. The panel is prone to bowing and delaminating if it becomes unglued. You will find padded seats, as well as caned ones.

Seat rim
A steam-bent, solid-wood or laminated hoop joined by a glued scarf joint. The rim is drilled to receive the rear-leg bolts and front-leg spigots. The scarf joint can split open if subjected to moisture.

Design variations
Typical examples of bent-wood chairs.
1 Side chair with pressed plywood seat.
2 Thonet bentwood rocker with caned seat and back.

❶

❷

METAL CHAIRS

Wrought iron had long been used to produce hand-made furniture, but it was not until the Industrial Revolution that metal, in the form of cast iron, became a viable material for mass-produced goods. Iron founders were able to produce both massive and intricately decorative castings in any number of matching parts. The weight of cast iron limited its use primarily to garden furniture, but some designs are now reproduced in cast aluminium.

Cast iron is strong in compression but not in tension. Steel, a later development, has great tensile strength and can be manufactured into relatively lightweight tubular sections. The designers of the Bauhaus school in the early twentieth century used bent tubing to create chair structures, harnessing the strength of steel to produce cantilevered frames. These chairs soon became design classics.

Metal furniture is generally tougher than that made of wood, but cast iron is relatively brittle and will crack if struck hard. Steel furniture, on the other hand, is more resilient, and components are more likely to bend than break. Metals are generally rot-proof, but may corrode if not protected with a surface coating, usually paint or chromium plating.

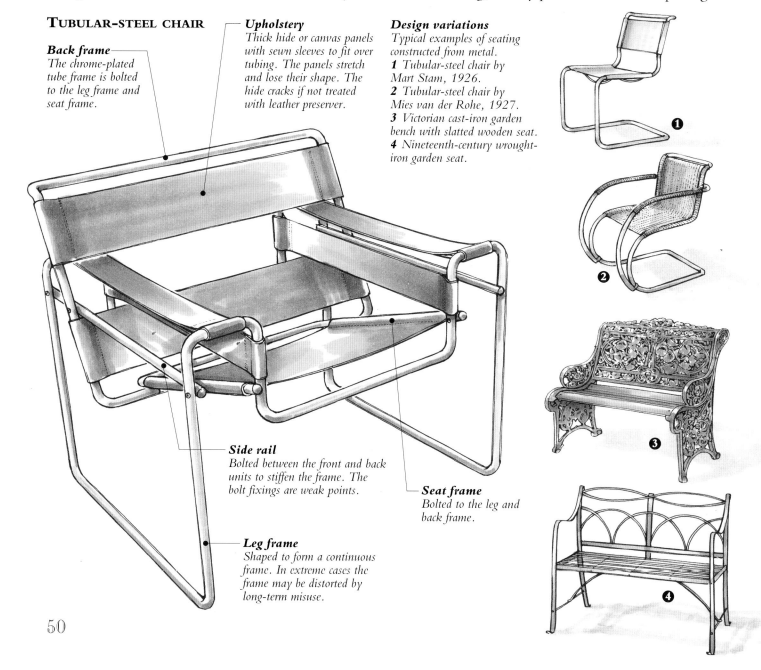

TUBULAR-STEEL CHAIR

Back frame
The chrome-plated tube frame is bolted to the leg frame and seat frame.

Upholstery
Thick hide or canvas panels with sewn sleeves to fit over tubing. The panels stretch and lose their shape. The hide cracks if not treated with leather preserver.

Design variations
Typical examples of seating constructed from metal.
1 Tubular-steel chair by Mart Stam, 1926.
2 Tubular-steel chair by Mies van der Rohe, 1927.
3 Victorian cast-iron garden bench with slatted wooden seat.
4 Nineteenth-century wrought-iron garden seat.

Side rail
Bolted between the front and back units to stiffen the frame. The bolt fixings are weak points.

Seat frame
Bolted to the leg and back frame.

Leg frame
Shaped to form a continuous frame. In extreme cases the frame may be distorted by long-term misuse.

MENDING LOOSE JOINTS

The condition of a chair frame is to a large extent dependent on the amount and type of use it has sustained, as well as the quality of the materials and manufacture. In the course of time an old frame-constructed chair will develop loose joints, caused by a weakening of the glue and the inevitable strain on the frame. Loose joints should be attended to promptly, as the wood forming the joint is likely to be compressed locally as the chair is racked, thus making the fit worse.

The splayed components and tapered socket joints of Windsor-style chairs tend to absorb stresses better than those of more conventional frame chairs. Shrinkage of the wood, however, will cause these joints to weaken, and it is not uncommon for the turned stretcher rails to work loose from the legs. Only the front legs of a bentwood chair are glued into the seat frame – all the other joints are screwed or bolted – and these can work loose, leading to worn fixings holes.

Regluing joints

It is usually possible to spring the frame to work or inject glue into a weak joint, but it is better to take the frame apart to make a thorough repair.

1 Gluing a stretcher rail

Spring the legs of a stick chair apart, and prop them with a piece of wood. Cut V-notches in the ends of the prop to help locate it. If the end of the rail has been crushed and is a loose fit in the leg socket, wrap it in a wet cloth to swell the grain. When it is suitably swollen, allow it to dry, then apply glue to the joint and clamp the frame.

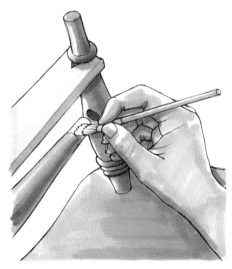

2 Trimming the rail

If the joint is only slightly loose, just trimming the end of the rail will allow it to sit snugly in the tapered hole.

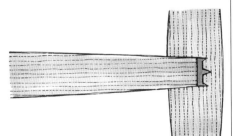

Gluing a seat rail

The mortise-and-tenon joints between the back legs and the side seat rails of a frame chair are particularly prone to stress. If the back frame feels loose, this is an indication that the joints are weak and need attention.

Although it is preferable to dismantle the joints, do not strip an upholstered seat unless it is necessary.

1 Injecting glue into a joint

Working from the underside, drill a hole into the leg or rails from inside the frame and inject glue into the joint. Clamp the frame until set.

2 Reinforcing a corner

Frame chairs are usually fitted with corner blocks to support the joints. If the original blocks are loose, remove them and clean up the faces, then reglue and screw them back into place. If blocks were not fitted, make them from hardwood about 25mm (1in) thick. Mark and cut them to fit the angle, and drill countersunk holes for the fixings screws. Glue and fix them in place.

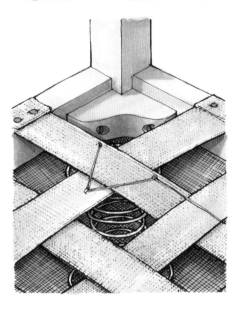

Bolted joints

The back-leg assembly of a typical bentwood chair is fixed to the seat rim with coach bolts. The joint is held tight by a square nut, prevented from unscrewing by a tabbed washer.

Tightening the bolt

If the joint is loose, perhaps because of shrinking wood, straighten the washer tab with a screwdriver and tighten the nut with a spanner. Do not overtighten, as the head of the bolt can crush into the wood. Bend the tab back into place to lock the nut.

Screwed joints

The back rails, arm rests, side brackets and hooped rails of bentwood chairs are fixed with either exposed or plugged woodscrews. Simply retightening the screws may be sufficient to secure the joint. If the fixing has failed, for instance between the hooped rail and front legs, you can try fitting a larger-gauge screw, but if the hole has stripped it will need to be filled and redrilled.

1 Filling a screw hole

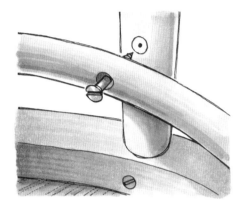

Remove the hoop, or the leg if it is loose. Glue a short length of dowel in the old screw hole, and trim the end flush when set. Drill a pilot hole exactly in the centre of the plug and reassemble the frame, using new screws if these are needed.

2 Tightening a plugged screw

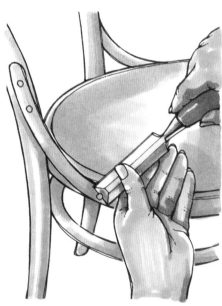

Where the fixings are on the outside of the chair frame, the screw holes are often hidden by wooden plugs. Carefully chisel these out with a small gouge or drill them with a dowel bit, and tighten up the screws. Use a plug-cutting bit to make neat side-grain plugs from a matching piece of wood, and glue them in place. When set, chisel the plugs flush, colour them to match the frame, and finish as required.

Screwed seat frames

Chairs with caned seats often have the seat frame glued and screwed into notches cut into the back legs. This fitting has a tendency to fail.

Tightening the joint

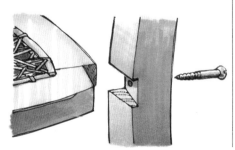

If the screw has stripped its thread, clean and reglue the joint, and replace the screw with one of a larger gauge, or plug the hole and redrill.

DISMANTLING A CHAIR

In order to carry out structural repairs, it is often easier to dismantle the chair first. However, if part of the frame is really secure, leave that part intact, unless it prevents another repair being made. Label the joints with patches of self-adhesive tape so you can quickly identify the parts when reassembling.

Secondary fixings

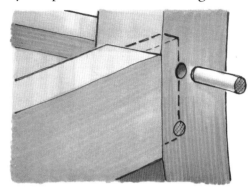

Joints are usually designed to be secure with glue alone, but some may be pinned with cross-dowels to reinforce the joints. Drill out any dowel pins, using a bit of the appropriate size. Punch a centre mark on the dowel to guide the drill tip.

Plugged fittings

Screws may be used, and are often covered with wooden plugs. Remove the screw from a plugged fitting when it is exposed.

Removing nails

Nails which were used to make a crude repair to a weak joint may be hidden with filler. Look for any shallow sink marks around the joint, where filler may have been used. Pull out accessible nails with a a pair of pincers.

Making a hollow drill

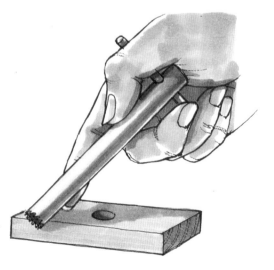

A hollow drill will clear wood from around sunken nails, so you can remove them with pliers. Make saw cuts across the end of a short length of 12mm (½in) steel tubing. Shape 'saw teeth' between the cuts with a fine file. Fit a tommy bar and use a guide block for hand-work, or alternatively use a drill press.

Metal brackets

Metal straps and brackets may be screwed to the frames to reinforce weak joints. Unless they are neatly fitted and discreetly placed, it is better to remove them and repair the joints and frame members.

Seat frames

Remove any upholstery that may prevent you dismantling the chair. Study the construction of the frame to determine the best way to take it apart. The back and front leg frames are usually made as complete subassemblies, and are removed first.

Dismantling a chair frame

Knock apart the weak joints of a chair with sharp taps from a hammer or a rubber mallet. Always hold a block of softwood between a hammer and the workpiece. Clamp the frame of the chair in a vice or onto the bench. To prevent racking the frame and binding the joints, work alternately from one side of the frame to the other.

Using fast-action cramps

It is possible to push the joints of a light frame apart with the help of fast-action cramps. Set the arms in reverse on the bar, and place the cramp between the opposing rails to apply the necessary force.

Using cramps on a single joint

For a single joint, hold the seat rail in the vice and apply the force between the bench top and the joint. A car jack could be used in a similar way.

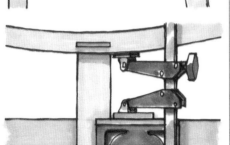

Back frames

Most chair frames have the back rails tenoned into the legs. The vertical splats or bars are usually stub-tenoned into the top rail and bottom rail, if fitted, or into the seat rail. Dismantle this type by removing the legs first.

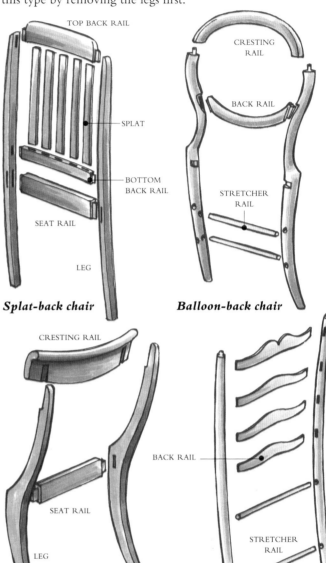

TOP BACK RAIL

CRESTING RAIL

SPLAT

BACK RAIL

BOTTOM BACK RAIL

SEAT RAIL

STRETCHER RAIL

LEG

Splat-back chair

Balloon-back chair

CRESTING RAIL

BACK RAIL

SEAT RAIL

STRETCHER RAIL

LEG

Empire-style chair

Ladder-back chair

Back-frame styles

Chairs with legs shaped into the back rail, such as balloon-backs, have a cresting rail stub-tenoned or doweled to the ends of the legs. The lower part of the hoop is tenoned into the sides of the legs. Remove the cresting rail, using pairs of shallow hardwood wedges to ease the joint apart. Take great care not to break the short grain around the joint. You may need to soften the glue first (see page 54).

If the single-curve cresting rails on Empire-style chairs are held by stopped dovetail housings, tap the underside edge of the back to release the joint. Similar-shape backs may be held with screws. The shaped rails of ladder-back chairs are housed in mortises in the back legs.

Releasing glued joints

Most old furniture is held together by animal glue, which is water-soluble and therefore reversible. If a glued joint needs to be dismantled but resists being tapped apart, apply wet rags around the joint until the glue softens. The application of steam speeds up the operation, particularly if it is introduced into the joint. Either operation is likely to affect the finish, which will have to be repaired.

Making a steam applicator

You can make a steam applicator by fitting a 150mm (6in) length of 3mm (⅛in) diameter aluminium or brass tubing through two wine-bottle corks. Attach one end of the tube to a length of silicone tubing, and fit this onto a length of the metal tubing fitted into a cork shaped to fit the spout of a domestic kettle. Both types of tubing can be purchased from model shops or some hardware stores.

Using a steam applicator
Drill a slightly oversize hole into the joint from inside the frame, and carefully introduce the steam around and into the joint with the applicator. Do not overfill the kettle, and wear protective gloves. After a few minutes, remove the applicator and tap the joint apart.

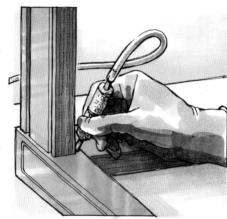

Heating the work

Dry heat, applied with a hair dryer, hot-air gun or electric heater, can also soften animal glues. This method is best suited to joints that are not surrounded by thick wood.

Applying the heat
Concentrate the heat on the joint in order to weaken the glue. Work the joint as the glue softens. You will need to make good the finish if it is not already stripped.

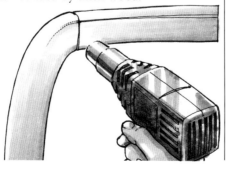

Using methylated spirit

Old animal glue can also be broken down by the application of methylated spirit. When it is applied into the wood by a hypodermic syringe, it can be used to release joints that would be damaged by other methods.

1 Preparing the joint
Where a joint has partly opened, methylated spirit can be easily applied into the joint. Where there is no gap, drill a discreet fine hole into the joint.

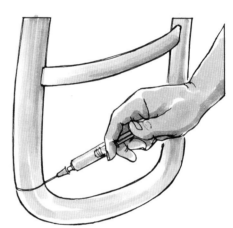

2 Injecting methylated spirit
Turn the work so that the liquid, aided by gravity, will run into the cavities of, for instance, a mortise joint. Inject the meths into the joint, to be absorbed by the wood. Do not flood the surface, as the meths will attack a shellac finish.

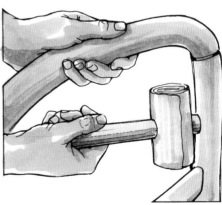

3 Loosening the joint
Continue to apply the meths periodically until the joint loosens as the glue begins to crystallize; this may take anything from five minutes to two hours to work. Rock the parts carefully to loosen them, then tap the joint apart.

Old repairs

An old chair may have been repaired in the past, and if this was carried out relatively recently, the restorer may have used one of the modern adhesives such as PVA woodworking glue, resin glue, or even an epoxy adhesive.

PVA glue, though not reversible, can be softened with water, which usually enables the joint to be knocked apart. Waterproof resin and epoxy glues cannot be softened, but if the joint was not thoroughly cleaned at the time of the repair, even small traces of the old animal glue may allow the joint to be weakened with the aid of steam or meths.

REPAIRING JOINTS

Chair joints are susceptible to wear and tear from the forces applied to the structure. Mortise-and-tenon joints are typically used for frame chairs. Early frames were not glued, relying on pegs and the close fit of the parts to hold them fast. This method was eventually superseded by glued joints as the designs and techniques became more refined. Dowel joints first appeared on chairs around the middle of the nineteenth century, and are now commonly used in the construction of this type of utilitarian framed furniture.

Joints starved of glue, exposed to damp or over-stressed will weaken, and movement will accelerate deterioration, eventually damaging the wood. Gap-filling glues may help, but refitting the joints may be necessary. Broken joints will need to be rebuilt.

Dowel joints

Dowels can be found in chair seat frames, in the ends of the back legs at the joint with a cresting rail, and possibly where an arm is fitted on a carver chair. Dowels are also sometimes used to replace a broken tenon. Dowel joints are strong, but it is possible for the dowels to shear if unduly stressed.

If the joint has failed due to loss of glue adhesion, clean as much old glue as possible off the parts and reglue the joint. The dowels will need to be remade if the joint is broken.

1 Mending dowel joints

If the broken dowel pegs cannot be pulled out with pliers, trim them flush with a saw. Find the centres of the dowels and drill them out, using a slightly undersize dowel bit. Pick out the remaining waste with a small gouge, to ensure that the original wood is not removed and the angle of the hole is not changed. Where possible, use a drill press to keep the bit true, and check the depth of the hole.

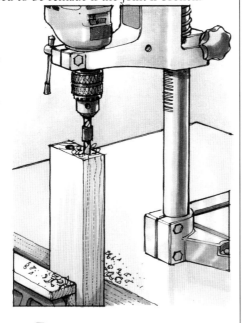

2 Preparing the dowels

Cut the doweling so that it finishes 2mm (1/16in) shorter than the combined length of the holes in each part. Chamfer the ends and cut a groove along the length of each dowel, to allow any air and excess glue to escape. Apply glue into the holes and to the shoulders, insert the dowels and finally clamp the joint (see page 62).

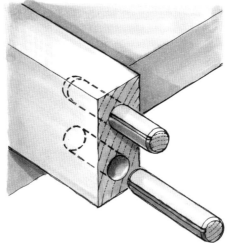

Worn mortise-and-tenons

The mortise-and-tenon joints between the seat rails and back frame are prone to racking. This can result in the side-grain edges of the tenon crushing against the tougher end grain of the mortise in the leg.

1 Retrimming the tenon

Cut across the line of the shoulder and then use a chisel to trim the worn edges of the tenon true.

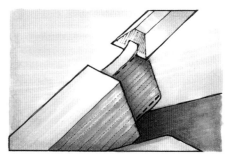

2 Trimming the repair

Glue oversized strips of the same wood to the prepared edges. When set, pare them down with a chisel to produce a tenon of the correct size.

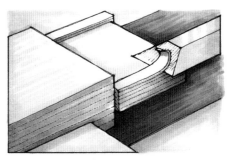

3 Reshaping the mortise

If the mortise has also become distorted, it can be squared up by chopping out the ends of the slot.

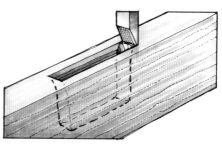

4 Trimming to size

Glue in new pieces of wood, with the grain following the length of the leg. When set, plane the surfaces flush and chop out the waste to make the required mortise.

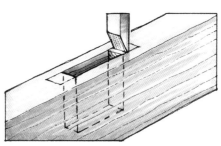

Broken mortise-and-tenons

Although a mortise-and-tenon is a strong joint, it is still possible for parts to fail. This may be due to insect infestation, naturally weak wood or excessive strain applied to the frame. Cut away the damaged wood, but try to retain as much of the original material as possible.

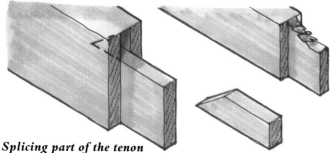

Splicing part of the tenon

Remove the damaged portion of the tenon with a saw, cutting it flush with the shoulder. Using a chisel no wider than the tenon, undercut the shoulder at an angle of 45 degrees. This allows new wood to be jointed into the rail without showing on the edge. Cut a new piece of matching wood to the thickness of the tenon, and shape it to fit the cut-out, leaving it oversize on width and length. Glue the wood in place and, when set, trim to size.

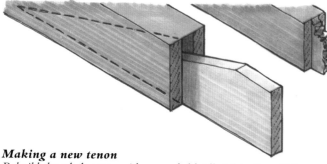

Making a new tenon

Rebuild the whole tenon with an angled bridle joint. Cut off the broken end of the tenon flush with the shoulders. Set a mortise gauge to the width of the tenon, and scribe the end and underside of the rail. Make the length of the bridle about three times the width of the tenon.

Set the wood in the vice at the required angle and carefully saw down the guide lines on the waste side, paring out the waste with a chisel. Cut a new tenon-piece slightly oversize on width and length, and glue into the rail. Trim to size when set.

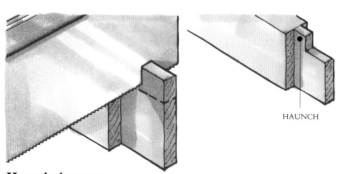

HAUNCH

Haunched tenons

If the tenon being repaired is haunched, rebuild the tenon as described and then mark and cut the haunch to fit the mortise.

Mitred ends

Where two rails are set at right angles to one another in the leg, the tenon ends are usually mitred where they meet. Set the rails at an angle in the vice and pare the ends of the tenons to 45 degrees.

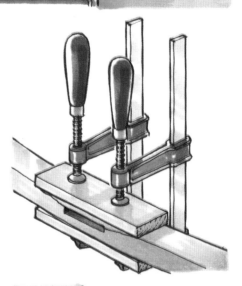

45°

Split mortise

Excess strain on a mortise that is set close to the surface of a component can sometimes result in the side splitting out. Repair this failure as soon as possible, to stop dirt getting into the break.

Work glue into the split and clamp it tightly. Place wood packing under the cramp heads to spread the clamping forces and also protect the surface of the wood.

Broken mortise

Where the wood from a split mortise is missing or the broken material will not fit together, new wood must be let in.

Mark out the area of the recess for the new wood, aiming to leave as much of the original as possible. Chop and pare out the waste up to the marked lines with a chisel, to leave a flat-bottomed housing. Cut and glue a patch of matching wood into place. When set, plane the surfaces flush, mark and chop out the mortise, then stain and finish.

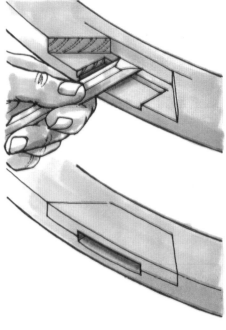

Stick-chair joints

The joints used on stick chairs are a cross between a mortise-and-tenon and a dowel. The turned end of one component (the tenon) is fitted into a through hole or stopped socket (the mortise) drilled in the other. If the tenon member is slack, it may be possible to tighten it with a wedge.

Although wedging helps secure a joint and may have been used originally for some joints, try to use other methods if at all possible, as they make joints difficult for future restorers to dismantle, and can cause splitting.

Through joints

The joints that pass through wood can be wedged securely from above. Saw a slot in the end of the tenoned member, stopping short of the shoulder line. Cut a 3mm (⅛in) hardwood wedge to the same width as the slot. Apply glue and assemble the joint, drive in the wedge and trim it flush when set.

Stopped joints

To wedge the joint in a stopped hole, first introduce the wedge into the slot. This method is known as fox-wedging. Saw the slot for the wedge. Apply glue to the joint and insert the wedge partly into the slot. Assemble the components and clamp up, forcing the wedge into the end and causing the tenon to spread in the hole. Use a web cramp to make assembly easier; it will accommodate the various angles and round shapes of the components.

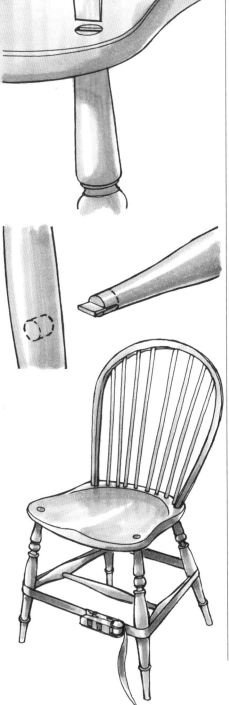

Bentwood hoop

The wood fibres of a bentwood chair have been artificially bent and will tend to straighten, causing components to lose their shape and weak joints to spring open.

Mending a scarf joint

If the scarf joint of a bentwood hoop should fail, clean up the meeting faces with warm water, then wrap damp cloths over the joint for a few hours to soften the wood fibres. Make shaped softwood clamping blocks to follow the contour of the rail, and wax the block surfaces to prevent them sticking. Apply glue to the joint and clamp the wood back into shape.

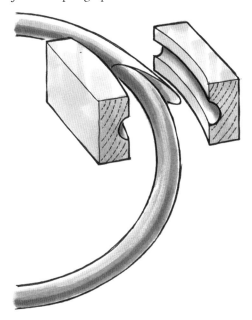

Repairing a front-leg joint

The front legs of bentwood chairs are glued into holes drilled into the seat rim. Screws or blocks fitted inside the rim may also be used to reinforce the joint.

Making a repair

If the joints of the chair frame are allowed to move, the strain on the front legs can make the top joints work loose. If the glue has failed, simply reglue the joint, but if it is very loose, pack out the leg, using veneer wrapped round the spigot at the top of the leg. Glue the veneer with the grain running vertically; trim to fit when set.

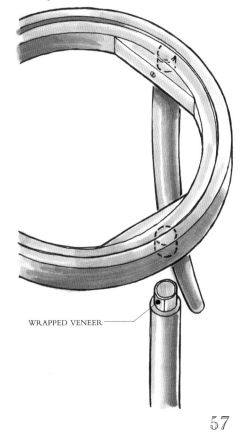

WRAPPED VENEER

REPAIRING LEGS

The main function of a chair is simply to support a person in a comfortable sitting position, but chair makers have always sought to make chairs attractive, either by the use of proportion and materials, or by elaborate decorative treatments.

Although dining chairs are mainly seen from the back, they are designed to be viewed from the front in the same manner as side chairs, which are placed against a wall. The front legs and chair back are often ornately worked, while the lower parts of the back legs and frame are left plain.

Chair legs can break because of naturally weak wood, infestation by woodworm, or from excessive shaping, all of which can result in weak sections. The method of repair will depend on whether they are turned, square-cut or carved.

Short-grain repair

Legs that have been cut from a wide board to produce a strongly curved shape will suffer from weak short grain. If the break is clean and provides a suitable gluing area, just bond the broken surfaces together.

Gluing a clean break

Apply glue to both broken surfaces and set in cramps. As there is a tendency for the parts to slide on the glue, use a sash cramp to restrict the movement.

A break near the end of the leg could also be reinforced with a dowel to make an invisible repair (see right).

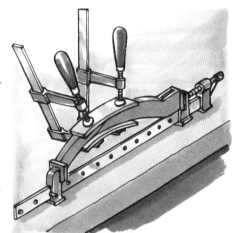

Rebuilding a sabre leg

When part of a sabre leg is beyond repair, scarf-joint a new piece of wood to the old leg. Leave the new wood oversize, rather than shaping it precisely first.

1 Jointing new wood

Cut off the damaged section, and plane smooth the cut edge of the leg to give a long gluing surface. Glue on the new piece with the grain following the old wood.

2 Shaping the repair

Mark out the profile, using the other leg as a template, and cut the leg to shape. Plane and then spokeshave the repair to the finished size.

Turned legs

Chair makers have long used turnery for the making of chair components, from the simple Windsor-style chairs to the elaborate shapes found on many old frame chairs. Although they are generally strong, these turned legs can still be badly weakened by deep-cut decorative turning or faulty wood.

A break that has occurred near the top of a turned leg or one near the foot can be repaired by drilling and inserting a long dowel from the end.

Doweling from the end

Glue and clamp the broken end into place, matching the broken faces precisely. When set, drill a hole down the centre of the leg to take the doweling reinforcement. Make the diameter as large as possible, but leave at least 3mm (⅛in) of wood around the dowel at the narrowest part of the turning. Either turn your own doweling, or make the hole suit a standard-size dowel. The length of the hole should extend well beyond the break. Prepare the dowel by chamfering the end and running a groove down its length. Glue up the repair and trim the dowel when set.

Deep-cut turned legs are liable to break if made from brittle wood.

Stopped-dowel repair

Broken turned legs that receive tenoned seat rails cannot be repaired with a dowel through the top, as the repair will show. In this case a hidden stopped dowel is required.

1 Drilling the stopped hole

With the seat rails in place, drill into the broken end of the upper part of the leg. Drill the hole as deep as possible without weakening the tenon joints. The diameter should leave at least 3mm (⅛in) of wood all round at the narrowest point.

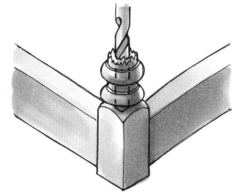

2 Cutting the broken section

Mark a registration line across the proposed cut, then cut off the broken turned section close to the shoulder line, using a fine-tooth saw.

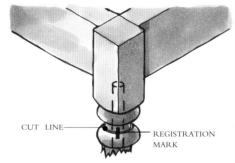

CUT LINE
REGISTRATION MARK

3 Gluing the broken end

Glue and clamp the broken ends together. Using the hole as a guide, drill the lower part of the leg. Use a drill press to ensure the hole follows the central axis.

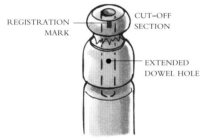

REGISTRATION MARK
CUT-OFF SECTION
EXTENDED DOWEL HOLE

4 Gluing the joint

As the assembled leg will be shorter by the thickness of the saw cut, you will need to trim the end of the other leg or make a packing collar out of matching veneer; this is used to fill the gap when the parts are glued together. Prepare the dowel, glue and assemble the parts, aligning the registration marks, and clamp together.

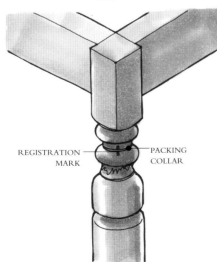

REGISTRATION MARK
PACKING COLLAR

Making turned parts

When part of a leg is beyond repair, it can be replaced with a new piece. For plain turning the new wood should be scarf-jointed to the original and turned *in situ*; decorative features can be turned separately and glued onto the leg.

1 Preparing the wood

Cut off the damaged portion on a shoulder line of a decorative feature. Mark the end of the leg with a centre-finding gauge, and drill a hole in the end, as wide as possible without weakening the wood. Prepare an oversized square section of matching wood for turning. Mark the diagonals on each end and scribe a circle that touches all four sides, then plane down the corners to produce an octagonal section.

CARD TEMPLATE
SPIGOT LENGTH

2 Making a template

Copy the shape to be turned from the undamaged leg, using a needle template. For greater accuracy, carefully mark out and cut a card template, including a spigot to fit the hole drilled in the leg. Set up and trim the wood on the lathe to form a cylinder slightly larger than the widest part of the turning. Use calipers to check the diameter.

NEW SECTION
SPIGOT
ORIGINAL SECTION

3 Turning to shape

Mark the position of the details on the work, using the template as a guide. Turn the part to shape, including the spigot, and check the contour as the work progresses. Cut a groove in the spigot and glue the completed part into the leg. Colour and finish the repair.

Repairing a square leg

Cut off the damaged end of the square leg of an upholstered chair at rail level. Glue a new end with a turned spigot into a hole drilled in the top of the original leg, and recut the mortise.

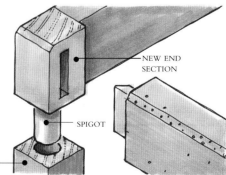

NEW END SECTION
SPIGOT
ORIGINAL LEG

Making a new turned leg

Where the extent of the damage is excessive, you may find it easier to replace the leg entirely. If you have a lathe you can undertake the work yourself, otherwise you can have the leg made by a specialist.

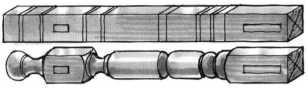

1 Marking out the turning

Make a template of the required profile. If the chair frame is mortise-and-tenoned, mark out the mortises in the leg before shaping on the lathe. Cut the mortises after turning, as the wood might otherwise split. The leg generally remains square where the rails are jointed.

2 Turning the leg full-length

If the whole leg is cylindrically turned, fit temporary soft-wood blocks into the mortises to prevent the edges tearing out. Turn the leg to shape and finish.

Drilling turned legs

The socket joints in the legs of stick-type chairs are usually set at an angle. Once a leg has been turned to shape, clamp it in a jig to hold it at the required angle (see opposite). Use a sliding bevel to set the angle, before drilling the hole with a drill press.

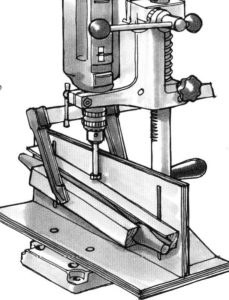

Cabriole legs

The delightful S-shape cabriole legs introduced in the late seventeenth century became a popular style for chairs as well as tables and cabinets. As an expression of the chair maker's skill, various patterns were produced, some relatively plain, others ornate. Repairs to genuine period chairs of this type should be left to professionals, but reproduction chair legs could be tackled; an example with a turned club foot is shown here.

Making a cabriole leg

Although this may not be immediately apparent, the shapely cabriole leg is cut from one square-sectioned piece of wood, except for the knee blocks, which are made separately. To manufacture a replacement for a leg beyond repair, take the shape from one of the remaining good legs, to ensure that the subtle curves match. This leg will need to be removed and the knee blocks unglued.

KNEE

POST BLOCK

MORTISE

KNEE BLOCK (EAR PIECE)

ANKLE

FOOT

45°

GUIDE BLOCK

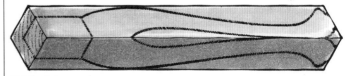

1 Making a template

Clamp the leg by the post block onto a piece of thin plywood, with one mortised side held face-down. Carefully mark round the profile with a purpose-made guide block. Cut out the template to create a smooth S-shape curve.

2 Marking out

Mark the shape on two adjacent inside faces of a square-section leg blank prepared to length and width. Make the width of the blank slightly more than the dimension across the knee.

3 Turning a club foot

Mark diagonal lines on each end of the wood to find the centre. Mount the work in a lathe and turn the club-foot detail to shape.

6 Finishing the leg

Assemble the chair frame and plane the post block flush with the rails, then shape the corner and cut a rebate in the top for a drop-in seat, if one is required. Glue the knee blocks into place and work the back of the leg into a smooth transition curve. Finally stain and finish the new leg.

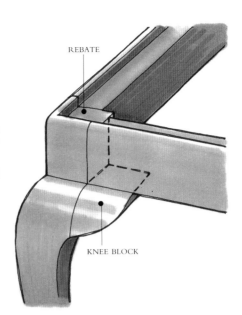

REBATE

KNEE BLOCK

4 Cutting to shape

Using a bow saw, or preferably a bandsaw fitted with a narrow blade, cut the leg profile. Closely follow the marked lines on one face, then temporarily tape the off-cut pieces back into place. Turn the work to present the remaining marked face uppermost – the underside waste keeps the work steady – and cut the second profile to produce a square-section version of the leg. Cut the mortises.

5 Shaping the leg

Make card templates, taken from different sections of an existing leg, to use as guides for shaping. Mount the new leg in a sash cramp gripped in a bench vice and shape the leg, using spoke-shaves, rasps, files and scrapers.

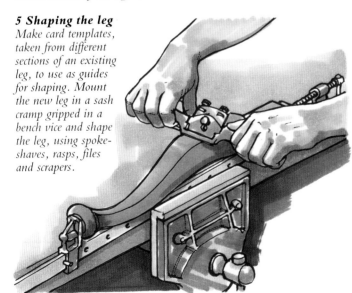

MAKING A DRILLING JIG

Turned legs can be held in a vice between V-shape blocks, but a purpose-made jig will make both setting-up and drilling easier.

Cut a baseboard and backboard from 12mm (½in) thick plywood. Cut the parts to suit the size of the work, and plane the edges square. Cut 6mm (¼in) slots in the backboard to take machine screws. Screw and glue the bottom edge of the back to the centre line of the base. Stiffen the joint with corner blocks at the rear. Cut a V-block the same length as the jig, and cut short slots at each end where it crosses the slots in the backboard. Clamp the V-block to the back with countersunk machine screws fitted with wing nuts. Make a short V-block to hold the work steady in the jig with the aid of a cramp or two. The backboard can either be calibrated with angled lines, or you can set the long V-block to the required angle with a sliding bevel. Clamp the jig to the base of a drill press. Position the work under the drill bit as required.

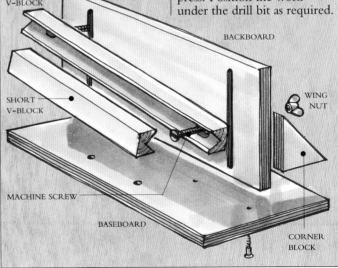

LONG V-BLOCK

BACKBOARD

SHORT V-BLOCK

WING NUT

MACHINE SCREW

BASEBOARD

CORNER BLOCK

Repairing a broken foot

Short grain can cause part of a turned club foot to break away. If the part is missing, rebuild it with a new piece of wood glued in place.

Fitting the block

Plane the broken edge smooth. Cut a block of matching wood to mate with the prepared face, and glue it in place. Mark out and carve the block to the original shape.

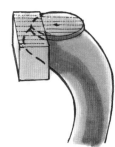

LEVELLING CHAIR LEGS

Chairs with uneven legs are annoying to sit on, and can be damaged if the frame is continuously racked under load. Where a new leg has been fitted, you will need to cut it to match the length of the others. For original legs that are uneven, perhaps due to the solid seat of a Windsor chair having warped, it will be necessary to identify the problem and trim the appropriate leg or legs to make the chair stable.

1 Trimming a new leg

Place the chair level on a flat surface, with the longer leg overhanging the edge. Mark the leg to the required angle and length with a pencil, using a ruler to help project the cutting line from the surface. Saw or pare the leg to length, and bevel the edges with a chisel or file.

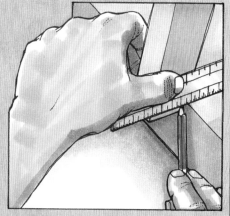

2 Dealing with uneven legs

Stand the chair on a flat surface and prop the leg or legs with pieces of thin card or veneer until the frame appears to be upright. Take the propping from underneath the shortest leg and, while keeping the chair steady, mark a pencil line on the other three legs, using the removed packing as a guide. Trim the marked legs.

CLAMPING CHAIR FRAMES

Whether regluing a loose joint or reassembling a dismantled chair, it will be necessary to apply pressure to the joints to ensure a tight fit and a secure bond. Chair frames come in all shapes and sizes, and sometimes require ingenious methods to clamp them together. Conventional metal sash cramps and G-cramps, ratchet straps, normally used to secure loads on automobiles, and even string can all be used for clamping.

Softening blocks

Whatever the device used to apply the force, it is essential to protect the chair frame from bruising, using softwood blocks or other relatively soft materials placed between the cramp heads and the work. In some instances shaped softening blocks will be needed, not only to protect the surface but also to allow the clamping forces to be applied in line with the joint. The examples below indicate the direction of the clamping force with an arrow.

Square frames

Rectilinear frames are usually the simplest to clamp, and require only flat softwood blocks placed at the corners. However, the back blocks of a curved back leg need to be shaped to follow the contour.

When a strap or tourniquet is used, shaped blocks are needed to protect the corners.

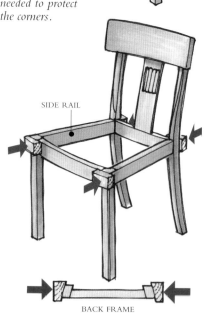

SIDE RAIL

BACK FRAME

FRONT FRAME

Tapered frames

The clamping forces should run parallel to the tenon, which normally follows the line of the rail. Make angled blocks to set the cramp in line with the rail. Cut the angles to compensate for the shape of the legs. When assembling a complete frame, clamp the front and back frames first. When set, clamp the side rails in place.

Rounded legs
Rounded shapes are more difficult to grip, and will require specially contoured blocks.

Making corner blocks
Cut the blocks to match the curve of the leg profile. As curved blocks will tend to slip as the pressure is applied, make them with an extension that can be held with a small cramp.

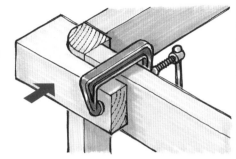

Using straps
Nylon straps, made for attaching loads to car roof racks, can be used to clamp frames together. Ratchet-operated heavy-duty types are available, as well as purpose-made web cramps, which are designed for woodwork.

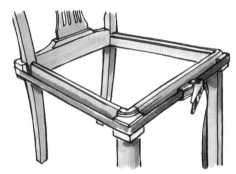

Curved rails
Chairs with strongly curved rails can be awkward to clamp, as there is no square shoulder on which to place the cramp head. In many cases straps can be used successfully without the need for utilizing special blocks.

Making a saddle
You can make an adjustable saddle for a compound-curve cresting rail on a chair back. Cut two flat-steel bars to the width of the chair back and bend them to accommodate the curve of the back seen in plan. Drill holes through the ends and bolt a V-groove block of wood at each end.

Cut off the top corners to provide a flat surface ready for clamping. Face the groove with thick felt. Place a stiff length of wood under the seat rail for the cramps to pull against, keeping the clamping force square to the joint.

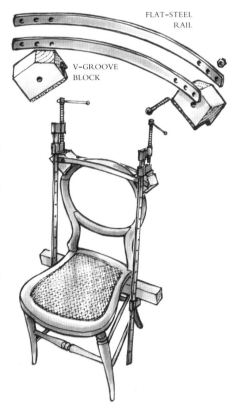

FLAT-STEEL RAIL

V-GROOVE BLOCK

REPAIRING RAILS

Seat and stretcher rails are important structural members. If damaged in any way, they will inevitably weaken a chair.

When making repairs, always try to use as much of the original rail as possible, even for chairs with upholstered rails that are not exposed. In this case, for an important chair, rebuild the rail to restore its integrity, grafting the old wood on the inside face to preserve the period character. In most cases it is best to replace the rail entirely – a perished rail that has been strengthened with glue-impregnated hessian will not hold nails for long.

Rail styles
Rails are usually rectangular in section and jointed to the legs with mortise-and-tenons, although dowels are sometimes used. Chairs with caned seats are lighter in construction and have the seat rails jointed together to make a flat frame.

Most chairs have straight seat rails, but some may have the front rail decoratively shaped along the lower edge, while others may be curved in plan as well as in side elevation. Curved rails require a larger piece of wood from which to cut the shape, and can be weak due to short grain.

Making a tenoned side rail
When a rail is beyond repair and needs to be replaced, take the dimensions from the old or remaining rail of the chair.

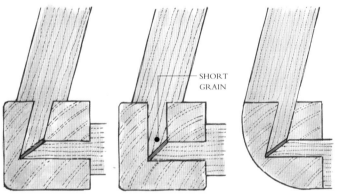

SHORT GRAIN

Marking out the rail
Prepare the wood to size and mark out and cut the tenons at each end, noting the details from the old example. The tenon usually runs parallel with the rail, and on a tapered-seat chair the mortise in the leg is cut at an angle. Sometimes the mortise is cut square to the face of the leg, and the tenon is angled. This is not good practice, as the tenon is weakened by short grain. If this is the case, carefully select the new wood for the rail.

The tenon is usually placed in the centre of the rail, but is sometimes set to one side. This is called a barefaced tenon, and is used where the conventional method would weaken the leg.

Making front rails

Front rails are often more ornate than side rails, and usually require larger sections of wood to accommodate the shape.

1 Making a curved rail

If possible, use the old rail as a template and mark out the plan shape on the new wood; or draw the shape, including the tenons, and transfer this shape to the wood. Cut the rail to shape on a bandsaw. Mark the shoulder lines of the tenons on the faces, and cut the joints.

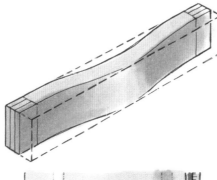

2 Routing the rail

For a visible rail, smooth the front surface with spoke-shaves, scrapers and abrasive paper ready for finishing. Cut a rebate in the top edge for chairs with drop-in seats, using a router; and if the rail has beaded moulding details, cut these using a scratch stock or router.

MOULDED EDGE
ROUTER
REBATE
RAIL
SUPPORT FOR ROUTER

Making Regency-style rails

Regency-style chairs with sabre legs may have thick front rails that are fixed to the side frames with twin tenons. Mark and cut the new tenons to match the mortises in the leg. If the front edge is rounded over, mark the contour on each end of the rail and then plane it to shape. Finish with a shaped sanding block.

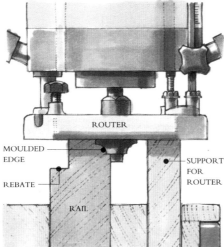

Broken stretcher rails

Stretcher rails are relatively light in section and, as they are close to the floor, are sometimes broken. Where a break forms a natural scarf joint, simply apply glue and clamp or bind the repair. If the wood has sheared close to the leg or is beyond repair due to woodworm, make a new rail.

Remaking a tenoned rail

A tenoned rail is rectangular in section and tenoned into the leg. If the chair frame cannot be taken apart, fitting a new rail can be a problem. This can be overcome by cutting the rail to shoulder length and fitting separate tenons. Clean out the mortises and prepare the rail to size. Cut angled bridle joints in the underside at each end (see page 56). Cut matching tenon pieces and glue them into the legs, then glue the rail to the tenon pieces.

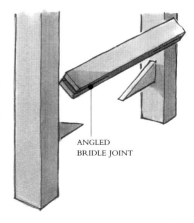

ANGLED BRIDLE JOINT

Broken turned stretcher

Where the end of the rail has broken close to the leg, cut the end of the rail square and glue on a short length of doweling or a turned piece to make up the missing end. Drill a deep hole into the end and glue in a dowel to reinforce the joint.

A chair with a turned under-frame will usually enable you to fit the rail by springing the legs apart. The repair should be virtually hidden by the leg socket.

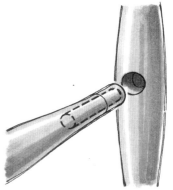

Split turned rail

Where a substantial part of a rail is damaged beyond repair, cut it back to sound wood and plane it to a shallow angle. Graft on a new section and turn it to the finished shape.

Cane-chair rail

The line of closely spaced holes in the rails of caned chairs tends to weaken the wood, causing it to split. Strip out the old cane (see page 68), work glue into the split and clamp it together. Drill the rail and fit two or three glued dowels into the inner edge between the holes to reinforce the repair.

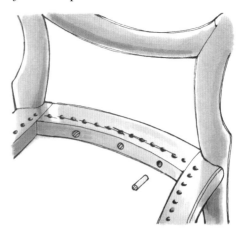

REPAIRING BACKS

Much of the character of a chair is found in the back rest, from simple, flat or turned slats or sticks to elaborately shaped, carved or pierced splats, all capped with a shaped cresting rail.

Chair backs can be angular and have very little curvature, or they can have sweeping curved shapes that link up with the arms. Dramatically curved shapes are inherently weak if cut from solid wood, and are often found broken. So too are cresting-rail joints and pierced back splats, where thin sections leave little material for strength.

Most broken components of chair backs can be repaired, as it involves nothing more than regluing a weak joint, mending a split or patch-repairing a broken piece. But remaking a cresting rail shaped into a double curve is best left to a professional. It will need a large piece of wood, and the correct species for an old chair could be difficult to find.

Broken cresting rails

The typical damage that occurs to a cresting rail is determined by its shape or method of manufacture, following certain period styles. The cresting rail of a comb-back Windsor chair, for example, is usually curved and embellished with a simple sawn profile. The lobe details at the ends are often broken off as a result of short grain.

1 Marking out the shape

Make a thin-card template of the profile by drawing round the unbroken end. If both ends are broken, trace the remaining parts and complete the outline, by using drawing instruments or by drawing it freehand. Cut out the shape with a craft knife or scissors.

2 Making the repair

Plane the broken surface smooth and prepare a block of matching wood to fit the resulting angle, leaving the new wood oversize. Glue the block in place and when set, plane or pare the front and back faces flush. Cut the profile using a coping saw, and shape it with a file and abrasive paper.

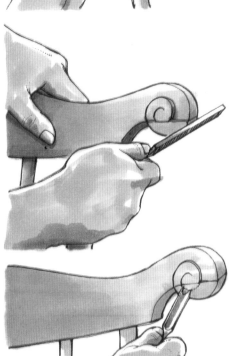

3 Decoration

For a simple carved motif, a spiral for example, draw the shape on the new wood and carve the detail, following the existing pattern.

Damaged cresting-rail joints

Cresting rails are sometimes relatively fine, even though the original piece of solid wood from which each was cut was considerably more robust. Having so much wood removed results in typical short-grain problems and small weak joints where the rails meet the legs.

Mortise-and-tenon joints are usually used to join the legs to the cresting rails. Breaks can occur in the ends of the slender legs, where the tenons are stressed, or in the cresting rail around the mortises for the legs, or the back splat, if fitted.

1 Repairing a tenon

Remove the cresting rail (see page 54). If the top end of the leg is split away but the tenon is still intact, simply clean the faces thoroughly and glue the parts together.

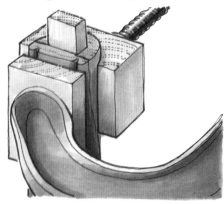

2 Replacing a tenon

If the tenon has sheared off, replace it with a new tenon mortised into the ends of the leg. Trim the stump flush with the shoulder, and cut a mortise in the leg to match the mortise in the rail, taking great care to match the angle. Cut and glue a new tenon-piece into the leg.

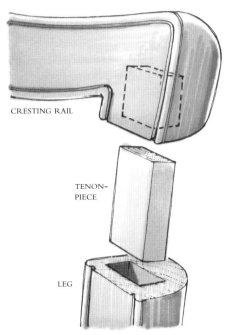

CRESTING RAIL

TENON-PIECE

LEG

Repairing a mortise

The short grain in the back rail often causes the mortise to split out. If the broken part cannot be glued in place, rebuild the wood. Plane the broken surface flat and glue on a matching piece of wood. Pare and file the patch to the contour of the rail. Mark and carefully recut the mortise, using what remains of the old mortise to guide the chisel.

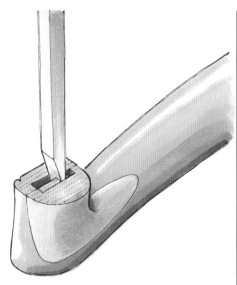

Repairing a back-splat mortise

If the broken part is missing, rebuild the damaged cresting rail with new matching wood. Either plane the broken surface smooth and splice on new wood, or cut a housing that tapers at each end to let in a new piece. Shape the patch to the profile of the rail when the glue has set.

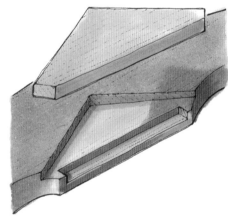

Empire-style backs

The backs of sabre-leg chairs were topped with bold single-curved cresting rails jointed to the legs with shallow dovetail housings. The joint is prone to short-grain failure caused by the curve in the rail.

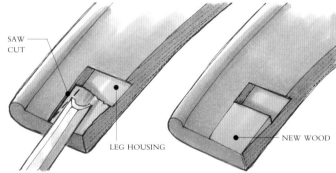

SAW CUT

LEG HOUSING

NEW WOOD

Making an invisible repair

In order to disguise the edge of the patch-repair, cut a tapered housing in the back rest. Glue in a piece of new wood and plane the surface to the contour of the back, running to a feathered edge at the corner. Cut a dovetail shoulder on the inner edge to match the leg joint.

Balloon-back joints

Cresting rails of nineteenth-century balloon-back chairs were often doweled to the tops of the legs so as to overcome the problems associated with short grain. Dowels provide long-grain strength to bridge the jointing faces, but the weak surrounding wood often breaks when stressed.

1 Rebuilding a broken end

Plane the broken surface flat. Glue on a slightly oversize block of roughly shaped matching wood, with the grain following that of the rail. Tape it in place or bind it firmly with waxed string.

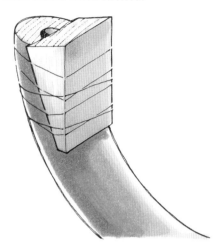

2 Making the dowel hole

When set, plane the end flat. Mark the diameter of the hole on the end and, using a gouge, pare away the wood to accommodate the dowel. Take care to follow the angle of the hole.

3 Shaping the new block

Check the rail for fit and glue into place, using a saddle to assist clamping (see page 63). When set, carve and file the block to the contour and section of the back leg and rail.

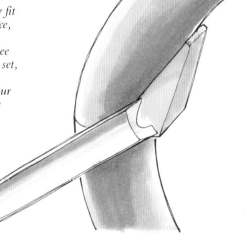

Split back splat

Back splats are made from relatively thin panels of wood tenoned into the underside of the cresting rail and the top edge of the seat rail. Fretted splats are particularly prone to splitting along the grain, and chairs are often found with pieces missing.

1 Making a template

The pattern of the back splat is generally symmetrical about the centre line. Hold a piece of thin card against the back face of the splat. Mark out and then cut a template from the related portion opposite the damaged part. The template will need to be reversed when used for marking out.

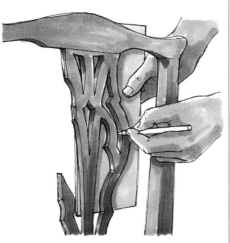

2 Fitting a patch repair

Plane or pare the broken edge or edges flat. Prepare a piece of matching wood slightly thicker than the splat, and glue it to the prepared edges. Tape, bind or clamp in place until set.

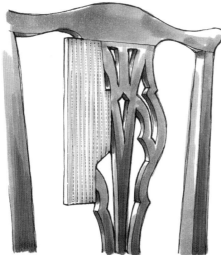

3 Shaping the patch

Mark out the shape from the template. Drill and saw out the waste close to the lines. Pare and file the surfaces to shape, and carve any surface detailing. Sand the surfaces with fine abrasive paper before matching the colour and finishing.

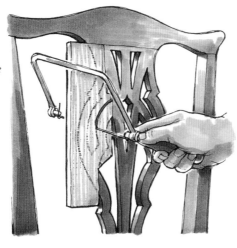

Windsor chair back

The thin sticks that form the back support on Windsor chairs are fairly vulnerable. Replacements can be made by hand or machine. They usually have a slight taper, and it may be necessary to dismantle the back to fit them.

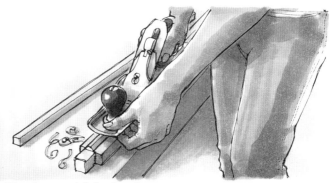

1 Shaping a stick by hand

Mark the diagonals and finished diameters on each end of a square-sectioned length of wood prepared to size. Clamp the wood in a V-block between end stops. Plane each face down to the smaller diameter to form a taper. Continue shaping the stick by turning and planing off the corners until rounded. Finish by rubbing with abrasive paper wrapped face-down around the stick.

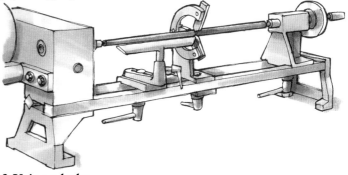

2 Using a lathe

Plane the stick octagonal as above, then set it between centres in a lathe. With the lathe running at a slow speed, turn the stick to a round taper. If the stick is long and light in section, you may need to support it with a steadying attachment to stop it whipping.

3 Trimming the end

Mark the length of the stick from the back assembly, ensuring it is held at the correct angle. If the holes in the bow are stopped, cut the stick to size; for through holes, leave it slightly over-length and trim to follow the profile of the bow after fitting.

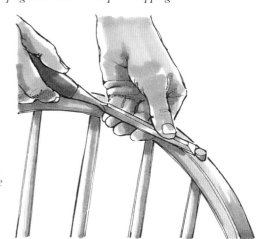

RECANING

Woven strips of cane have been used since the seventeenth century to form infill-panels for chair seats, backs and arms. The craft of caning has produced many weave variations, as well as special treatments for shaped frames. A 'spider's web', for example, features a floating oval or round block in the centre of the frame. Another common pattern is known as 'rising sun'.

Chairs with damaged panels, usually the seat, can look daunting to repair, but by following some basic principles the task is not as complex as it may first appear. However, chairs with shaped frames are best repaired by a specialist. The method for recaning a seat using the common six-way pattern is illustrated on the following pages, but the techniques can be applied to other frames.

Simple walnut-frame chair with broken cane seat

New cane will darken with age

Caning materials

Cane is a relatively tough material that will give long service if it is not unduly stressed. It is stripped from rattan to produce standard-width strands that are numbered from 1 to 6. The split cane has one glossy surface and is woven through the frame so that this always remains uppermost. The pegs, used to secure the canes in alternate holes, are cut to length from basket-weave cane or dowel of suitable diameter.

Select the width of cane in ascending order, according to three factors: the complexity of the woven pattern, the size of the frame and the spacing of the holes. A typical dining-chair seat will use number 2 for the front-to-back and side-to-side canes. Use a number 3 or 4 cane for the diagonal weave and number 6 cane for the edge beading, with number 2 cane used to tie it in place.

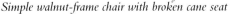

TYPICAL CANE SIZES FOR STANDARD SIX-WAY PATTERN						
Holes per 150mm (6in)	10	11	12	13	14	15
Size of cane	4	3-4	3	2-3	2	1-2
Beading	6 & 2	6 & 2	6 & 2	6 & 2	6 & 2	6 & 2

Preparing the seat frame

Where possible, take one or more photographs of the old damaged caning before stripping the frame, to help you set out the new work.

Cut out the old canework with a craft knife, following the inside of the frame. Cut away the beading cane and ties, and pull out the loose loops of cane. Drive out the pegs from below, using a hole-clearing tool, and pull out the remaining pieces of cane, ensuring that all the holes are clear.

Check the condition of the framework and joints, and make repairs as appropriate. Finally clean and revive or refinish the woodwork.

Preparing cane

Cane is sold by weight and supplied in coiled bundles. Soak two or three strips in warm water for a few minutes prior to use, keep them in a plastic bag until needed, and replenish them as the work progresses. Should a cane dry out while being worked, wipe it with a damp cloth.

Caning tools

You will need some basic tools from a standard wood-working kit, plus one or two improvised special tools.

Craft knife
For cutting out old caning and general trimming.

Side cutters
Used to cut canes to length.

Hole-clearing tool
Make this from a large wire nail with the point cut off, or a cut-down screwdriver. Used to drive out old pegs from the frame.

Pin hammer
Used to drive the hole-clearing tool and tap in new pegs.

Stiletto
An improvised tool made from a sack needle fitted with a handle, or a small screwdriver with a rounded and bent tip, which manipulates the woven cane.

Long-nosed pliers
Used to grip and pull the cane in tight spaces.

Temporary pegs
Used to hold the loose ends of the canes being worked. Long golf tees make good pegs, or use short lengths of tapered dowel.

Caning a seat frame

A number of woven patterns are found on old chairs, but the most successful, and therefore most common, is the six-way pattern described here. This has two pairs of canes that run back to front, two pairs from side to side, and two lengths that cross opposite diagonals. A seventh, beading stage is used to finish the edges. If each stage is followed methodically and the cane is neatly threaded, what appears to be a complex pattern can be achieved with relative ease.

First stage

The first stage is worked from the front to the back. Have the chair facing you, set at a comfortable working height.

Walnut-frame bedroom chair
Recaned in the six-way pattern with number 2 cane and number 3 cane on the diagonals.

Bentwood dining chair
Recaned with number 3 cane throughout, to provide extra strength for a larger round seat.

1 Finding the central hole

Count the number of holes in the back rail to find the centre. An uneven number will place a hole in the middle, and an even number will have a hole on each side of the centre. Place a temporary peg in the central hole or in a hole on one side of the centre, and place another peg opposite in the front rail.

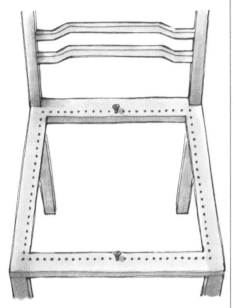

2 Starting the first cane

Pass the first length of number 2 cane through the back hole until its length is equal above and below the rail, and then secure it with a temporary peg.

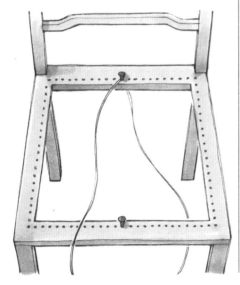

3 Working the first hole

Take the end of the half above the rail and pass it down the marked hole in the front rail, keeping the glossy surface uppermost. Give it a half-twist towards the adjacent hole on the left, and replace the temporary 'working' peg to hold it under slight tension.

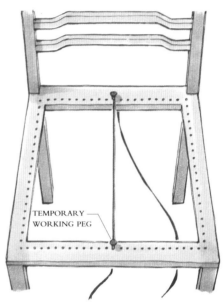

TEMPORARY WORKING PEG

4 Working the second hole

Pass the end up the next hole and again give it a half-twist so that it points towards the back rail with the glossy surface uppermost. Transfer the temporary peg into this hole.

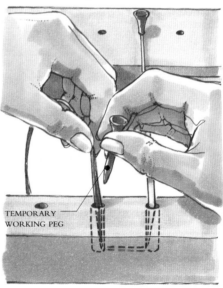

TEMPORARY WORKING PEG

5 Working the third hole

Take the cane across to the back rail and down the opposite hole. Give it a half-turn and, keeping the tension on the cane, move the working peg into this hole.

TEMPORARY WORKING PEG

6 Working the fourth hole

Pass the cane up through the next hole on the left, give it a half-twist and once more transfer the peg in readiness to repeat the process in the front rail.

7 Completing the first caning

Continue in this way until all the holes except the corner hole in one half of the back rail have been filled. Then thread the remaining half of the cane across the other half of the seat frame, again leaving the corner hole free.

8 Starting a new cane

In the event that the first cane is not long enough to complete all the holes, peg the end of the first cane, leaving about 75mm (3in) below the front or back rail. Start a new cane in the next hole on the opposite rail, again pegging it with surplus material below.

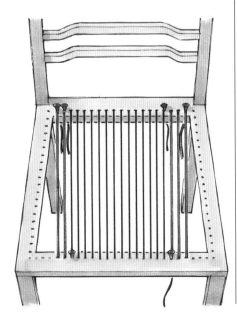

9 Tapered frames

Frames that are wider at the front than the back will have spare holes in the front rail when all the back holes are filled. Select holes in the side rails and peg short lengths of cane into them to run parallel with the existing caning. The corner holes are left clear at this stage.

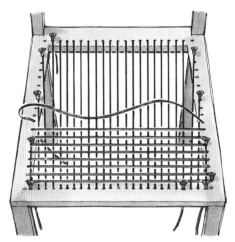

Second stage

This is run from side to side and worked across the frame in a similar manner to the first stage. It is not necessary to weave the cane, which simply overlays the front-to-back canes at right angles to them.

Working the cane

Leaving the front corner hole clear, peg the end of a length of cane into the first hole along the side. Leave a short length underneath for tying off later. Continue to work the cane across the frame, leaving the back corner holes clear when you reach the back of the seat.

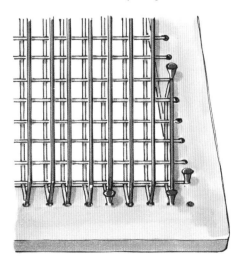

Third stage

This is worked from front to back and lies parallel with the first stage. Again, it is not woven but overlays stage two.

Working the cane

Follow the procedure used for the first stage, but work the cane to the right side and parallel with the first canes. Use the stiletto to manipulate the line of the first canes, to set each pair about 2mm ($\frac{1}{16}$in) apart. This places the canes in the right position for weaving the diagonals, and makes the fourth stage easier.

Fourth stage

This runs in front of and parallel with stage two, but is now woven through the front-to-back canes of the first and third stages. Peg the end of the cane into the same right-hand hole as stage two, leaving the corner hole free. Make sure the cane is not twisted by sliding it through your fingers; this will also help you manipulate the little nodules or knots found on cane, so they do not catch or tear.

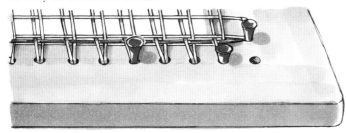

1 Weaving the cane

Work the cane across the seat in front of the second stage, taking each pair of front-to-back canes in turn. Weave the end over the first cane, under the second, over the third and under the fourth. Weave between no more than two or three pairs at a time, and then pull the cane through. Repeat this across the seat.

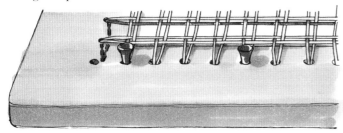

2 Returning the cane

On reaching the other side, pass the cane up through the next hole. Continue weaving the end, but this time under the first cane to the right, over the second, again working in front of the cane of stage two. Continue weaving from side to side in this way, always checking that the cane is not twisted and leaving the back corner holes clear.

Fifth stage

The first of the diagonal canes is now woven, this time starting from a corner hole and using a slightly wider number 3 or number 4 cane.

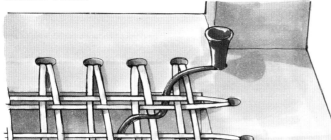

1 Weaving the cane

Starting at the rear right-hand corner hole, fasten the end of the cane. Ensuring the cane is not twisted, weave it towards the front rail. Pass the free end over the front-to-back pairs of canes and under the side-to-side pairs. Weave about four pairs of canes at a time, and then pull the cane through.

2 Spare holes

On tapered seats the diagonal cane will not meet the front corner hole, but will finish a few holes from it in the front rail. The empty holes will be filled when the other half of the seat frame is caned, and can be ignored at this stage.

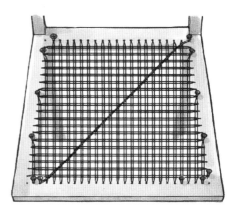

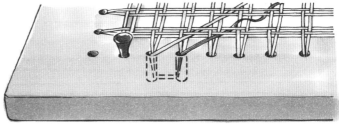

3 Returning the cane

Take the cane up through the next hole on the right and weave it in the same way towards the back, so that it runs parallel with the first cane and finishes in the same hole at the back.

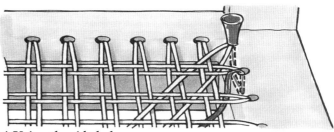

4 Using the side holes

Take the free end forward and up through the first adjacent hole in the side rail. Weave the cane diagonally under the side-to-side pairs and over the front-to-back pairs as before. Repeat until all the remaining front and side holes are filled, leaving the right-hand corner hole clear. Some side holes may be used twice on a tapered seat (see page 72).

5 Completing the stage

Fill the remainder as above, starting from the next hole in the back when an even number of holes is available in the front rail, or from the front for an odd number. Work the cane into the front left-hand corner hole twice, then take it on to the next side hole and complete the half. Leave the rear left-hand hole clear.

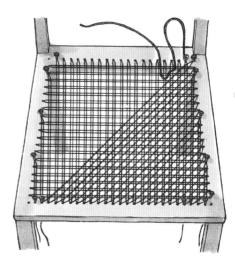

71

6 Tapered seats

In order to make the diagonal canes run parallel and not excessively distorted, it will sometimes be necessary to run two canes into the same side holes. Decide which holes to use as the work progresses. Whenever a hole is used twice, miss its opposite number on the other side and fill it at the next stage.

Sixth stage

This repeats the method used for the fifth stage, but starts from the rear left-hand corner hole and is worked from left to right.

Weaving the cane

Weave the cane under the front-to-back pairs of canes and over the side-to-side ones. Double up the canes in the corner holes. Fit two canes into the side holes missed at the fifth stage, to keep the panel balanced, and miss the opposite holes already fitted with two canes.

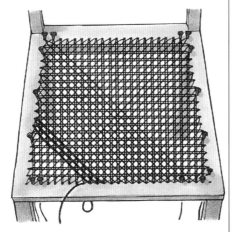

Plugging and beading

With the woven panel completed, the canes are fixed with pegs and the line of holes is covered with a beading cane. Only alternate holes are plugged, with the remainder left clear, including the corner holes and those adjacent to them. Work from each corner; rails with an even number of holes will have two clear or two plugged holes meeting in the middle.

1 Plugging the holes

Cut basket-cane or dowel pegs to be a tight fit in the holes and slightly shorter than the thickness of the frame. Starting at the third hole from the corner, tap a peg into alternate holes. Use a clearing tool to set them just below the surface. Remove any temporary pegs.

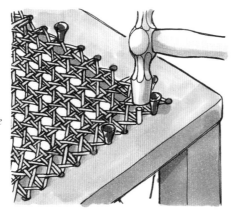

2 Trimming the loose ends

Cut off the loose ends from below the plugged holes. Where a hole to be left clear has a loose end in it, take the end up into the next hole to be pegged. Keeping the tension on the end, tap in a peg to secure it, then cut the cane flush with the top of the frame.

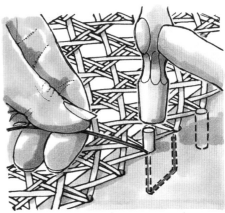

3 Preparing the beading

Cut four lengths of number 6 cane about 50mm (2in) longer than the seat rails. Trim one end of each to fit into the corner holes. It is not absolutely necessary to dampen the cane, though this will help it to follow the shape if the rails are curved.

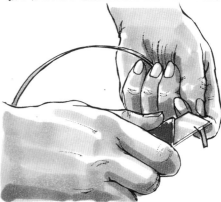

4 Fitting the beading

Pass the end of a long length of number 2 cane up through the rear corner hole. Bend the end forward following the line of holes. Insert the prepared end of a beading cane down into the same hole, bend it forward and secure the canes with a temporary peg.

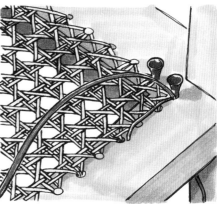

5 Tying the beading

Thread the loose end of the number 2 cane up the first clear hole, then loop it over the beading cane and back down the same hole. Pull the loop tight and repeat the procedure through the remaining holes.

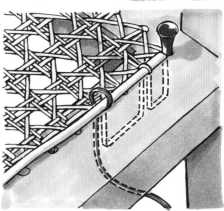

6 Fitting the end

On reaching the other corner, cut the number 6 beading cane to length and trim the end. Tuck it into the corner hole, complete the loop tie in the last hole, and take the free end of the cane diagonally across and up into the next clear hole in the front rail.

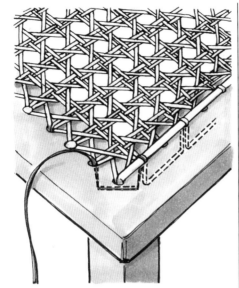

7 Fitting the front beading

Prepare the end of the next beading cane and insert it into the corner hole. Plug the hole to fix the ends, and position this new beading to cover the peg and line of holes when it is bent over. Continue to tie the beading as before, and repeat the process around the next side and back rails.

8 Finishing the beading

Remove the working peg from the first corner hole and insert the last prepared end of the beading cane. Pass the end of the number 2 cane up through the hole and plug it to secure all the ends. This peg is not hidden.

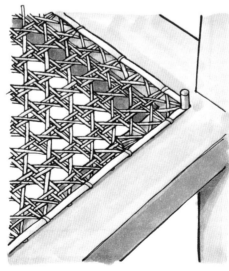

Using pre-woven cane

Making canework by hand is time-consuming, and many caned pieces of furniture are now fitted with pre-woven machine-made cane panels. The six-way pattern is frequently used; it is produced in a standard width and sold by length. Pre-woven cane is fixed into a groove machined in the frame, and is not threaded through holes.

You will need a panel of cane sufficient to cover the frame, a length of plugging cane or spline, a paper pattern and purpose-made hardwood wedges. Make a driving wedge about 100mm (4in) long, about 25mm (1in) wide and 3mm (⅛in) thick at the tip. Also make enough temporary fixing wedges to fill the groove: these should be 25mm (1in) long and the same width and thickness.

1 Stripping the old panel

Prise out the old cane from the groove in the frame, using a narrow chisel, and clean away the old glue. Select a spline or plugging cane slightly smaller than the groove width.

2 Making a groove pattern

Lay a sheet of stiff paper over the frame and take a rubbing of the groove with a wax crayon. Trim the pattern about 12mm (½in) larger than the outside line. Centre the pattern on the cane and cut the panel to shape.

3 Preparing the cane

Soak the panel for about 15 minutes in a bath of warm water. Cut the spline cane about 25mm (1in) longer than the total length of the groove for a curved shape, or cut and mitre separate lengths for rectilinear frames.

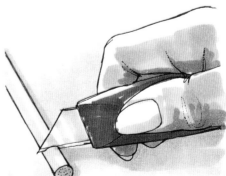

4 Fitting the cane

Place the panel shiny-side up onto the frame and pull out any strands of cane that run along the grooves. Starting at the centre of the back rail, drive the cane into the groove, using the long wedge and a hammer. Follow this with a temporary wedge to hold the cane in place. Fix the front edge in the same way, then the sides. Repeat the process, working alternately from back to front and from side to side from the centre to the corners.

5 Trimming the cane

With the cane well seated, the projecting ends can now be trimmed. Remove the temporary wedges one at a time and trim off the vertical ends of the canes level with the bottom of the groove, using a sharp chisel and mallet.

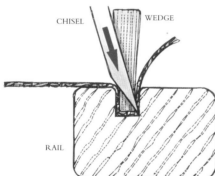

CHISEL   WEDGE

RAIL

6 Fixing the cane panel

Apply a bead of PVA glue into the groove and tap in a length of plugging cane or spline flush with the panel, using a rubber mallet. If the spline is in one piece, start at the back. When the ends meet, cut off the overlap to give a neat butt joint. For jointed splines, start at the corners. Wipe off surplus glue and allow the panel to dry and shrink tight.

RUSH SEATING

Rush cording is used for making the seats of some country chairs. Natural rush is available from specialists in various colours according to its origin, but it is not a very common material. Substitute materials, made from corded paper or twisted fibre, are generally available. All are sold by weight. About 1 to 2kg (2½ to 5 lb) will be sufficient for one chair seat. Artificial materials are easier to use than natural rush, as they are more consistent and available in continuous lengths. Their uniformity, however, lacks the traditional character of the real material.

Preparing rush

Dampen bundles of natural rush to make them pliable by either soaking them in a bath for about five minutes or by spraying them with water prior to working. Wrap them in damp cloth to keep them moist.

The rush is formed into an even cord by taking two or three lengths and twisting them together, always in a clockwise direction. This is only necessary for the top of the seat; when run underneath, the rush is not twisted. Expel air trapped in the rushes by squeezing and quickly running the hand down their length, forcing the air out. When joining a new length of cord, simply knot the ends over the last one under the seat.

Only lightly dampen corded paper and fibre materials if you need to work tight bends.

1 Working a tapered frame

To fill the front corners of chairs that are wider at the front than at the back, start by tying the end of the first cord to the inside of the left-hand side rail with string. Take the cord forward over and under the front rail (1), then up and over the side rail (2). Keeping the tension on the cord, pass it across to the opposite side rail. Take the cord over and under the rail (3), then over and under the front seat rail (4), and tie the end to the inside of the side rail.

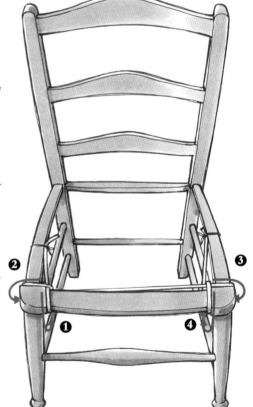

2 Filling the corners

Continue to tie and wrap separate cords in this way, until the space between them at the front is the same as the length of the back rail. If you are using natural rush, knot lengths together and twist them into a cord. Twist artificial cord as you work to prevent it unwinding.

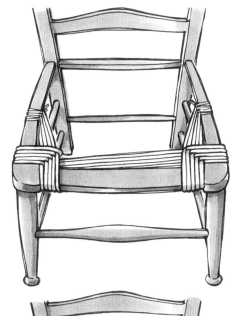

3 Filling the seat

Tie the end of a new length of cord to the left-hand side rail. Wrap it around the front of the frame as before, but continue over and under the back rail. Pass it up and over the right-hand side rail, then across and over the opposite rail. Take it over and under the back rail, and then forward and over the front rail. Fill the frame in this way, adding more cord when required.

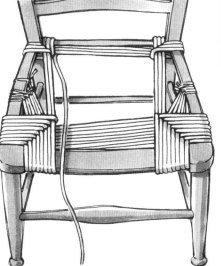

4 Packing the corners

When about eight rows are completed, temporarily tie off the working cord, then squeeze the cords woven together and regulate the weave, using a lever tool such as a wooden spatula handle or an old screwdriver. Turn the chair over and trim off any loose ends under the seat. Pack folded offcuts of rush or pieces of corrugated card between the top and bottom cords, to help support the seat.

5 Completing the seat

Continue weaving and packing the remainder of the seat. If the seat is wider than it is deep, the sides will be filled before the front and back rails. In this case, weave the cord in a figure-of-eight from front to back. Use a lever tool to help squeeze the last cords into place. Finally tie off the loose end of cord to the underside of the seat, trim it, and tuck it in neatly.

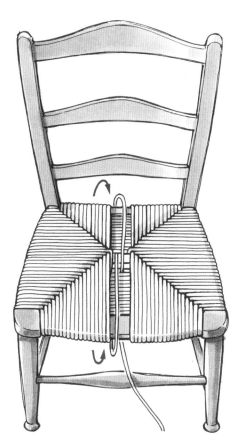

Inexpensive oak chair frames being restored using paper-rush cording

BASIC UPHOLSTERY

Traditional upholstery work is time-consuming, and requires a good eye and developed hand-craft skills to create pleasing, well-balanced work. For the amateur, stripping an old sprung seat can seem like an archaeological dig, with up to nine layers of material on the frame. On stripping the old stuffing and support, all that is left is a skeletal chair frame that can give little clue as to the final shape.

The beginner should start with manageable projects so as to learn the basic techniques. Careful notes, and possibly photographs taken as the chair is stripped, will help to make rebuilding the shape easier. The examples shown here deal primarily with dining chairs, which make a good introduction to traditional upholstery, from which most of the basic skills can be developed.

Tools and equipment

Upholstering a chair is a relatively clean activity, and can be undertaken in the house. Stripping old upholstery, however, is very dirty work, and should be done either in the open or in a workshop. Wear a mask to prevent inhaling dust.

You need enough space to enable the coverings to be laid out and the frame to be manoeuvred. Set the chair frame at a comfortable height on low trestles or on a worktop clamped in a folding bench. A raised lip all round the supporting surface will stop the frame slipping off.

Many woodwork tools can be used for upholstery, but you will also need a limited number of special handtools, available from upholstery suppliers, plus a sewing machine.

Webbing stretchers
Used to apply tension to the webbing when tacking to a frame.

Upholstery skewers
Skewers temporarily hold hessians and coverings in place.

Upholstery scissors
Strong scissors used to cut fabrics and webbing. Dressmaker's shears can also be used.

Upholsterer's hammer
A lightweight, small-headed hammer with two faces or one face and a claw. Some hammers have a magnetic face for picking up tacks. A cabinetmaker's pin hammer can be used instead.

Hide strainer
Special pliers with wide jaws for tensioning leather coverings. Also used to grip webbing or hessian.

Trimming knife
A sharp craft knife used to trim linings and coverings.

Ripping chisel
Used to drive out old tacks with a cabinetmaker's mallet. Otherwise, use an old screwdriver.

Needles
The needles used in upholstery work are: double-pointed straight or mattress needles; curved spring needles with a bayonet point; and curved or semi-circular needles, all available in a range of sizes.

Regulator
Used to manipulate the stuffing into position and shape. Use the flattened end to tuck in coverings.

Tack lifter
Made with an angled clawed tip, a tack lifter is used to extract tacks and decorative chair nails.

Staple gun
An alternative to the traditional tacking for fixing coverings. Also known as a hand tacker.

Upholstery materials

With a few exceptions, the materials used for upholstery have not outwardly changed in centuries, except that most modern materials are flame-retardant, to meet current safety standards.

Webbing
Fabric webbing forms the support platform for the seat, so use only good-quality cotton twill or jute. Rubber webbing is a resilient support for seat cushions.

Springs
Made in a range of wire gauges and sizes; the lower the gauge number, the firmer the spring. The heaviest are used for seats, the lighter for backs and arms.

Hessian
This is a coarse fabric made from jute and graded by weight. The heaviest grade covers coil springs or the webs of a drop-in seat frame; the intermediate grade and lightweight open-weave scrim cover the second stuffing.

Stuffings
Traditional stuffings are animal hair or vegetable fibre. Hair can often be reused if washed and teased. Fibre is coarse-textured and much cheaper than hair; it provides a reasonably resilient stuffing. Mats of rubberized hair are used in the seats and backs of some reproduction chairs.

Foam sheet
This flexible material combines the bulk of traditional stuffing with the resilience of springs. Foam sheet is made in soft, medium and firm grades of latex rubber or polyurethane plastic, and in a range of thicknesses.

Upholstery nails
These nails secure and finish the edges of heavy fabrics or leather coverings. Gimp pins are fine, small-headed nails used for fixing gimp or braid.

Adhesives
Contact adhesives for bonding upholstery foams are available in liquid or aerosol forms. Latex contact fabric adhesive can be used to fix braid in place of gimp pins.

Linings
Close-woven unbleached calico is used to cover the second stuffing of traditional upholstery and to make a lining over foam pads. Black calico is used to line the underside of seat frames to form a dust cover. Cambric is a fine wax-treated calico used for making feather-cushion cases.

Wadding
Cotton felt wadding about 25mm (1in) thick is used as a top stuffing or built up as a layered pad to stop hair stuffing coming through. Fine cotton or 'skin' wadding has a thin paper surface, and is laid under the top cover.

Top covers
Upholstery fabrics are available in a wide range of types, designs and colours. Always try to use the best quality you can afford.

Trimmings
The line of tacks securing the covering is usually trimmed with a decorative braid or gimp. A wide range of types is available.

Tacks
Improved tacks have a large head, usually range from 10mm (⅜in) to 16mm (⅝in), and are used for fixing webbing, and temporary tacking. Fine tacks have a smaller head, and range from 6mm (¼in) to 25mm (1in). The 10mm (⅜in) and 12mm (½in) sizes are used to fix linings and top covers.

Twines, threads and cords
Twine is used to tie the springs to the webbing and tie the stuffing into shape. Traditional fibre twines are dressed with beeswax to strengthen them and make them easier to work. Sewing threads and carpet thread come in a range of colours for sewing seams and piping, as well as for fixing braid. Lacing cord, or 'laycord', is used to tie springs together and to the frame, as is sisal string. Piping cord makes a neat beaded edge to seams.

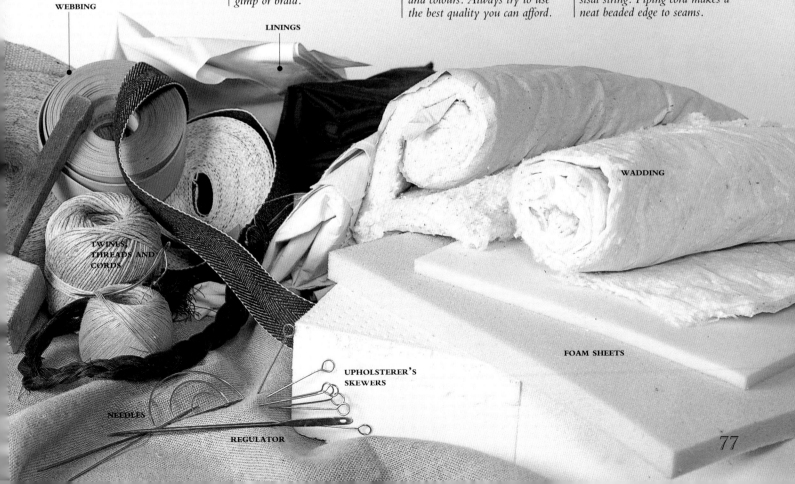

WEBBING

LININGS

WADDING

TWINES, THREADS AND CORDS

FOAM SHEETS

UPHOLSTERER'S SKEWERS

NEEDLES

REGULATOR

GENERAL REPAIRS

With regular attention, upholstery will last a considerable time. However, soft materials such as fabrics will wear. Even coverings on seldom-used chairs can degrade in strong sunlight, causing colours to fade and fibres to eventually weaken. Try to avoid direct sunlight when placing furniture in a room, and change its position from time to time. Regular cleaning with a vacuum cleaner, using suitable attachments, helps maintain the fabric in good condition. However, feather-filled cushions should be beaten, to avoid the possibility of drawing the feathers through the covering. Have any soiled upholstery dry-cleaned or use a proprietary fabric shampoo, following the manufacturer's instructions.

Old fibrous materials will weaken and stretch, and can allow the upholstery to gradually collapse or distort. Rips and tears occur, and piping can show wear. All of these problems can be rectified and will give the original upholstery a longer lease of life.

Sagging seats

A sagging seat usually indicates that the support webbing has stretched, or that perhaps one or two of the tacked ends have worked loose. Webbing fixed to the underside of a frame can be re-tensioned or reinforced with additional webs to provide an interim repair until the upholstery is remade.

1 Releasing the webbing
Turn the seat upside down on the bench and remove the dust cover, if fitted. Working on one slack web at a time, remove the fixing tacks from one end, using a ripping chisel or an old screwdriver.

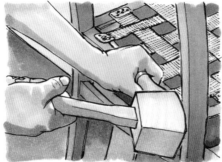

2 Re-tensioning the web
Unfold and grip the free end of the old webbing with a pair of hide-strainers. Hold it under tension and fix it with tacks (see page 77). If you can't get the special pliers, use standard ones, repositioning them after each tack is put in place.

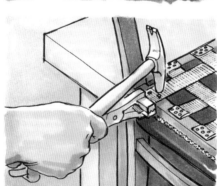

3 Reinforcing the webbing
Alternatively, tack and stretch new lengths of webbing across the underside of the seat, leaving the original in place. Position the webs slightly to one side to avoid hitting the old tacks (see page 82).

Torn covers

Tears and rips in fabrics tend to follow the warp and weft of the weave, forming a triangular flap. Coarse-textured fabrics can be sewn, but the stitching would be obvious on smooth coverings such as leather cloth. Bonding a patch of material under the tear reinforces the repair and will be less noticeable.

1 Fitting a patch
Cut a patch of a thin fabric such as canvas slightly larger than the torn area. Use a regulator or spoon handle to insert the patch evenly under the tear or rip.

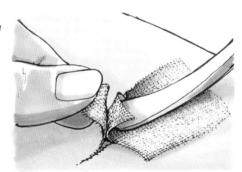

2 Gluing the tear
Peel back the loose flap of the covering, and temporarily hold it with a skewer or pin – use masking tape for leather. Carefully apply latex fabric adhesive under the edges of the tear and to the meeting faces of the flap and the new patch.

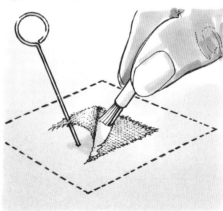

3 Pinning the flap
Turn the flap back into position and then mate up the torn edges, taking care not to spread the glue onto the surface. Use skewers to hold the fabric against the tension of the cover until the glue has set.

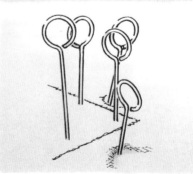

Worn piping

Piping is sewn into the seams of the covering; because it stands proud of the surface, it will almost invariably wear before the main covering. It can be replaced using hand stitching.

1 Cutting the fabrics

Try to match the original cloth in both texture and colour. If this is not possible, aim for an accurate colour match, unless you prefer a contrast. Cut diagonal strips of fabric 38mm (1½in) wide and stack them together, keeping the weave the same way round. Fabric cut 'on-the-cross' in this manner will follow curves smoothly.

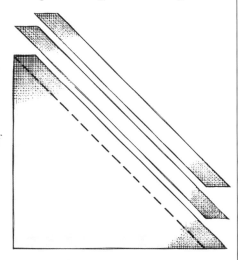

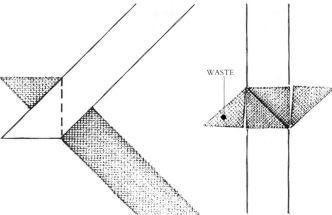

WASTE

2 Joining the fabric

Lay the end of one strip at 90 degrees to the end of the next, with their face sides together. Machine-stitch straight across to join them. Sew the remaining strips end to end in the same way, always with their 'right sides' together. Press the joins flat, and cut off the waste.

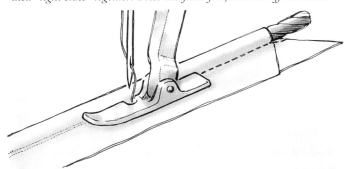

3 Forming the piping

Fold the strip of fabric in half lengthwise over a piece of piping cord of the appropriate size as you feed it through the sewing machine. Machine the seam close to the cord, using a special piping foot.

4 Stripping the old piping

Fix the covering in place with skewers. Using a dressmaker's thread-cutter or fine scissors, carefully cut the threads that hold the old piping along the seams.

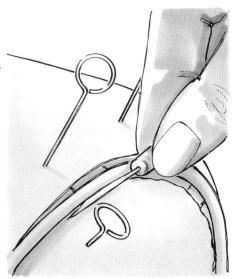

5 Fitting the new piping

Insert the piping into the seam and secure it with slip or ladder stitching (see page 80). Make the stitches about 12mm (½in) long for coarse fabrics and about 10mm (⅜in) or less for fine fabrics, to give a neat finish.

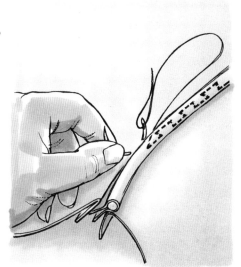

6 Working a curved edge

Where the piping follows a curved upholstery edge, cut notches in the flange.

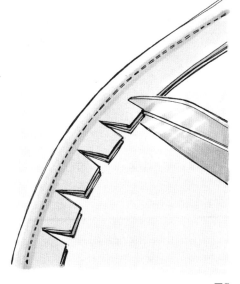

SLIP STITCHING

Also known as ladder stitching, this hand-sewn method is commonly used to close up a seam.

1 Making a slipknot

Using a 75mm (3in) curved needle, first make a small stitch at one end in the fold of the fabric and pull the thread through. Holding the thread taut, coil the short end over itself and the long thread, and pass the end through the loop formed in the process. Tighten the knot and slide it down the thread.

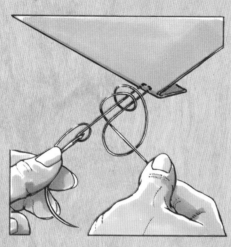

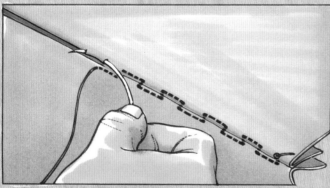

2 Making the stitch

Make the first stitch through the opposite fold of the seam, setting it back about 2mm (¹⁄₁₆in) from the knot position. Take the needle across to the other side and make the next stitch, again setting it back by about 2mm (¹⁄₁₆in) from where the first stitch emerged. Repeat this sequence, pulling the seam closed after every six stitches or so.

3 Making a French knot

Make a small stitch at the end of the seam, and wind the thread over the needle as it emerges. Pull the thread through and tighten it into a knot to secure the stitching. To prevent the knot coming undone, make two long stitches back and forth along the seam before you finally cut the thread.

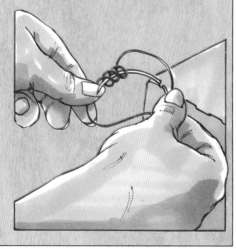

Worn rubber webbing

Slack or missing rubber webbing causes the cushions of an easy chair to sag. The webbing may be stapled, tacked in place, or held with special clips for wooden or metal frames. Webs should be spaced no more than their width apart, and should cover 50 per cent of the seat area.

1 Calculating the length

Rubber webbing must be cut shorter than the span of the frame, to provide the tension required. The standard 50mm (2in) webbing is usually reduced by 10 per cent in length for seats and 7.5 per cent for backs. This is deducted from the distance between the clips or end fixings.

2 Using clips for wood

Cut the webbing to length, ensuring that the ends are square. Secure the steel clips to the webbing ends by squeezing them in a vice. Slot the web into place with the rounded shoulder of the clip on the inside. The inner edge of the seat frame should be rounded to prevent wear on the webbing.

3 Using metal-tube clips

First cut the webbing to length. Using the old webbing as a guide, mark and then pierce holes through the ends of the new webbing. Fold the ends over the metal clips before fitting the staples and washers provided. Bend the ends of the staples over with pliers and hammer them flat on the underside.

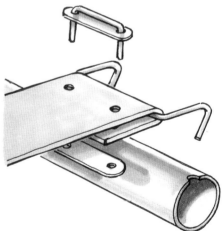

RE-COVERING A DROP-IN SEAT

Framed dining chairs are sometimes fitted with upholstered, drop-in seat pads that either rest in a rebate cut on the inside of the seat rails, or simply sit on the corner blocks used to brace the frame. These pads were traditionally stuffed with vegetable fibre or animal hair, but nowadays plastic or latex foams are also common. The actual base of the pad, upon which the upholstery is built, is often no more than a panel of plywood, but traditional upholstery uses a webbed wooden frame. If, after stripping the old upholstery, the frame is in a poor state, it could be simpler to make a new one than to repair it.

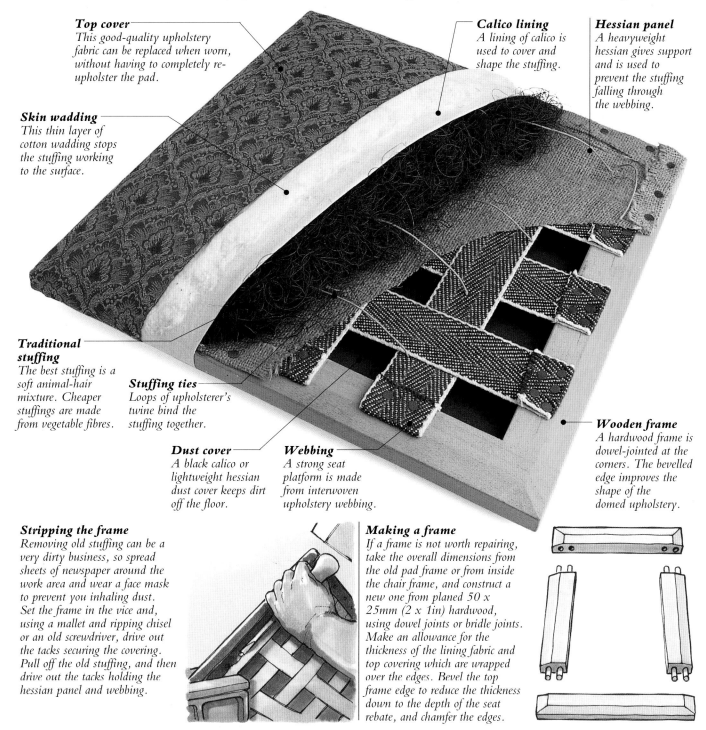

Top cover
This good-quality upholstery fabric can be replaced when worn, without having to completely re-upholster the pad.

Skin wadding
This thin layer of cotton wadding stops the stuffing working to the surface.

Calico lining
A lining of calico is used to cover and shape the stuffing.

Hessian panel
A heavyweight hessian gives support and is used to prevent the stuffing falling through the webbing.

Traditional stuffing
The best stuffing is a soft animal-hair mixture. Cheaper stuffings are made from vegetable fibres.

Stuffing ties
Loops of upholsterer's twine bind the stuffing together.

Dust cover
A black calico or lightweight hessian dust cover keeps dirt off the floor.

Webbing
A strong seat platform is made from interwoven upholstery webbing.

Wooden frame
A hardwood frame is dowel-jointed at the corners. The bevelled edge improves the shape of the domed upholstery.

Stripping the frame
Removing old stuffing can be a very dirty business, so spread sheets of newspaper around the work area and wear a face mask to prevent you inhaling dust. Set the frame in the vice and, using a mallet and ripping chisel or an old screwdriver, drive out the tacks securing the covering. Pull off the old stuffing, and then drive out the tacks holding the hessian panel and webbing.

Making a frame
If a frame is not worth repairing, take the overall dimensions from the old pad frame or from inside the chair frame, and construct a new one from planed 50 x 25mm (2 x 1in) hardwood, using dowel joints or bridle joints. Make an allowance for the thickness of the lining fabric and top covering which are wrapped over the edges. Bevel the top frame edge to reduce the thickness down to the depth of the seat rebate, and chamfer the edges.

81

Webbing the frame

The support for the seat is provided by stretched webbing run from front to back and from side to side, and nailed to the frame. Start with one length in the middle, and space the others about 25mm (1in) apart.

1 Fixing the webbing

Clamp the frame to the bench. Take the continuous roll of webbing and fold over the first 40mm (1½in). Tack the folded end to the centre of the back rail, about 12mm (½in) from the outer edge; use five 15mm (⅝in) improved tacks. Stagger the tacks in order not to split the rail.

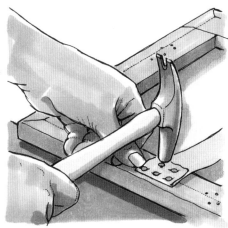

2 Stretching the webbing

Using a webbing stretcher, tension the web across the frame. Depending on the type being used, attach the webbing to the stretcher and lever down the handle to tension the webbing.

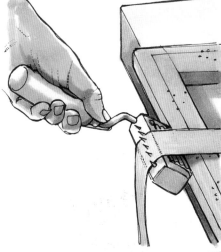

3 Fixing the end

Secure the webbing to the front rail with three tacks. Remove the stretcher and cut the webbing, leaving a 40mm (1½in) flap to fold over and fix with two more tacks. Stretch and fix the remaining front-to-back webbing in the same way, followed by the side-to-side webbing, which is interwoven with it.

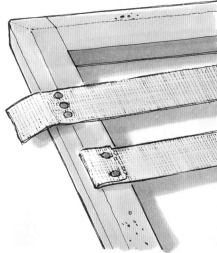

Fitting the hessian panel

A taut, heavyweight hessian panel is used to cover the webs and prevent the stuffing from falling through.

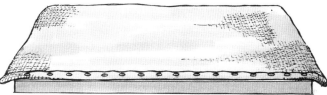

1 Tacking the front edge

Draw round the frame and cut the hessian 25mm (1in) larger all round. Fold over one edge and tack it to the front rail, spacing the tacks about 25mm (1in) apart.

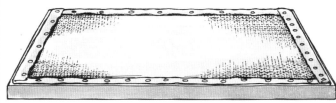

2 Fixing the back edge

Stretch the hessian to the back rail and, starting from the middle, fix it with tacks spaced about 50mm (2in) apart. Fold the hessian over and fix more tacks between those in the first row. Stretch and fix the hessian across the sides of frame in the same way.

Applying the stuffing

Traditional hair-and-fibre stuffing is attached to the hessian with loops of twine known as stuffing ties, and is built up to form a loose domed pile about 100 to 150mm (4 to 6in) high.

1 Making stuffing ties

Thread a large half-circle needle with No 1 twine. Start near one corner of the platform with a slip knot, then sew three or four rows of stuffing ties across the hessian, making each loop about 40mm (1½in) high. Finish with a double-hitch knot (see page 87).

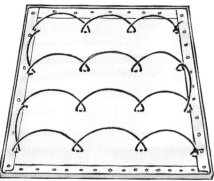

2 Adding the stuffing

Push handfuls of stuffing beneath the ties, teasing it out to form even rows. Fill the spaces between the rows with more stuffing, adding more to the centre until you have constructed an even dome shape.

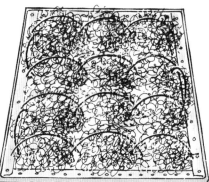

Covering with calico

Unbleached calico is an inexpensive material used as the first covering, to secure and shape the stuffing.

1 Fitting the calico

Cut or tear a panel of calico about 50 to 75mm (2 to 3in) larger than the seat frame on all sides. Lay the calico over the stuffing with its weave square to the front rail, and then hold the lining in place by temporarily tacking it to the outer edges of all four sides of the frame.

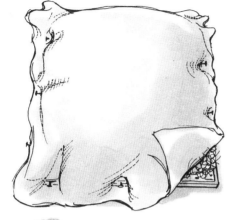

2 Secondary calico tacking

Support the frame on one corner, holding it between your arm and body to leave both hands free to attach the calico. Tension it with one hand while driving three or four temporary tacks into the underside of the frame. Tack all the other sides in the same way.

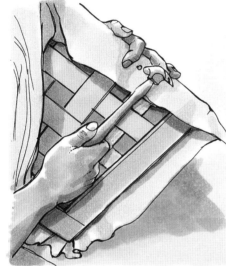

3 Tensioning the calico

Remove the tacks from the edges of the frame, then stretch the calico diagonally over each corner and tack it to the underside. Rest the frame on one edge and remove the upper tacks. Re-tension the fabric while running the flat of your free hand towards the edge to smooth out the stuffing.

4 Fixing the calico

Secure the covering with a neat row of 10mm (⅜in) tacks, working out from the centre to the corners. Tack the opposite edge of the calico, and then the other two sides. Make neat pleats at each corner, and fix these with tacks. Finally trim the cover close to the line of tacks.

5 Tearing the wadding

Place a layer of cotton 'skin' wadding over the calico lining, to prevent the stuffing materials working through the top cover. Holding the wadding down firmly with one hand, tear it to size, leaving a feathered edge all round.

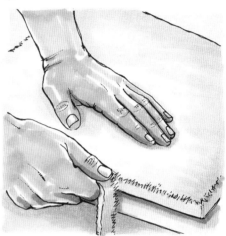

Fitting the top cover and dust cover

Mark the centre points on all four rails with a soft pencil. Cut the top covering fabric to shape, allowing an extra 50mm (2in) all round. Cut small V-notches in the edges of the fabric to mark the centre on all four sides. Lay the cover centrally over the pad and tack into place as for the calico lining.

Fitting a dust cover

Staple a cotton panel to the underside of the pad to cover the tacks. Use a similar method to that described for the hessian seat panel, but fold the edges under before stapling.

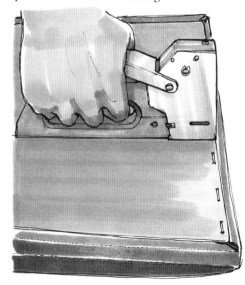

Using foam upholstery

When using a foam pad to cushion a framed drop-in seat, fit the webbing and cover the frame with a hessian panel as for a traditional stuffing. Plywood platforms need no preparation.

1 Cutting the foam

Place the frame or panel onto 25mm (1in) thick, firm-density foam. Draw round it with a felt-tip pen, then cut the foam 12mm (½in) larger all round. An ordinary bread knife will cut foam, but an electric carving knife is preferable.

2 Thickening the pad

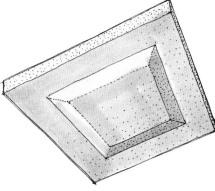

Cut a pad of 12mm (½in) thick foam to the same shape as the seat, but 60mm (2½in) smaller all round. Cut a shallow bevel on its edges, then bond it centrally to the underside of the larger pad. This will produce the required dome shape.

3 Taping the edge

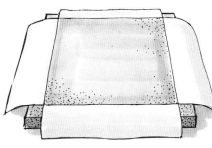

Glue 125mm (5in) wide strips of calico to the top of the pad so that they overlap the edges by 75mm (3in). These tacking strips will secure the foam and shape the edges into a curve.

4 Fixing the pad

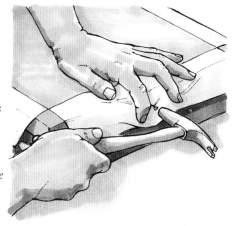

Place the pad on the centre of the frame or base panel, and then temporarily tack through the tape, as when tacking a calico cover. Tuck the edges of the foam under, to produce an even, curved profile. Tack or staple the tape to the underside. Fit the calico lining and top cover (see page 83).

Re-covering a pincushion pad

Unlike the drop-in seat pad, which is made as a separate unit, some chairs have a shallow pad that is fixed to the top of the seat frame. These are known as pincushion seats. The stuffing is built up on a webbing base in a similar way to that used for a drop-in seat, but the covering is trimmed with braid or finishing chair nails.

1 Stripping the old upholstery

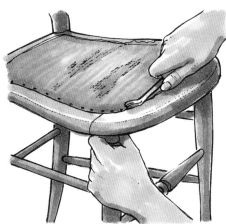

This type of pad is often used on elegant mahogany-framed side or bedroom chairs. Take care when removing the tacked materials not to split the brittle wood. Use a tack lifter or pincers, rather than driving tacks out with a ripping chisel.

2 Making the pad

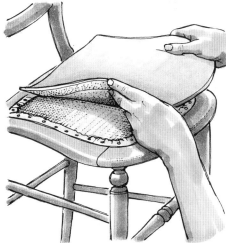

Tack webbing and a hessian panel to the frame as for a drop-in seat. Sew in stuffing ties in the same way, and build up a shallow dome of stuffing held with a calico covering tacked all round and then trimmed just inside the area of the pad. Alternatively, use a foam pad with the edges undercut at an angle in place of the traditional stuffing.

3 Fitting the top cover

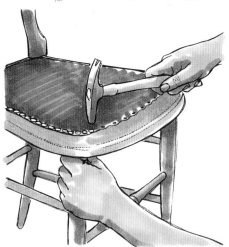

Cut the cover about 18mm (¾in) larger than the finished shape. Temporarily fix the cover into place with fine tacks, tucking the edges under all round. When the tension is even, tack the cover permanently. Finish the edges with close-fitting chair nails or sewn-on braid.

TRADITIONAL STUFFED-OVER SEAT

Stuffed-over seats are the thick seat pads enclosing most or all of the seat rails on dining chairs. The covering is either tacked off under the frame or fixed and trimmed on the face of the rails.

Early seats used a thick pad of stuffing built up on hessian-covered webbing fixed to the top of the frame. Later seats used coil springs. The webbing supports for the springs were tacked to the underside of the rails. The position of the webbing tack holes on a bare frame indicates whether springs were originally fitted to the seat, although they may have been added subsequently.

The stuffing is built up and then consolidated with stitching to form an edge roll that gives the overall shape. Where springs are not used, the stuffing is built on a flat hessian platform similar to that of a drop-in seat. The hessian panel of a sprung seat is shaped to cover the springs. This example deals with a sprung seat, but the methods for forming the stuffing are similar for both types.

Top cover
Upholstery-grade patterned or plain-coloured fabric, made from natural and man-made fibres in a wide range of types to suit all styles of work.

Medium hessian or scrim
Used to cover and retain the first layer of stuffing. Stitched through ties fasten the scrim to the heavy-weight hessian below, to consolidate the stuffing.

Skin wadding
A thin layer of cotton wadding gives a soft feel and prevents the stuffing from working its way through the covering.

Braid or gimp
A decorative trimming used to cover the line of tacks.

Calico lining
Used to cover the second stuffing.

Edge roll
A firm edge formed by compressing the stuffing with stitches through the hessian.

Second stuffing
More stuffing, held with stuffing ties, is used to build up the seat shape.

First stuffing
Hair or fibre stuffing built up to form a pad and held in place with stuffing ties.

Heavy-weight hessian
Used to cover the springs and support the stuffing.

Spring ties
Thick laycord used to link springs together and to tie them to the frame to stop them buckling.

Coil springs
Steel-wire 'double-cone' compression springs sewn to heavyweight hessian and webbing.

Dust cover
A lightweight fabric tacked to the underside of the rails to prevent dust falling to the floor.

Webbing
Interwoven cotton or jute webbing tacked to the underside of the rails as a seat support.

Preparing for work

Clear the bench or set up trestles to support the chair. If the frame is polished, lay strips of foam-backed carpet on the work surface to protect the finish.

Stripping the upholstery

Although it is possible to make good an upholstered seat without stripping all the materials, a new seat built from the frame up will give longer service.

1 Removing the covering

Start by removing the top cover. Carefully prise out or pull the tacks from face-fixed coverings; you can use a ripping chisel to clear the tacks that are holding coverings under the rails. Try to save the fabric to use as a pattern for the new cover.

2 Removing the stuffing

Peel off the skin wadding and untack the calico lining. Lift off the second stuffing layer to reveal the scrim-covered first stuffing. Cut the twine through-ties, remove the scrim-fixing tacks and cut the stuffing ties at the same time as you remove the stuffing.

3 Removing the springs

Remove the tacks, always following the grain, and cut the spring ties to enable you to lift off the heavyweight hessian. Strip out the spring-lacing cord and then cut the fixing twine to free the springs. Remove the underside dust cover, if that has not already been stripped, and then the webbing.

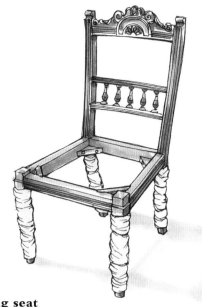

4 Preparing the frame

Make sure all the tacks are removed. Inspect the joints and rails, and repair them as required. Refurbish the wood finish and then bind the legs with a soft cloth to protect them while the upholstery work is completed.

Building a sprung seat

Start by webbing the frame. The amount of webbing will depend on the size of the chair. A good guide is to allow about the width of one finger between the webs at the back and sides, and two fingers at the front. The webs are tacked to the underside of the seat frame in a similar manner to that described for a drop-in seat (see page 82). Position the webs to provide all-round support to the base of the springs. Most often, four springs are placed symmetrically on the webbing. In order for the springs to exert equal pressure, arrange the twisted ends at the top of the coils to face the centre. If a fifth, central, spring is needed, place its twist facing forward.

1 Stitching the springs

Start at one corner or with the central spring, if used. With the chair standing upright or laid on its back, stitch the base of the spring to the webbing, using a curved spring needle threaded with No 1 thickness twine.

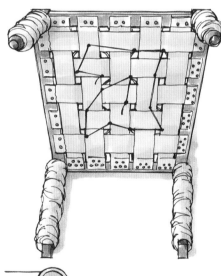

2 Starting the stitching

Pass the needle up through the webbing, close to the outside edge of the base of the spring. Pass it back through, close to the inside of the coil, and secure the spring with a slipknot.

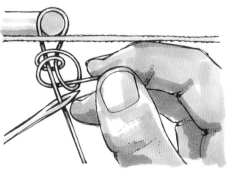

3 Using a half-hitch knot

Secure the remainder of the coil with two or three half-hitch knots stitched through the webbing and spaced equally apart. Move on to the next spring, and sew it to the webbing with three or four half-hitches.

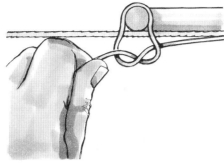

4 Using a double-hitch knot

Sew the other springs in place in the same way, and finally tie off the twine with a double-hitch knot on the last spring.

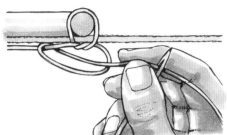

Tying the springs

In order for the springs to compress as one unit, the tops of the coils are tied together with lengths of laycord run from back to front and from side to side.

1 Fixing a cord

Partially drive 16mm (⅝in) improved tacks into the top edges of the seat frame in line with the springs. Cut the cord into lengths about twice the size of the seat. Knot a cord around a back tack about 225mm (9in) from the end, and then drive in a tack to fix it.

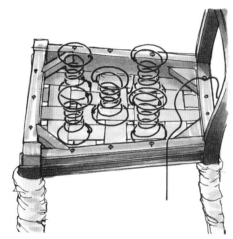

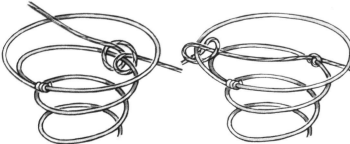

2 Tying the knots

Compress the rear spring by about 50mm (2in), and secure the second coil with a clove-hitch knot. Continue across and onto the top coil of the spring, and tie a lock-loop knot. Secure the next spring in the reverse order, and finally tie off the cord on the opposite tack.

3 Lacing the springs

Lace all the springs from front to back and from side to side in this way, keeping the tension even. Where cords cross, bind them together with a lock loop. Tie the loose ends of each cord to the top coil of the spring with a double-hitch, so that they are held at a slight angle.

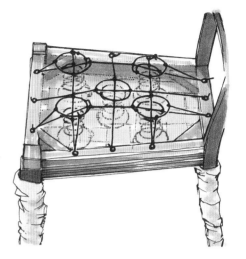

Covering the springs

Heavyweight hessian fabric is used to cover the springs evenly and to provide a sound base for the stuffing.

1 Fitting the hessian

Cut the hessian panel about 25mm (1in) larger than the seat. Tension the fabric over the springs without compressing them, and fix it to the top of the rails with light tacking. When the cover is even, fold over the edges and tack it permanently.

2 Stitching the springs

Sew the tops of the springs to the hessian cover, employing the same method as when tying them to the webbing.

87

Building the first stuffing

Once the foundation of webbing and springs is in place, the hair or fibre stuffing materials can be added.

1 Sewing stuffing ties

Using a curved needle, sew a row of stuffing ties about 60mm (2½in) from the bottom edge of the sloping face of the hessian and across the middle (see page 82).

2 Placing the stuffing

Pack rolls of stuffing under the ties to form a firm edge, and build up the centre to around 100mm (4in) deep, using more stuffing. Manipulate the stuffing to make it consistent and even in density and shape.

3 Covering with scrim

Cut an oversized panel of scrim to cover the stuffing, drape it evenly over the seat, and then temporarily tack it to each rail. Make a diagonal cut in the back corners to fit the covering around the back legs. Trim the surplus and fold in the spare scrim fabric at the ends.

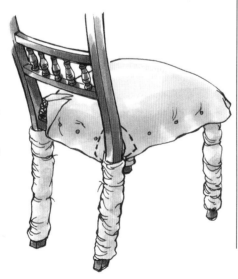

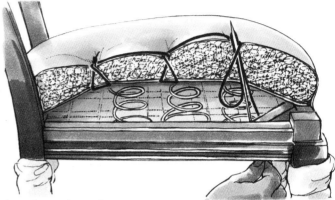

4 Making through ties

Using a mattress needle and No 1 twine, stitch ties through the stuffing to hold it in place. Starting in one corner of the covering, push the needle down through the stuffing and hessian covering the springs. Take the threaded end about 18mm (¾in) forward, passing it back up to the point of entry and securing with a slip knot.

Continue to make the ties around the seat with 100mm (4in) stitches above and 18mm (¾in) below, finishing in the middle of the seat. Do not catch the springs.

5 Tacking the seat

Starting at the front, remove a few of the temporary tacks at a time and, if required, push more stuffing under the scrim to firm up the edge. Tuck the edge of the scrim under the stuffing and tack it temporarily to the bevel on the top edge of the seat. Following a thread to keep the tension even, close-tack it to the rail, working round all four sides.

6 Pleating the corners

Pack the corners with stuffing until hard. Tuck in the scrim to form neat pleats at the front corner, and tack the edges to secure them.

Forming an edge roll

In order to give the seat a well-defined shape and provide a firm support, blind stitches are used to consolidate the sides before an edge roll is formed.

1 Using a regulator

Moving the stuffing about with a regulator helps to reinforce and even out the edges. Insert the regulator through the scrim, and employ a stirring action to gather the fibre round the spike and pack it into position.

2 Blind stitching

Starting about 40mm (1½in) from one of the back legs, insert a mattress needle threaded with No 2 or No 3 twine into the edge just above the tack line, at an angle of 45 degrees.

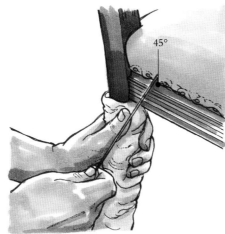

45°

3 Knotting the stitch

Pull the needle through, but not all the way out. With the eye still in the stuffing, angle it towards the back corner, and push it backwards so that the eye emerges close to the tack line. Pull the needle out, tie the end of the thread with a slip-knot and pull taut.

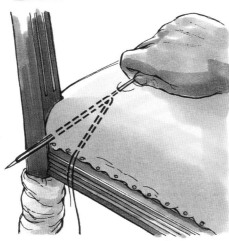

4 Making the next stitch

Insert the needle about 50mm (2in) along from the first stitch, again at about 45 degrees, and pull it through to the eye as before. Push the needle backwards to emerge about 25mm (1in) from the point of entry.

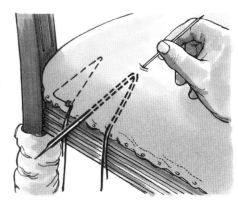

5 Tying the thread

Before pulling the needle out, wind the thread secured by the slipknot three times in a clockwise direction around the needle. Pull the needle through the loops to knot the thread tightly.

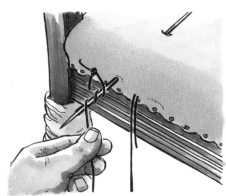

6 Completing the stitching

Continue in this way along the side, the front, the other side and then the back, securing the ends of the thread with a double-hitch knot. Make a second row of stitches in a similar way, about 12mm (½in) above the first row. Model the shape with a regulator.

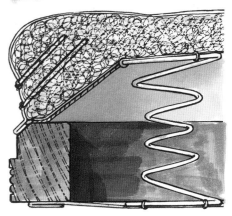

7 Forming the edge roll

Work the edge into an even line, using a regulator. Mark parallel stitch lines about 22mm (⅞in) from the edge on the top and sides. Starting at the side, make a series of 25mm (1in) long stitches to pass right through the edge, and finally knot them as described previously.

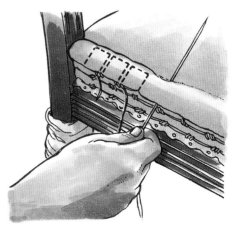

Second stuffing

Add more stuffing by sewing a series of stuffing ties across the seat and packing them to form an even shape, as described for making a drop-in seat (see page 82). The stuffing should be 50mm (2in) thick, and should taper to the edge without overhanging the edge roll.

Tear a calico panel about 100mm (4in) larger than the seat, to cover it. Lay the calico in place and smooth it into an even dome shape. Tack it temporarily, working from the centre on all four sides. The edges are not tucked underneath, but are cut level with the tacks when they are finally fixed.

Making the back corners

Fold the fabric over at the corners and make a diagonal cut towards the leg. Fold the spare material under and tuck the covering around the leg before tacking it into place.

Stuffed corners

There are two methods of making corners, depending on the leg shape.

1 Forming rounded corners

For rounded corners, make two even pleats on each side of the corner. Tension the fabric across the corner and fix it with a tack, then fold the pleats underneath.

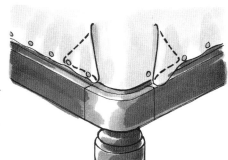

2 Forming square corners

To form a square corner, make a single pleat, tacking the spare fabric to the front rail.

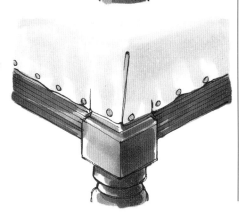

Fitting the covering

The calico lining is now covered with one or two layers of wadding, torn to the shape of the seat. This is then overlaid with the top covering fabric, fitted in the same way as the calico, except that the spare material at the pleated corners is cut away from the inside of the folds, to give a neater appearance to the thicker fabric. In some cases the pleats may need to be closed with a neat line of slip stitches (see page 80).

Finishing the edges

To finish off the tacked edges, use a decorative braid bonded in place with a fabric adhesive.

Gluing the braid

Fold back the end of the braid and tack it level with the back of the leg, using two gimp pins. Apply latex adhesive to the back of the braid and then press it into place around the seat. Fasten the other end with a gimp pin. Fix a length of braid to the back rail in the same way.

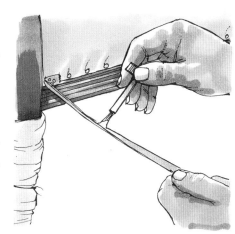

Sewing the braid

Braid can also be sewn into place using a small curved needle and fine thread. Make small stitches along the top and bottom edges.

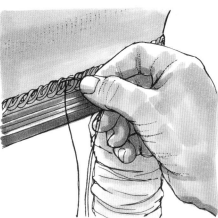

Using upholstery nails

Nails can be used instead of braid. Alternatively, you can pin braid in place with chair nails. Space the nails to follow a straight and even line. For close nailing, ensure that the heads touch. Tap any misaligned nail heads sideways before driving them home.

LEATHER UPHOLSTERY

Leather is a high-quality upholstery material that improves with age, provided it is regularly cleaned and nourished. When used to cover conventional stuffed upholstery, leather is normally fastened to a chair frame with upholstery nails. Alternatively, wide seat and back panels are cut from relatively thick hide, and are then sewn to form cylindrical sleeves that are slipped over a tubular-steel frame.

Maintaining leather

Most leathers used for upholstery since the 1920s are fully-finished; being water-resistant, they are relatively easy to maintain. However, earlier, aniline-finished leathers are not water-resistant, and stain relatively easily.

1 Cleaning finished leathers

Make up a cleaning solution from a non-alkaline soap (use non-perfumed pure toilet soap) and water. Do not use a detergent such as washing-up liquid, as this can lead to long-term deterioration of the surface. Work up a lather with a wrung-out soft cloth, taking great care not to soak the leather.

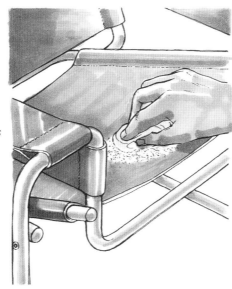

2 Finishing the surface

Wipe the surface with a clean damp cloth, and leave it to dry thoroughly. Apply thin coats of hide food to finish and nourish the clean leather, and polish with a soft cloth.

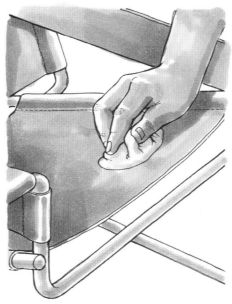

Identifying and treating aniline leather

To detect whether old furniture leather is aniline, drip a small amount of water onto an inconspicuous part of the upholstery. If the water is quickly absorbed though the surface, the leather is almost certainly aniline, and will subsequently require a great deal of care through regular maintenance.

Cleaning and finishing

Regular wiping with a soft cloth dampened with warm soapy water helps keep the leather clean. A hide food can be used on aniline leather, but only extremely sparingly. A better finish for aniline leather is pure soft beeswax. Do not use waxes that contain any silicone.

Dealing with cracks

Cracking occurs when leather loses its natural oils, through neglect and being stored in an unsympathetic environment. Although you cannot eliminate or even disguise surface cracking, regular treatment with a leather dressing will at least recondition the fibres and prevent further damage.

Treating the leather

Apply hide-food cream once a month over a six-month period, cleaning between applications to prevent a build-up on the surface; or apply a proprietary liquid leather dressing, following the manufacturer's instructions.

Stitching leather

'Slung' leather seats, backs and arm straps on chairs are usually made from two layers of thick leather bonded back-to-back and sewn together along their edges, employing a saddler's stitch. If the stitching has failed, you can replace it using two harness needles.

1 Preparing for sewing

Match the new thread to the original, cut it no more than 1.8m (6ft) long, and draw it through a block of beeswax. Taper the ends and thread each end through a needle, then push the needles right through the thread to form a loop to lock the needles.

2 Starting the seam

Strip the old thread from the seam. Insert one needle about three holes in from one end, and pull the thread through until it is an even length on both sides.

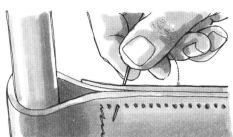

3 First stitches

Working towards the end, insert both needles in the next hole from each side of the seam. Make sure that the right-hand needle passes over the left-hand needle as they go through. Pull the thread tight.

4 Stitching the seam

At the end, work back along the entire seam, now inserting the needles left over right through each hole. Pull the stitches tight as you go.

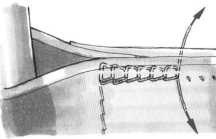

5 Finishing off

At the other end of the seam, work back right over left for three or four holes to secure the thread. Cut the thread with a sharp knife.

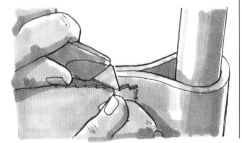

METAL-FURNITURE REPAIRS

Metal furniture is relatively uncommon and, being made from a strong material, the need for repair is rare. If a metal chair is damaged, it is usually not so easy to restore as furniture made of wood. Even so, it is possible to work metal with a limited range of basic workshop tools, and it can be glued. Making a repair as good as new, however, requires the services of a specialist.

Cast-iron repairs

Cast-iron furniture can suffer from brittle fractures. The surfaces of the break usually fit back together well, and can be glued. If a decorative, non-structural piece of metal has broken off, gluing it back in place is probably sufficient.

1 Gluing the break

Check the fit and make sure that the surfaces of the break are clean. Using tiny quantities of super-glue, press the pieces back in position. When set, run more glue sparingly around the join, allowing capillary action to draw it in. Gel types of superglue need only be applied to the surfaces, and will take up any slight unevenness.

2 Using epoxy adhesive

If you are using an epoxy-resin adhesive, warm both parts with a hair dryer or fan heater. Cover both surfaces of the break with an even film of glue. Press together, check the fit and remove any glue that might squeeze out. Hold the parts together with adhesive tape or string until set.

3 Using reinforcing dowels

For a stronger joint, drill both parts and insert roughened metal dowels. Put a spot of paint on the centre of one end to position and align the holes. Set the other part in place to transfer the mark.

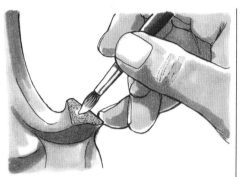

Making missing parts

If a broken piece is missing, but the shape is basically two-dimensional, consider making a replacement, using casting resin. If a similar part exists, perhaps on another piece of furniture, it may be possible to make a mould from it, using a material such as plaster, rubber or glass fibre. Some castings are moulded on one face only, the other being flat. If the casting is moulded on both faces, you will need to make a split mould.

1 Making a mould box

Lay the component from which the casting will be taken on a board. Make a wooden frame that encloses the area to be moulded, or use modelling clay. Cut notches in a wooden frame where the parts of the component extend out of the sides. Paint the frame and seal the notches with modelling clay.

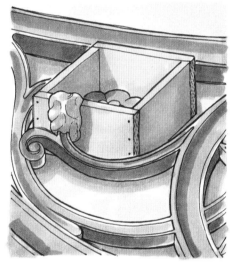

2 Making the mould

Coat the surfaces, including the component, with a release agent such as petroleum jelly. Half-fill the framed area with plaster of Paris. Make two holes in the surface to form registration points in the mould and, when dry, coat the surface with petroleum jelly.

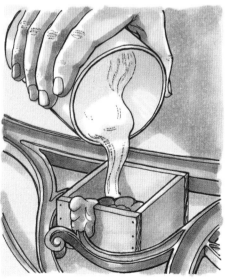

3 Completing the mould

Mix and pour more plaster of Paris to cover the remaining half of the moulding and fill the frame. Leave to dry thoroughly, then dismantle the mould, leaving two reverse-moulding halves of the shape to be cast. Fill all but one exit hole in mouldings where the original casting extends beyond the mould. Apply a release agent to the surfaces.

4 Making the casting

Clamp the two halves together with strong elastic bands. Mix casting resin according to the manufacturer's specification and pour it into the mould. When set, remove from the mould and clean up the edges with a file.

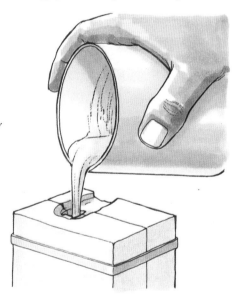

5 Fitting the casting

Prepare the joining surfaces between the old and new materials by cutting and filing them both flat. Bond the new moulding in place with epoxy resin. A metal dowel can be included to strengthen the joint.

Repairing load-bearing parts

It is possible to weld cast iron, but this is a job for a professional. It might prove possible to brace a component with a flat back by bolting on a steel splint, but this must be done carefully to avoid an ugly result.

1 Using steel plate

Mark the shape of the component on the plate and cut out the profile using a drill, hacksaw and files. Ensure the splint spans the break to give good support on each side.

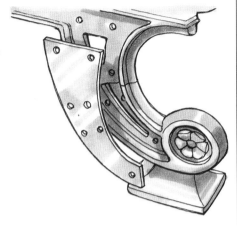

 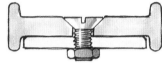

2 Fixing the plate

Clamp the brace in place and drill bolt holes through the sound sections of the casting and reinforcement. Ideally, cut threads in the bracing and use countersunk bolts for a neat finish. Otherwise, drill plain holes and use through bolts secured with nuts. Thoroughly paint the metal to protect and disguise the repair.

Dismantling bolted joints

Cast-iron furniture is usually made in components held together with bolts. It is easier to repair bolted components if you dismantle the furniture first.

Dealing with corroded threads

Where threads have corroded, it pays to apply penetrating oil before you attempt to free them. Let the oil soak in for at least 10 minutes.

Using heat

If the fixing resists the lubrication treatment, try heating the nuts with a gas torch. Allow to cool and apply more penetrating oil.

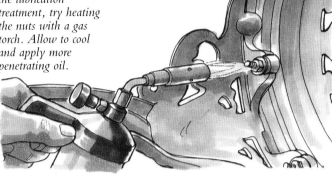

Dealing with worn nuts

If the flats of the nut have become rounded, use a plier wrench to grip the nut or refile the flats.

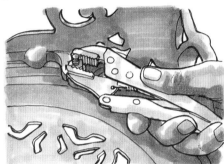

Dealing with broken bolts

If a bolt or stud has sheared off, it may be possible to remove it with a special extractor tool. Drill an appropriate-size hole in the bolt as accurately centred as possible. Insert the extractor screw and turn it anti-clockwise with a spanner.

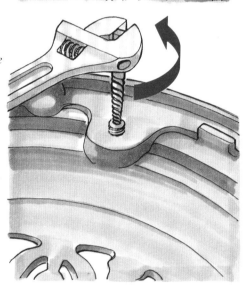

Drilling a broken bolt

Alternatively, drill down the centre of the stump, then pick out the remains of the bolt from the threaded hole.

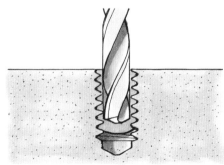

Tubular-steel repairs

Steel is tougher than cast iron and will usually bend considerably before breaking; it may even be possible to bend it back into line. However, years of repeated bending and straightening will inevitably cause steel to crack.

Dealing with distortion

Metal tubing that is overstressed will distort. To correct the problem it is necessary to support the frame securely, in order to bend only that part that needs straightening.

Clamping the frame

Assuming the leg of a chair is bent out of line, brace the frame with a notched batten and sash cramps placed at the point of the bend. Use a fast-action cramp set in reverse, or possibly a car jack, to apply a controlled force to straighten the tube. It will probably be necessary to over-straighten the part to allow for spring in the tube.

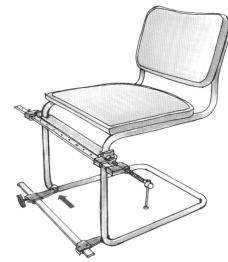

Mending cracks

Cracks in steel tubing can be repaired by welding, but it takes skill to avoid burning through. Also, the heat will probably soften the metal and certainly damage the finish. Brazing will not burn holes but, as it takes longer, it heats the metal more.

1 Bracing the repair

If the break is in a straight section, it may be possible to insert a piece of smaller diameter tube to jig the repair. This reduces the risk of burning through and strengthens the joint to compensate for softening of the metal, and makes it unnecessary to weld all round. The joint could also be secured with epoxy-resin adhesive.

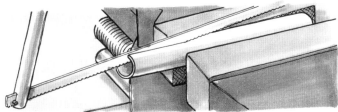

2 Cutting the tube

Cut the inner tube about 75mm (3in) long, and round over the ends with a hammer. If the diameter is difficult to match, cut a slit in a slightly larger diameter piece that will squeeze down to fit.

Wrought iron

This is very tough and malleable, and must be worked with handtools. It should be possible to straighten wrought iron without risk of breaking. If a component should fail, repair it by welding, brazing or riveting.

Wrought iron is not readily available, but mild steel is a reasonable substitute for replacement parts; indeed, much of what is called wrought iron today is in fact mild steel.

Thin-section wrought iron is used to make elegant garden seating

Repairing a riveted joint

Joints between wrought-iron components are often made using rivets which, when worn, will weaken the frame.

Replacing rivets

Drill out or cut old rivets and replace them with new soft-iron ones. Support the work on an anvil or heavy metal plate and, using a ball-peen hammer, forge the end of the rivet to fill a countersunk hole drilled in the metal. Alternatively, form the rivet into a rounded head.

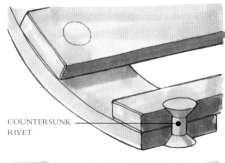

COUNTERSUNK RIVET

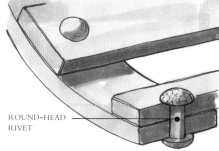

ROUND-HEAD RIVET

TABLES

A TABLE IN ITS BASIC FORM IS SIMPLY A FLAT
top supported on a base or legs at the
appropriate height for its purpose. From this
principle a whole range of types and shapes
have been produced, such as dining tables in
all their variants, side tables, console tables,
sofa tables, writing tables, card tables and tea
tables. Some include ingenious methods for
extending the surface, and their tops and bases
can be made in various shapes, providing us
with a rich design choice.

Most tables are made from solid wood, but
some, particularly the smaller types, are often
veneered and inlaid with decorative motifs,
which require different restoration techniques.

TABLE CONSTRUCTION

Traditional tables are primarily functional pieces of furniture. Some are quite plain, while others are fitted with simple or elaborate folding frames and tops. Typical designs include frame, draw-leaf, drop-leaf and pedestal tables.

Frame tables

The majority of frame tables are based on a simple jointed frame with legs placed at each corner. The method of construction – using mortise-and-tenon or dowel joints – ensures a rigid frame, provided the sections are not too thin.

The rails of a table act as beams to support the load, and need to be as deep or wide as possible to resist bending. Rails are therefore generally wider than they are thick, and are set vertically on edge.

In order to sit at a dining table, there must be sufficient clearance for your knees. This tends to restrict the width of the rails, and therefore the span of the frame. To overcome the problem, extra legs are used to support the rails of long tables.

In order to accommodate a drawer, two end rails are set horizontally into the frame to provide an opening while tying the legs together. The upper rail is usually dovetailed into the top of the leg, and the lower rail is stub-tenoned into the inside face. A central crossrail stiffens the frame.

Lightweight tables, such as decorative side tables or tea tables, are made from thinner sections, often simply jointed and screwed together. In the case of bamboo pieces, the butt-jointed frame is held by nothing more than glue and long thin nails.

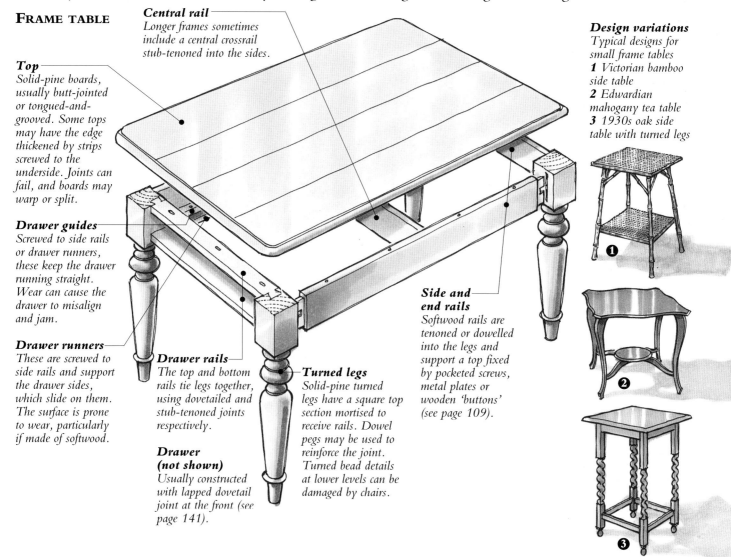

FRAME TABLE

Central rail
Longer frames sometimes include a central crossrail stub-tenoned into the sides.

Top
Solid-pine boards, usually butt-jointed or tongued-and-grooved. Some tops may have the edge thickened by strips screwed to the underside. Joints can fail, and boards may warp or split.

Drawer guides
Screwed to side rails or drawer runners, these keep the drawer running straight. Wear can cause the drawer to misalign and jam.

Drawer runners
These are screwed to side rails and support the drawer sides, which slide on them. The surface is prone to wear, particularly if made of softwood.

Drawer rails
The top and bottom rails tie legs together, using dovetailed and stub-tenoned joints respectively.

Drawer (not shown)
Usually constructed with lapped dovetail joint at the front (see page 141).

Turned legs
Solid-pine turned legs have a square top section mortised to receive rails. Dowel pegs may be used to reinforce the joint. Turned bead details at lower levels can be damaged by chairs.

Side and end rails
Softwood rails are tenoned or dowelled into the legs and support a top fixed by pocketed screws, metal plates or wooden 'buttons' (see page 109).

Design variations
Typical designs for small frame tables
1 Victorian bamboo side table
2 Edwardian mahogany tea table
3 1930s oak side table with turned legs

❶

❷

❸

Extending tables

Dining is an important activity in family life, and on occasions can require a large table. When room is restricted, it is useful to have a smaller table that can extend. Draw-leaf extending tables, developed in the sixteenth century, proved an enduring type that became particularly popular in the 1930s. Many designs were inspired by oak trestle or framed refectory tables, which featured turned legs and low stretcher rails.

Basically a simple sliding system based on a stable four-legged or trestle underframe, a typical draw-leaf table comprises a single top that can rise and fall slightly to allow a pull-out 'leaf' to extend from each end as required. The sturdy framed construction of these tables rarely needs repair, but the working elements of the top can wear.

Another extending design, popular in Victorian times, uses a system of sliding frames that telescope together. The two complete halves of the table, when pulled apart, allow separate top panels to be dropped in across the frame. Short integral pegs locate in holes in the meeting edge, and the whole top is clamped together with metal fittings. Larger tables have a central pair of legs to support the extended frame, and some have a screw mechanism for extending the table. Wear can occur on the sliding system, and the wheeled castors fitted to the legs can fail.

DRAW-LEAF TABLE

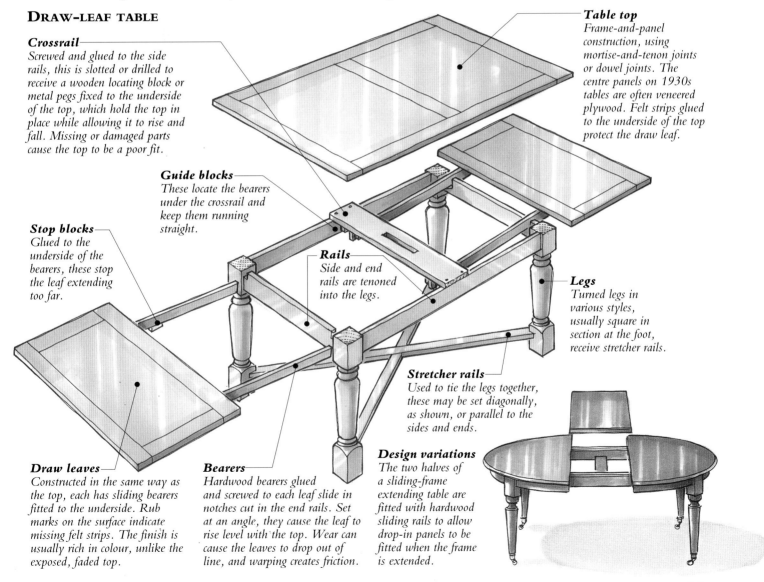

Crossrail
Screwed and glued to the side rails, this is slotted or drilled to receive a wooden locating block or metal pegs fixed to the underside of the top, which hold the top in place while allowing it to rise and fall. Missing or damaged parts cause the top to be a poor fit.

Table top
Frame-and-panel construction, using mortise-and-tenon joints or dowel joints. The centre panels on 1930s tables are often veneered plywood. Felt strips glued to the underside of the top protect the draw leaf.

Guide blocks
These locate the bearers under the crossrail and keep them running straight.

Stop blocks
Glued to the underside of the bearers, these stop the leaf extending too far.

Rails
Side and end rails are tenoned into the legs.

Legs
Turned legs in various styles, usually square in section at the foot, receive stretcher rails.

Draw leaves
Constructed in the same way as the top, each has sliding bearers fitted to the underside. Rub marks on the surface indicate missing felt strips. The finish is usually rich in colour, unlike the exposed, faded top.

Bearers
Hardwood bearers glued and screwed to each leaf slide in notches cut in the end rails. Set at an angle, they cause the leaf to rise level with the top. Wear can cause the leaves to drop out of line, and warping creates friction.

Stretcher rails
Used to tie the legs together, these may be set diagonally, as shown, or parallel to the sides and ends.

Design variations
The two halves of a sliding-frame extending table are fitted with hardwood sliding rails to allow drop-in panels to be fitted when the frame is extended.

Drop-leaf tables

Tables with hinged flaps have a long history; the gate-leg table is the most common. Most designs have a similar frame configuration, with a central four-legged main frame from which leg frames or 'gates' are pivoted to support the flaps. Tops are usually oval or round, incorporating a flap that folds down on each side of the main frame. Solid-oak mass-produced gate-leg tables were popular in the 1930s, and usually featured barley-twist legs.

Pembroke tables and sofa tables also feature drop-leaf tops. These are usually rectangular, with the flaps on the long sides of the Pembroke, and at the ends of the sofa type. Drawers are fitted at the ends and sides respectively. The flaps are held open by cantilevered wooden brackets attached by knuckle-joint hinges cut in the wood. Small card or tea tables sometimes use folding frames or a single leg jointed to a hinged rail to form an alternative gate-leg design, the latter style also being used for dining tables. The legs are turned, square-tapered, cabriole or sabre-shape, and most are fitted with castors.

Drop-leaf tables usually feature a rule joint where the flaps meet the fixed table top, forming an attractive edge detail that masks the hinges. Typical problems include warped tops, loose gates, split table legs, and binding rule joints.

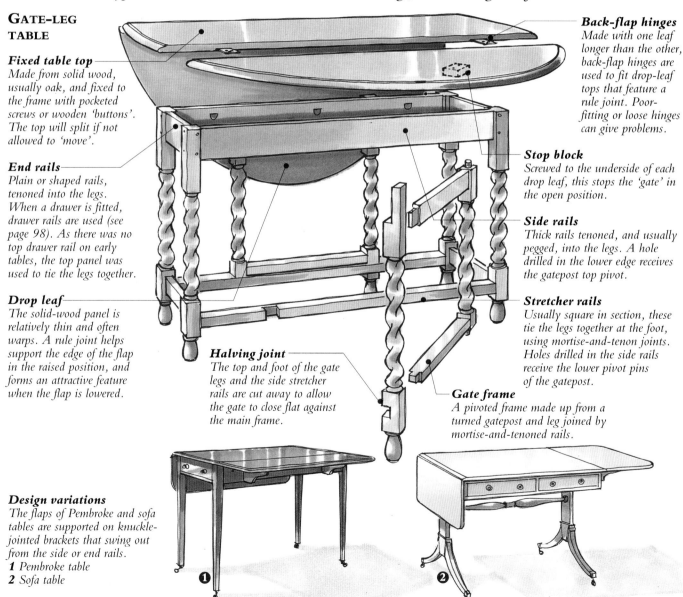

GATE-LEG TABLE

Fixed table top
Made from solid wood, usually oak, and fixed to the frame with pocketed screws or wooden 'buttons'. The top will split if not allowed to 'move'.

End rails
Plain or shaped rails, tenoned into the legs. When a drawer is fitted, drawer rails are used (see page 98). As there was no top drawer rail on early tables, the top panel was used to tie the legs together.

Drop leaf
The solid-wood panel is relatively thin and often warps. A rule joint helps support the edge of the flap in the raised position, and forms an attractive feature when the flap is lowered.

Halving joint
The top and foot of the gate legs and the side stretcher rails are cut away to allow the gate to close flat against the main frame.

Back-flap hinges
Made with one leaf longer than the other, back-flap hinges are used to fit drop-leaf tops that feature a rule joint. Poor-fitting or loose hinges can give problems.

Stop block
Screwed to the underside of each drop leaf, this stops the 'gate' in the open position.

Side rails
Thick rails tenoned, and usually pegged, into the legs. A hole drilled in the lower edge receives the gatepost top pivot.

Stretcher rails
Usually square in section, these tie the legs together at the foot, using mortise-and-tenon joints. Holes drilled in the side rails receive the lower pivot pins of the gatepost.

Gate frame
A pivoted frame made up from a turned gatepost and leg joined by mortise-and-tenoned rails.

Design variations
The flaps of Pembroke and sofa tables are supported on knuckle-jointed brackets that swing out from the side or end rails.
1 Pembroke table
2 Sofa table

Pedestal tables

These tables feature a central turned column which is supported on three curvaceous splayed legs, jointed into the column with dovetail housings.

Pedestal tables usually have round tops that are either fixed in place or made to tilt into the vertical position when not in use. Some small tea tables were also made to revolve. Tables made with fixed tops have a simple block mounting, either fitted to the column with a mortise-and-tenon joint or screwed together with a coarse wooden thread.

The revolving and tilting top incorporates a wooden 'cage' or gallery held in place by a wedge passed through the column. The typical tilting table top is fitted with two parallel bearers screwed to the underside, that help to keep the top flat and serve to locate it on the mounting-block pivots.

The splayed-leg pedestal base is also used for larger tables. Rectangular dining tables sometimes use two or three pedestal bases to support the top, which can be extended with drop-in panels held with metal fittings.

Heavy-looking round dining tables with solid or veneered tops mounted on pedestal bases were fashionable in the Victorian era. Their columns are made from glued staves, forming faceted or round hollow pillars, mounted on three- or four-cornered platform bases that are veneered to match. Castors are usually fitted to the bases.

PEDESTAL TABLE

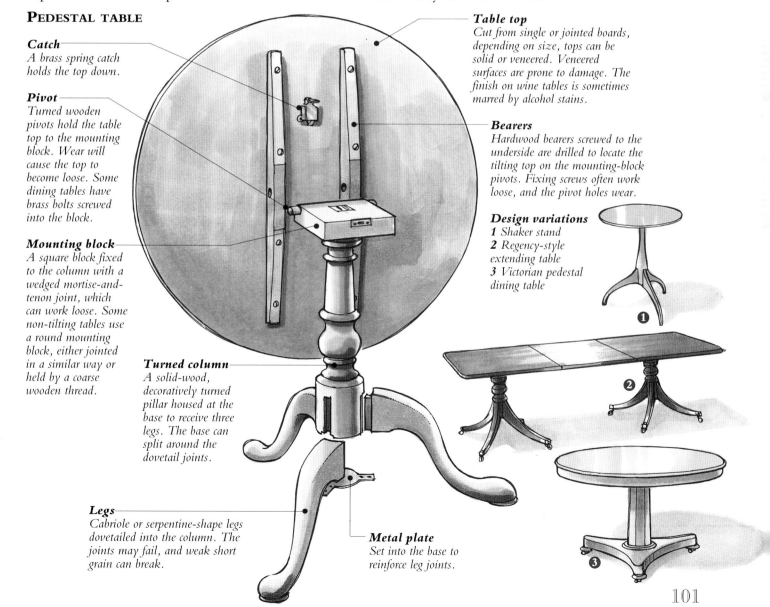

Catch
A brass spring catch holds the top down.

Pivot
Turned wooden pivots hold the table top to the mounting block. Wear will cause the top to become loose. Some dining tables have brass bolts screwed into the block.

Mounting block
A square block fixed to the column with a wedged mortise-and-tenon joint, which can work loose. Some non-tilting tables use a round mounting block, either jointed in a similar way or held by a coarse wooden thread.

Turned column
A solid-wood, decoratively turned pillar housed at the base to receive three legs. The base can split around the dovetail joints.

Legs
Cabriole or serpentine-shape legs dovetailed into the column. The joints may fail, and weak short grain can break.

Table top
Cut from single or jointed boards, depending on size, tops can be solid or veneered. Veneered surfaces are prone to damage. The finish on wine tables is sometimes marred by alcohol stains.

Bearers
Hardwood bearers screwed to the underside are drilled to locate the tilting top on the mounting-block pivots. Fixing screws often work loose, and the pivot holes wear.

Design variations
1 Shaker stand
2 Regency-style extending table
3 Victorian pedestal dining table

Metal plate
Set into the base to reinforce leg joints.

101

DISMANTLING TABLES

Frame-constructed tables which use mortise-and-tenon or dowel joints can be dismantled in a similar way to chair frames, using steam or methylated spirit to break down the glue (see page 54). The top is first removed, to expose the frame (see page 109). Draw-leaf and drop-leaf tables are basically frame tables, and can be taken apart in more or less the same way.

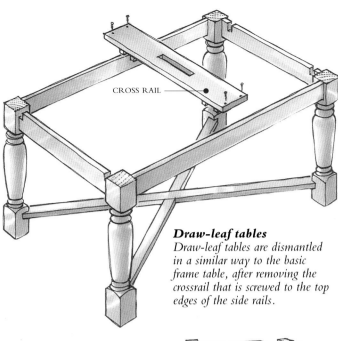

CROSS RAIL

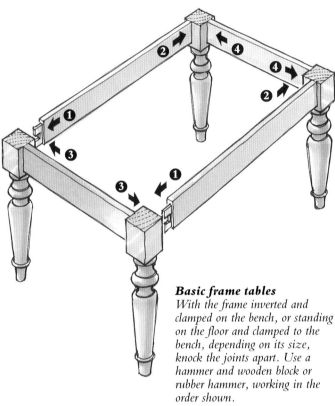

Basic frame tables
With the frame inverted and clamped on the bench, or standing on the floor and clamped to the bench, depending on its size, knock the joints apart. Use a hammer and wooden block or rubber hammer, working in the order shown.

Draw-leaf tables
Draw-leaf tables are dismantled in a similar way to the basic frame table, after removing the crossrail that is screwed to the top edges of the side rails.

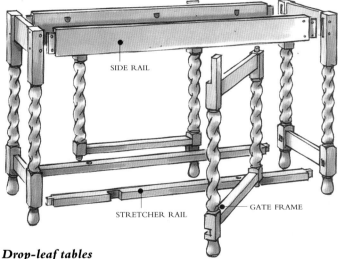

SIDE RAIL

STRETCHER RAIL   GATE FRAME

Frame fitted with drawers
When drawers are fitted, it is first necessary to remove the top drawer rail that is dovetailed into the top of the frame. The joints can then be dismantled as above. Check the order of assembly, as you may have to remove drawer runners and guides beforehand.

Drop-leaf tables
Dismantle the main frame in a similar way to the basic frame table, but working on the rails and stretchers together. Once the side rails and stretchers are freed from the legs, the 'gate' frames can be removed for dismantling, if required.

Releasing pegged tenons
Gate-leg tables are often constructed using mortise-and-tenon joints that have been reinforced with cross-dowels or pegs. Drill out the pegs before you attempt to dismantle the joints.

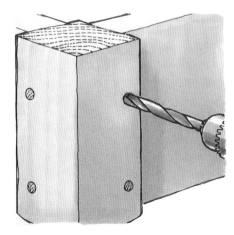

Pedestal tables

The method of construction of pedestal tables requires a different approach to dismantling, depending on the size and design of the assembly.

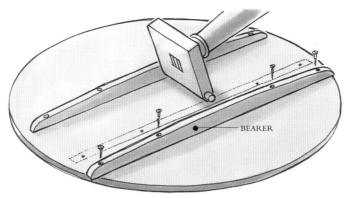

Small pedestal-table top

Unscrew and remove one bearer from the underside of a small table, to free the top from the mounting block pivots.

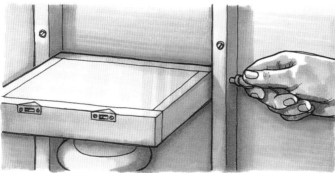

Dining-table top

For a large top on a pedestal base, tilt the top and support the edge, then unscrew the brass thumb screws and lift off the top.

A dining-table top is fixed to the block with thumb screws and a catch

Dismantling a mounting block

Support the mounting block of a small table on an open bench vice, and drive out the tenon with a wooden block and hammer. On pedestal dining tables, release the retaining bolt securing the top block.

Unscrewing the reinforcing plate

In order to dismantle a tripod base, first remove the metal plate that ties the three legs to the central column. If the screws are rusty, make sure the screwdriver is a snug fit in the slots before you attempt to turn them.

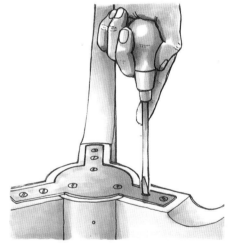

Removing a tripod leg

If a loose dovetail-jointed leg cannot be wiggled free, tap it out. Shape a saddle block to follow the curved leg, and clamp it in place to protect the leg and provide a striking surface.

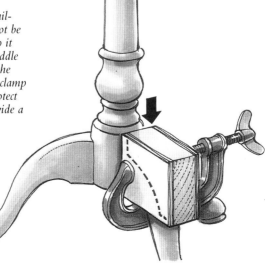

103

MENDING JOINTS

Most large tables are made from substantial sections of wood and proportionately large joints. However, legs that are not tied by stretcher rails can exert considerable leverage on the joints when dragged across the floor. In time this can cause the joints to fail or break, and the legs

themselves can also split. If a table frame racks when leaned against, the joints are probably weak. Mortise-and-tenon joints, commonly used for a wide range of frame tables, can be reglued or repaired in a similar way to chair joints (see pages 55-6). Other joints require specific repairs.

Bamboo tables

The nailed-and-glued butt joints of bamboo tables are relatively weak. If the natural shiny surface of bamboo is not abraded locally to provide a key for the glue, the bond will not be so strong. As bamboo is hollow, the ends are plugged with softwood to receive the nail fixing. If the joint has been allowed to 'work', the nail can lose its grip.

Regluing a joint

Prise the joint open sufficiently to clean the surfaces with water. Pull out the old nail if it has worked loose. If necessary, abrade the side face of the bamboo with a fine file in the vicinity of the joint. Apply glue and re-nail the joint.

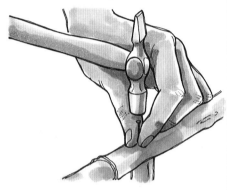

Replugging cane

Remove the component, and drill or chisel out the old worn plug. Turn or whittle a softwood plug to fit into the end of the cane, and glue it in place. Shape the end to match the contour of the joint shoulder, using a half-round file or fret saw. Glue and nail the joint.

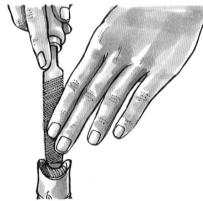

Mending braces

Small-section bamboo braces set diagonally across the corners are usually nailed through their sides close to the ends. Splits often occur where the nail hole has weakened the cane. Pull out the nail and glue the split. Drill a tight-fitting clearance hole for a new nail, and reassemble the joint.

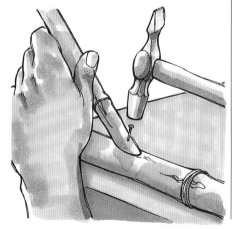

Pedestal tables

The components of tilt-top pedestal tables are more stressed than those of conventional framed types, with the result that these tables often have wobbly tops and legs. Tea and wine tables of this type are relatively light in construction, with the top held by two bearers screwed to the underside. Because the tops are so thin, the fixing screws are comparatively short and prone to strip. In addition, shrinkage in the wood can cause the legs and top block to work loose.

Tightening loose bearers

First try fitting a larger-gauge screw of the correct length in the worn hole. If this fails, plug the screw hole with matching wood and refit the original screw. Drill a pilot hole in the plug to suit the screw size (see page 52).

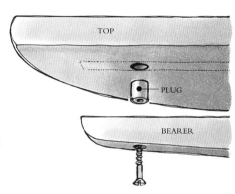

TOP

PLUG

BEARER

Securing a loose mounting block

If the mounting block is loose, check the mortise-and-tenon joint. If it is only slightly slack and will not pull free, drill one or two small holes down the sides of the tenon and inject glue into the joint.

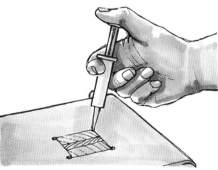

Wedging the tenon

If possible, knock the joint apart and cut out the original wedge. If the joint has been assembled without a wedge, make a saw cut in the tenon to receive one cut from hardwood. Glue and assemble the components, and drive in the wedge to secure the joint.

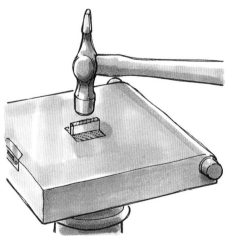

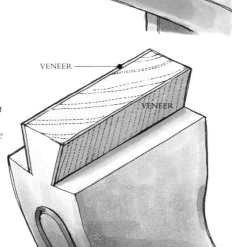

Tightening a bolted block
Large dining tables with hollow pedestals have the block bolted through to the base with a threaded rod. Tighten the nut found underneath the base to clamp the block onto the column. These are often handmade square nuts that can only be tightened fully by tapping with a cold chisel.

Refitting a loose tripod leg
The dovetail housings which join the legs to the column often work loose due to shrinkage. Remove the leg, and clean and inspect the joint. If the wood is sound, glue a thin strip of veneer to one or both faces of the dovetail and trim it to fit the housing. Reglue when it is a snug fit (see below).

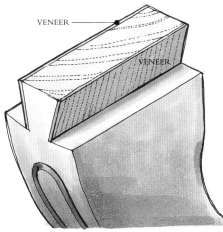

VENEER

VENEER

Repairing split pedestals
The tripod underframes of delicate wine and tea tables are usually fitted with metal plates to prevent the legs splaying outward. However, when the reinforcing plate has been omitted or lost, it is not uncommon to find tables with splits near the base of the central column. It pays to do something about a split of this nature before a leg breaks off completely.

Gluing the split
Flex the legs gently to work some glue into the split, then apply a tourniquet of string to the legs. Cut shaped plywood blocks that hook over the toe of each table leg. Line the blocks with thick felt to protect the polish.

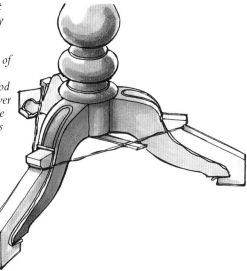

Repairing mechanical joints
There are very few types of table that do not have moving parts or mechanical joints which allow the top to fold, slide or pivot. The majority of these components are made from wood so, if the table has seen long service, they are bound to be a little slack or misaligned as a result of wear.

Repairing a binding rule joint
The special back-flap hinges cause most of the problems associated with rule joints. It is essential that the hinge knuckle is positioned directly below the square shoulder of the joint if it is to function smoothly. A poorly fitted hinge can throw the flap out of alignment, causing the rule joint to stick or 'bind' as you attempt to move it. Before you do anything else, try lubricating the joint with white candle wax.

Rule joint between top and flap

Recessing the hinges
If the rule joint binds when the flap is almost horizontal, check that the hinges are in good condition and screwed firmly in their recesses. If necessary, pare the recesses slightly to make sure the hinge flaps are perfectly flush with the underside of the table top.

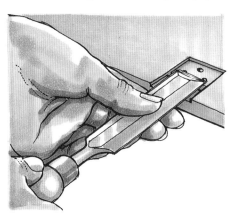

Packing out the hinges
If the joint binds just before the flap hangs vertically, the hinge flaps may be recessed too deeply. In this case, slip some thin-card packing behind the hinges.

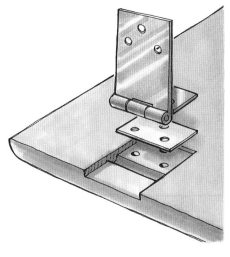

Repairing loose gates

Since they are made entirely of wood, there is almost bound to be a degree of slack in the pivoting joints of an old table gate, but excessively worn or even broken pivots should be repaired before an accident occurs.

The shorter gatepost has an integral pivot pin at each end. The bottom pin invariably pivots in a hole drilled in the stretcher rail. The upper pin fits into a hole in one of the deep side rails that support the table top. Some tables are designed so that the gate can be attached after assembly; the top pivot is held in place by a block of wood screwed to the side of the table rail. This type can be removed for repair by simply unscrewing the block.

In other cases, the gate is located as the main table frame is assembled; unless you saw through both pivots (see below), the table frame has to be dismantled before the gate can be removed.

Removable gate

Captive gate

1 Releasing the gate

Saw through both pivots, then slide the gate sideways to remove it.

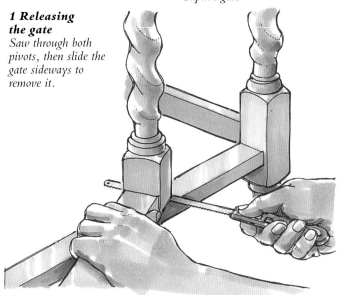

2 Renewing the pivots

Plane the ends of the gatepost square, and drill a hole in each end for chamfered dowels. Glue them in place.

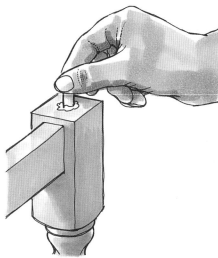

3 Making a tapered block

Make a tapered block of wood, drilled with a new pivot hole. Align the new and old pivot holes, and then draw round the block to mark a notch on the side of the table rail.

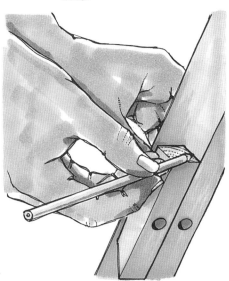

4 Fitting the gate

Cut the notch in the rail, insert the tapered block and fix it with screws. Unscrew the block and slip it over the new dowel on top of the gate post. Drop the bottom dowel into the hole in the stretcher rail, slide the gate-post sideways, and screw the block to the table rail.

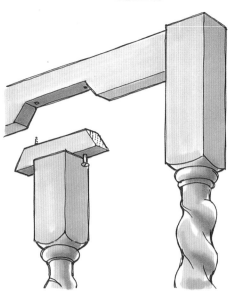

Mending a split gate leg

The halving joint cut into a folding gate allows it to lie flush with the table underframe. Unfortunately, the joint is also a weak point that can promote a split if the gate is dragged clumsily across the floor.

Gluing a split

Carefully flex the leg until you can brush glue into the split, then apply a G-cramp and softening blocks until the adhesive sets.

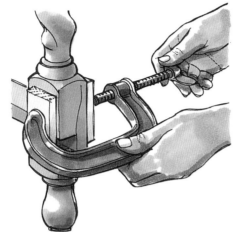

Repairing a slack knuckle joint

A Pembroke-table flap is supported on a hinged bracket that is cantilevered from a wooden knuckle joint. If this joint becomes slack, it allows the table flap to droop. One solution is to replace the knuckle-joint pivot pin with one of a slightly larger diameter.

1 Removing the pivot pin

Remove both halves of the knuckle joint and clamp them to a board, making sure the two halves are aligned perfectly. Stand the board on edge so that you can drive out the pin, using stiff metal rod.

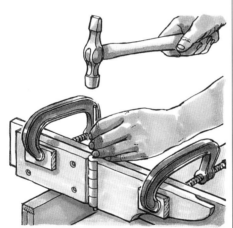

2 Inserting a new pin

Bore out the hole left by the pin, using a bit approximately 1mm (¹⁄₁₆in) larger. Choose a drill bit that matches the diameter of steel or brass rod, from which you can make a replacement pivot pin. Drive in the new pin, and file each end flush.

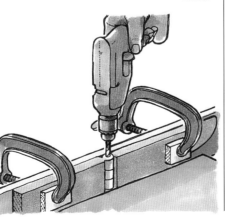

Remaking pedestal-table pivots

To correct a wobbly pedestal-table top, first make sure that the mounting block is fixed securely to the column and that the bearers are screwed firmly to the underside of the table top (see page 104). Next, inspect the pivots for signs of wear.

Dining-table pivots

Withdraw the metal pivot bolts, with the dining-table top tilted and held steady, then lift off the top.

Servicing the pivots

Tighten the screws that secure the small threaded 'nuts' to the block, and lightly oil the shaft of each bolt. If any of the parts are badly worn or missing, you can order replacement pivots from a specialist supplier.

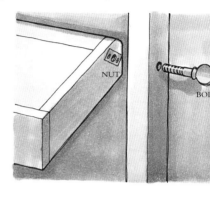

Small-table pivots

Worn pivot pins on smaller pedestal tables can be lined with brass tubing, provided the holes in the bearers have not become oval. If this is the case, replace the bearers.

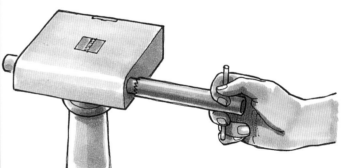

1 Reshaping worn pivots

Select brass tube that fits snugly in the holes in the bearers, and file the worn pins until they fit the bore of the tubing. For a perfect fit, make a hollow drill from a length of the same tubing (see page 52), and use that to finally reshape the wooden pins.

2 Lining the pivots

Cut and file the tube linings to length. Smear the reshaped pivots with epoxy-resin glue and slide on the linings, wiping off surplus adhesive with methylated spirit.

107

Renovating draw-leaf tables

Most of the problems associated with draw-leaf tables are related to the condition of the bearers that are screwed to the underside of each leaf.

Easing a sticking leaf

Rub the bearers with candle wax to ensure they run smoothly. If that does not solve the problem, inspect the guide blocks and make sure the bearers themselves are straight.

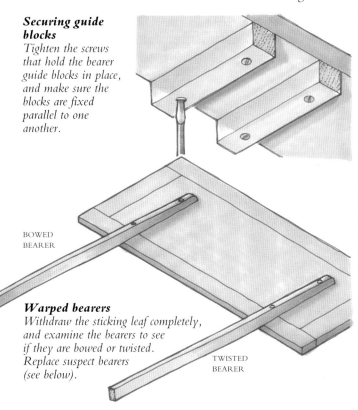

Securing guide blocks
Tighten the screws that hold the bearer guide blocks in place, and make sure the blocks are fixed parallel to one another.

BOWED
BEARER

Warped bearers
Withdraw the sticking leaf completely, and examine the bearers to see if they are bowed or twisted. Replace suspect bearers (see below).

TWISTED
BEARER

Curing a drooping leaf

If a leaf is drooping, try tightening the screws that hold the bearers to the underside. If there is no improvement, the bearers may be worn or bowed, and need replacing.

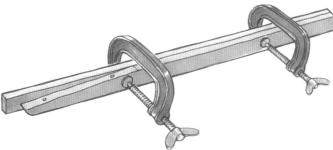

Making new bearers
Choose a straight grain piece of timber, and plane it to size to match the existing bearers. Remove one bearer in good condition, and clamp it to the side of the prepared wood so that you can mark the required slope on one end. Shape the new bearer and screw it to the leaf.

Replacing stop blocks

When stop blocks are missing, there is nothing to prevent a leaf being withdrawn too far. It is not a great inconvenience, but since it is so simple to rectify, replacements may be fitted while the table is in the workshop.

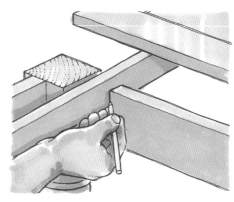

1 Positioning the blocks
Withdraw the leaf until it is in the required position in relation to the fixed top, and then mark the bearers where they pass through the table rail.

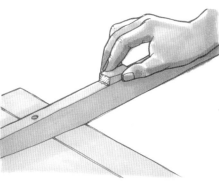

2 Gluing blocks to the bearers
Lay the leaf aside on the workbench, and rub glued blocks up to the marked lines on the underside of each bearer.

Dealing with a scratched leaf

When a leaf is marred with parallel scratches, it pays to examine the underside of the main table top carefully before you go to the trouble of refinishing.

A strip of baize is normally glued to the underside of the top at each end, to protect the surface of the leaf as it is withdrawn. In all probability, the protective strip has peeled off, allowing the polish to become scored as the leaf was moved in and out.

Replacing the protective strip
Turn the top upside down, and rake out the gaps between panels to remove any debris that could be scratching the finish. Make sure there are no panel pins or other nails embedded in the wood, then use a sharp chisel to scrape old adhesive from the top before gluing a new strip of baize at each end.

TABLE TOPS

Until the introduction of veneer, all table tops were made from solid boards. Small tables could be cut from a single wide board, but larger tops were made by gluing a number of boards together. Wide boards are prone to warping and, because wood expands and contracts, splits can occur if movement is restricted. Veneered tops are not as robust as those made from solid boards – the thin surface layer of wood which is bonded to a solid core is prone to damage.

How tops are fixed

Tables are basically made as two distinct elements, the underframe or base, and the top. It is usually easier to make repairs if the two are first separated. This is not a problem, as most tops are attached from beneath with screws. Furniture makers have long recognized that solid wood will move with changes in humidity, and this is particularly apparent on wide panels such as table tops. Boards expand and contract more across their width than in their length; this presents a problem when the underframe rails, which do not appreciably change in length, are fixed across the width of a table top. Various methods of attachment have been used to overcome the risk of splitting; examples are shown below. If a top has split, check the fixings and, if necessary, modify them to allow for movement.

Pocket screws

Angled pockets, drilled or chiselled into the inside faces of the rails, are commonly used to make a cheap fixing. The screw hole may be oversize to allow for movement, or, better still, slotted.

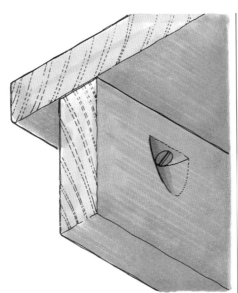

Button fixing

A traditional method utilizes wooden 'buttons' to hold the top in place while allowing it to move. The tongue locates in a groove cut on the inside of the rail. Remake missing buttons to match. Note that the side-rail buttons are not butted against the rail, to allow for movement.

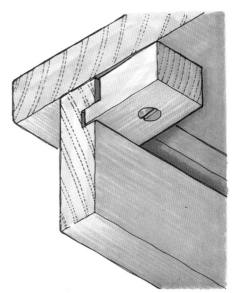

Counterbored screws

Counterbored holes are sometimes drilled into the edges of rails, allowing relatively short screws to fasten the top. Unless the shank-clearance hole is slightly oversize, the movement of a solid-wood top is restricted. Cutting the hole to form a tapered slot will help.

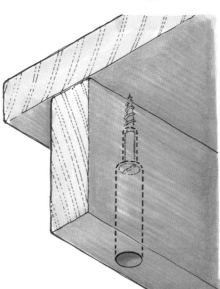

Shrinkage plates

Nowadays it is usual to fit metal shrinkage plates. Flat plates are let into the top edge of the rails, or angled plates are screwed to the inside. To allow the top to move, the plates are slotted in two directions; insert screws into whichever slot runs at right angles to the grain.

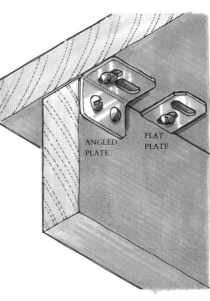

ANGLED PLATE

FLAT PLATE

Split table tops

Splits occur along the grain of the wood or, if the top is made from glued boards, along the joints. Splits following the grain tend to meander and taper from the edge, making them awkward to repair without a fair amount of preparation (see page 137). Simply gluing and clamping the split closed is likely to stress the wood, which could then split in a similar way at another point. Unless they are particularly unsightly, these faults could be accepted as part of the table's character. Failed joints, however, form a straight break that can be readily repaired. The method will depend on how the boards are joined.

Butt-jointed top

The boards of most old tables were simply planed straight and square, then glued together. If the glue has failed, dismantle the top and carefully scrape or wash the joint clean. Check the fit, and glue and clamp the boards together (see right).

1 Truing the joint

If the jointing edges do not mate properly, skim them with a plane. Set the two halves back-to-back in a vice, with the edges flush. Using a long, finely set plane, trim the edges straight. A very slight hollow or concave edge is acceptable, but not a convex one.

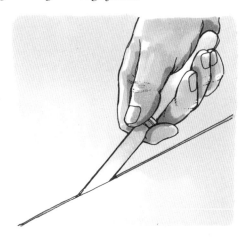

2 Using a guide fence

To help keep the joints square, you can make a simple wooden guide fence from hardwood and fix it to the body of the plane with a small cramp.

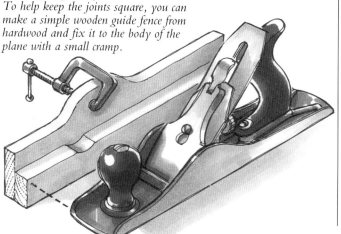

Tongue-and-groove joint

Some joints are reinforced with a strip of wood or 'tongue', let into stopped grooves cut in the edges. For strength, the tongue is cut from plywood or solid wood, with the grain running across its width.

Regluing the joint

If the glue has failed, pull the joint apart. You may need to dampen the joint with water or steam to remove the tongue entirely (see page 54). Clean the jointing faces and apply glue with a brush, then assemble and clamp the parts (see opposite).

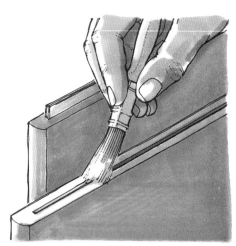

Doweled joints

Short dowels, placed at regular intervals, are another method often used to strengthen edge-to-edge joints.

Locating the dowels

To determine the exact positions of all the reinforcing dowels, pass the blade of a table knife along the gap between the boards.

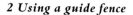

Repairing a dowelled joint

If the dowels remain glued, break down the bond (see page 54). Clean up the gluing surfaces and reglue the boards. Otherwise, cut the dowels with a fine saw through the gap between the boards, redrill the edge and fit new dowels.

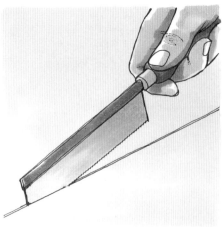

Gluing boards

Most joints in old furniture are held together with water-soluble animal glue. Since it allows joints to be dismantled in the future, some furniture repairers still prefer to use this traditional glue, even though it needs to be prepared before use and applied hot. PVA woodworking adhesive is now commonly used for all kinds of furniture making and, although not fully reversible, is a strong, ready-to-use glue.

Whichever glue you decide to use, always apply it to both jointing faces, to ensure even distribution and penetration. Hot-setting animal glue is traditionally spread with a brush, but modern cold-setting adhesives can also be spread along edge-to-edge joints, using a rubber roller.

Clamping boards

Before applying glue, assemble and lightly clamp the parts to ensure the joints fit well. To make the process as quick and efficient as possible, always prepare the gluing area in advance with cramps, softening blocks to protect the workpiece, glue and applicator, wiping cloth and metal straightedge all to hand.

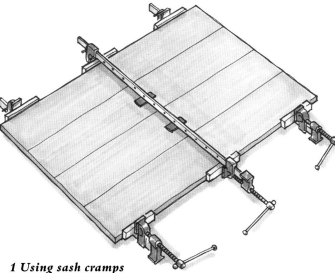

1 Using sash cramps
You need at least three cramps to glue up a table top – two placed below and one above – to even out the tendency for the panel to bow under pressure. Place softwood blocks between the work and cramp heads, to spread the clamping forces and protect the edge from bruising.

2 Levelling the joint
Apply light pressure to the boards, squeezing out excess glue. Check that the surfaces on butt-jointed boards are flush by feeling the surface. If necessary, tap the joints level with a hammer and block of wood, then tighten the cramps.

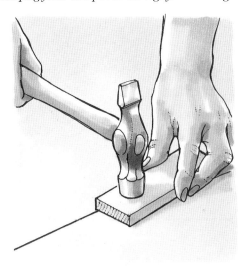

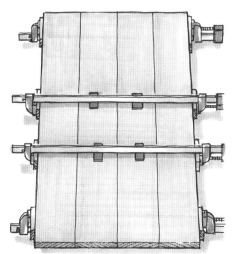

3 Checking for distortion
Wipe surplus glue from the surface with a damp cloth. Check with a straightedge that the surface is not being bowed by the cramps. Adjust the cramps to alter the angle of forces, or add another cramp if you need to correct any misalignment.

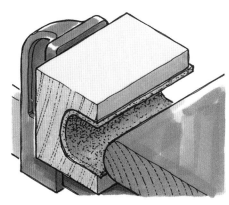

4 Softening blocks
Moulded-edge table tops need shaped blocks to distribute the pressure evenly across the edge profile. Make these from several pieces of softwood or shape them from solid wood. Glue a lining of thick felt or carpet inside, to protect delicate mouldings.

5 Clamping round tops
To compensate for the shaped edge of a round or oval top, make a pair of cradles to fit the curve of the top where it will be clamped.

111

Warped wood

When a tree is sawn into boards, it holds a high percentage of water in its cell structure. In order to make the wood usable, the level of moisture must be reduced by a process known as seasoning. This is traditionally effected by slow natural air-drying; by contrast, more modern methods employ highly sensitive and controllable kilns that prepare the wood in a fraction of the time. When fully dried and seasoned, the moisture content is relatively low and the wood is more or less stable. However, wood continues to react to its surroundings and will expand and contract if exposed to higher or lower humidity; this movement is greater across its width and thickness than in its length.

Warped table tops

Relatively thin tops cut from wide boards are prone to warping. Unframed panels, such as the flaps of a drop-leaf table, are not easy to repair successfully, and you may have to live with the distortion. Tops of framed tables can sometimes be taken apart, remade and pulled flat against a sturdy underframe. As moisture is more readily absorbed by unfinished wood, try sealing the back of a table top with a wood finish, to help reduce the tendency to warp.

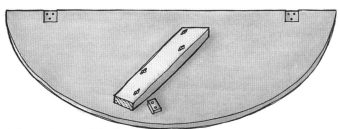

Flattening a table flap
It may be possible to flatten a thin bowed flap of a gate-leaf table by screwing a stiff batten to the underside. Planing the face of the batten slightly convex will help. Set the batten diagonally to clear the gate, and make slotted screw holes to allow for movement.

Cutting the back

A more drastic method of dealing with warped boards involves making a series of cuts along the grain, using a power saw or router, and inserting packing strips.

1 Making the cuts
Cut the grooves about 18mm (¾in) apart and two-thirds the thickness of the top. Stop the grooves short of the ends of the boards, unless you intend using an applied lipping to cover the repair.

2 Fitting the strips
To flatten the top, clamp it between stiff battens. Cut strips of matching wood to fit the grooves, and glue them in place. Leave until the adhesive has cured before removing the clamping battens, then plane the new strips flush.

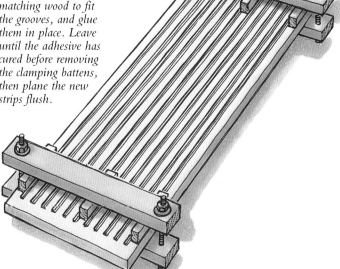

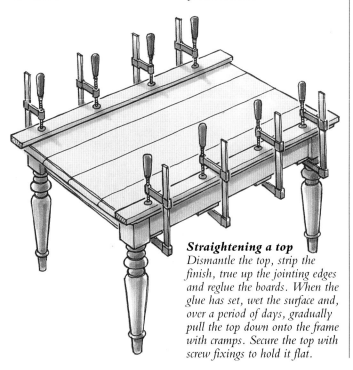

Straightening a top
Dismantle the top, strip the finish, true up the jointing edges and reglue the boards. When the glue has set, wet the surface and, over a period of days, gradually pull the top down onto the frame with cramps. Secure the top with screw fixings to hold it flat.

MARBLE TOPS

MOULDED EDGES

The edges of table tops are often moulded to provide a decorative detail. These are worked into the edge of a solid-wood top, or an applied lipping is glued to a veneered top. The corners are particularly vulnerable to damage; raise small dents with steam (see page 23) and repair broken edges with patches of wood (see page 136).

Small pedestal tables are sometimes made with tops that have raised edges. Some of these tops were originally shaped on a lathe, and you may be able to employ the same method to integrate a patch repair to a damaged edge. Decorative 'pie-crust' edges are carved from solid wood or are built up with applied mouldings. In either case, unless you are an experienced woodcarver, repairs are best left to professional restorers. However, the basic stages involved in remaking the edge are shown below:

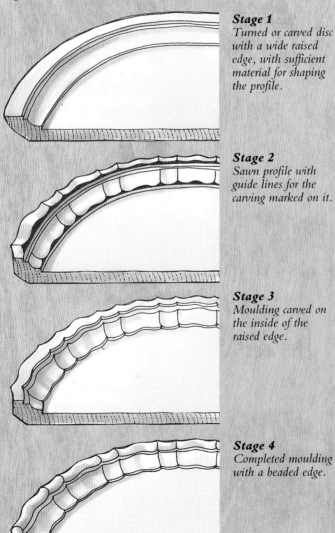

Stage 1
Turned or carved disc with a wide raised edge, with sufficient material for shaping the profile.

Stage 2
Sawn profile with guide lines for the carving marked on it.

Stage 3
Moulding carved on the inside of the raised edge.

Stage 4
Completed moulding with a beaded edge.

Marble is a fine-grained, crystalline, limestone rock, found in a wide range of colours and usually featuring striking veined markings. It takes a high polish and provides a functional and attractive surface. In the past, furniture makers used marble for table tops, particularly for side tables and washstands. White marble is perhaps the most common, but pink and black marbles are also used.

Marble table tops are not usually fixed in place, but simply rest on the underframe. As they are relatively brittle in slab form, handle these tops carefully when removing them. Chipped or cracked marble can normally be repaired successfully.

Maintaining marble tops
Being porous, marble easily absorbs dirt and stains – this is particularly noticeable on white marble – but it is not difficult to maintain, provided it is protected with a wax marble polish, available from specialist suppliers. However, acidic foodstuffs and drinks should be wiped away promptly, as they tend to etch the surface, leaving rough patches. Stains can usually be removed by applying an absorbent poultice containing a suitable solvent. Make a poultice from soft white tissue soaked in water, or use an absorbent powder such as whiting.

Cleaning marble
Dust the surface regularly, and occasionally wash it with a solution of mild soap and water containing a few drops of ammonia. Dry the surface with a soft cloth or a chamois leather, and apply a thin coat of wax marble polish.

Removing light water-based stains
Apply a thick layer of prepared poultice over the stain. Leave this in place for the water to activate the stain, which will be absorbed by the poultice as it dries. Remove the poultice, rinse the surface and dry with a soft cloth.

Removing oily stains

Make a poultice, using a solvent such as alcohol, lighter fluid or acetone, and apply it to the stain. Cover it with a piece of polythene sheet, taped in place to prevent the solvent evaporating too quickly. Repeat the process if necessary, and then finish off.

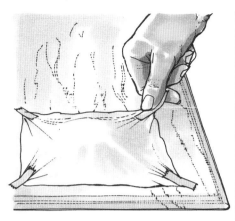

Bleaching white marble

For persistent or strong stains, use a solution of 3 parts distilled water to 1 part 100-volume hydrogen peroxide, plus a few drops of ammonia. Brush this onto the stain, leave until it works, then wash the surface thoroughly. Leave to dry, and repeat the process if required.

Smoothing the surface

If marble is scratched or etched, rub out the rough patch with very fine, 'flour'-grade wet-and-dry paper lubricated with water. For deeper marks, start with two or three coarser grade papers and then use progressively finer grades (see page 23).

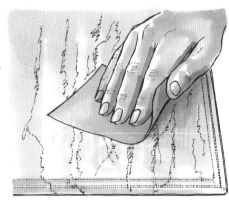

Polishing the surface

Apply a marble wax as a polish or, for a high shine, burnish the surface hard with a coarse cloth dampened with a solution of oxalic acid (see page 25). Wash the acid from the surface, and finish with marble wax.

Mending broken marble

If a marble top fractures, repair it promptly before the break becomes discoloured. Clean old breaks before making repairs.

You can bond a broken marble top using a two-part epoxy-resin adhesive. Check that the broken edges mate properly, and prepare the equipment needed to hold the parts together. Depending on the size and type of break, you may require woodworking cramps, elastic bands, cord or self-adhesive tape.

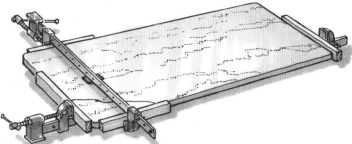

Bonding the edges

Mix the two-part adhesive according to the maker's instructions, and apply a thin film to both parts. Clamp them together, ensuring that the surface is flush. Carefully wipe off excess glue with acetone or methylated spirit. Leave to set hard.

Filling the surface

Should the repair require filling, make a coloured cement using epoxy adhesive mixed with marble dust scraped from the rough back of the table top. Talc or whiting can be used for white marble. Fill the crack and, when set, rub smooth with fine abrasive paper. Finish by applying wax polish.

Repairing a chipped edge

Clean the surface thoroughly, then fill the chipped edge as neatly as possible with a mixture of epoxy glue and marble dust. Tape a strip of stiff polythene plastic to contain the filler. When set, peel off the plastic, then shape and smooth the repair with very fine abrasive papers.

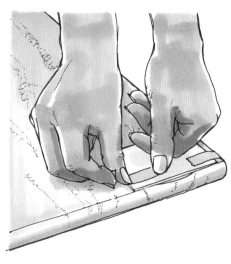

Veneered table tops

Veneer is a very thin sheet of wood sliced from the log for bonding to a stiff backing known as groundwork. In the past, pine boards and solid mahogany were used for the groundwork, but modern veneered panels are made from stable, man-made laminated boards or particle boards.

Veneered furniture has a reputation for being inferior to that made from 'solid' wood. However, veneering makes it possible to construct furniture from certain exotic woods that would hardly be practicable if used in their solid form.

Veneering also makes sense economically, since it utilizes comparatively little wood. Although craftsmen of the past may not have been overly concerned with preserving diminishing resources, they recognized the variety and beauty of veneer, and used it to produce refined and decorative furniture that is highly valued today.

How veneer is cut

The appearance of veneer is not only governed by the natural colour of the wood, but also by how it is cut from the log. The figure, or surface pattern, is produced by the orientation of the cell structure which forms the grain of the wood. Common types of grain are straight grain, irregular grain, wavy grain and interlocked grain.

Until veneer-slicing machines were developed, all veneers were sawn from the log and, by today's standards, were relatively thick. The thickness of the veneer can be a useful guide for dating furniture, since the use of saw-cut veneer declined in the nineteenth century as it was superseded by thinner, machine-cut veneer.

There are basically three methods used to produce machine-sliced veneer: rotary cutting, half-round cutting and flat slicing. Before the veneer is cut, the wood is softened by immersing the log in boiling water or treating it with steam, the length of time depending on the species of wood.

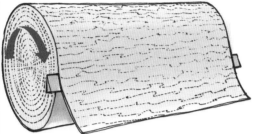

Rotary cutting
The log is mounted in a giant lathe, and the veneer is peeled off by a knife blade running the length of the machine. This method produces a wide continuous veneer that displays a variable figure. It is an economical process, used for producing constructional veneers employed in plywood manufacture, but some decorative veneers such as bird's-eye maple are also produced in this way.

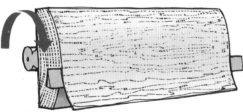

Half-round cutting
This is a variation of rotary cutting where a half-log is mounted off-centre between the lathe centres. It produces a wide decorative veneer with a similar figure to flat-sliced, crown-cut veneer. The half-log is sometimes mounted with the heartwood facing outwards. This is known as back-cutting, and is used for slicing decorative butt and curl veneers.

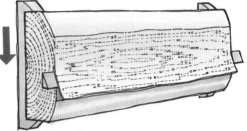

Flat slicing – for crown-cut veneers
Used for cutting decorative veneers, the flat-slicing method uses a sliding frame to hold a log, which has been cut down its length to form 'flitches'. The frame moves across the knife blade, which slices the veneer. The character of the figure is determined by the way the log is cut and how it is mounted in the frame. When a half-log is mounted heart-side down and cut tangentially, it produces crown-cut veneer.

Flat slicing – for quarter-cut veneers
When the veneer is cut more or less perpendicular to the growth rings of a flitch, it produces the quarter-cut striped figure of woods with interlocked grain and the distinctive 'ray' figure of oak veneer.

ROTARY-CUT BIRD'S-EYE MAPLE

HALF-ROUND CUT KINGWOOD

FLAT-SLICED CROWN-CUT ASH

FLAT-SLICED QUARTER-CUT OAK

115

TYPES OF VENEER

The character and appearance of veneer are not only dependent on the species of the wood, but also on the part of the tree from which it is cut, and the method used to slice the log. No two pieces of veneer are ever exactly the same, but those types illustrated here show a typical selection, all of which may be used in repairing and replacing damaged or missing veneers on panels and table tops. Even odd-grained or defective veneers may be used.

Buying veneer

When veneered furniture is damaged, try to retain the original veneer to make the repair. If parts of the veneer are missing or the damaged veneer is unusable, buy new material that is a close match in thickness, grain pattern and colour. This may not be an easy task, not least because the original veneer has probably been stained, or bleached by light, making identification and colour-matching difficult.

Crown-cut veneer
When a log is cut tangentially, the veneer displays a bold, attractive figure that features sweeping curves down the leaf centre, as well as a striped pattern along the edges.

Striped veneer
Wood that is cut radially will display a striped figure. Ribbon-figure veneer has subtle stripes produced by the changing direction of the cell structure found in woods with interlocked grain.

Curly-figured veneer
A decorative veneer with distinctive bands of light and dark tones that run across the width of the leaf, produced from wavy-grain woods such as sycamore and ash.

Ray-figured veneer
Woods that have a distinctive radial cell structure produce unique and decorative veneers when quarter-cut. When the rays are cut and exposed, a striking flecked figure is displayed.

If you provide a good sample of the old veneer, specialist suppliers will identify the species and should be able to select a close match of new veneer. Most materials can be purchased by mail order, but if you have a local specialist you can take part of the furniture with you for identification.

Veneer is sold as cut pieces or full leaves, the latter varying in length and width depending on species, and valued accordingly. Burr veneers are supplied as irregular shapes, and curl veneers are trimmed and usually tapered. Full leaves are sold singly or in bundles of consecutive veneers, in multiples of four. Packs of assorted veneers containing relatively small pieces are useful for marquetry. If you need to match a thick veneer, as found on older pieces of furniture, this is usually made up by laminating thin modern veneers until the desired thickness is achieved.

Curl veneer
Curl veneer is cut from the 'fork' of a tree where the trunk divides. It produces a lustrous feather-like figure formed by the diverging grain cells.

Butt veneer
The natural irregular growth of wood cut from the stump of a tree produces a random-pattern, highly-figured decorative veneer.

Burr veneer
Burrs are growths on the side of a trunk which display a unique and attractive pattern of swirls and dots when cut into veneer. Burr veneer is only available in small sections, and is fragile until bonded to the groundwork.

Freak veneer
Woods with irregular grain or some defect are used to produce random-pattern decorative veneers. They are cut using the rotary method.

117

Built-up patterns

Furniture makers often divide the area of a panel into sections, in order to utilize smaller pieces of veneer or add interest, building up a pattern by varying the direction of the grain. Typical arrangements are book-matching, butt-matching, quartered diagonal and quartered reverse diagonal. The most simple arrangements can be laid by hand, using a veneer hammer, but in most cases you will find it easier and more efficient to use cauls (see page 123).

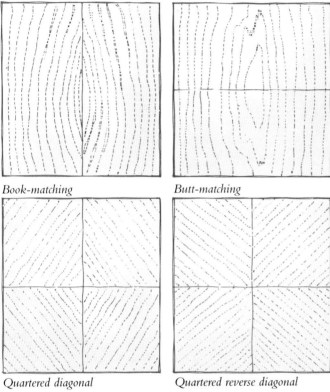

Book-matching

Butt-matching

Quartered diagonal

Quartered reverse diagonal

Coffee table surfaced with quartered veneer

REPAIRING VENEERED SURFACES

A veneered top or panel is no less serviceable than a solid one, provided the veneer is well laid and finished. However, like a solid top, it can be damaged by an impact from a hard object. Poor workmanship, inferior materials and, in some cases, adverse environmental conditions can cause veneer to blister or lift, which in turn can lead to chipped edges. Should the veneer become damaged, do not ignore the problem, as it can make repairs more difficult later, particularly if broken pieces are lost.

All the techniques described in this chapter also apply to repairing veneered chests and cabinets.

Raising a dent

Carefully consider whether to raise a dent in veneer. If the damage is acceptable, it may be best left alone.

Raise a shallow dent in a similar way to that described for a solid top (see page 23). Treat the damage with the minimum amount of moisture, and stop when the surface is flush.

Pressing the surface

Because water and steam will soften the glue holding the veneer, it is necessary to keep the laminate under pressure to prevent it lifting. Cover the repair with a piece of polythene sheet and a wooden block, and press it down with heavy weights or cramps.

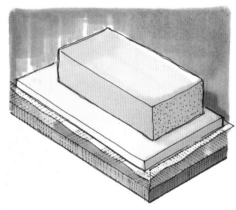

Dealing with blisters

Blisters are often the result of a breakdown or insufficient spread of the glue bonding the veneer to the groundwork. In some cases water may have been allowed to saturate the veneer, causing the veneer to buckle. Although some blisters are obvious to the eye, you can also detect loose patches of veneer by tapping the surface with the tips of your fingernails. A change in tone denotes the weak spots.

Repairing an old blister

The cavity of an old split blister is likely to be contaminated with dirt. Soften the veneer and any remaining glue with a damp cloth, and heat before regluing. Scrape the underside of the blister with a scalpel, apply glue and press flat.

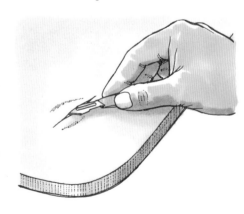

1 Flattening a blister

Apply a damp cloth to the blister, and heat it with an electric iron. As the veneer and glue start to soften, press the blister into place. Remove the cloth and press the surface with the iron, then leave to cool. Provided there is sufficient glue, the veneer will remain flat.

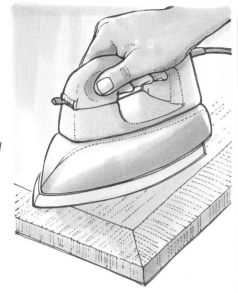

2 Adding glue

If the blister is starved of glue, you will need to introduce some. Dampen the veneer, then make a fine knife-cut through the blister, following the grain. Work PVA or animal glue under the veneer, using a palette knife or brush. Press the blister flat, wipe away excess glue and tape the cut.

3 Clamping the repair

Cover the area with polythene sheet and then clamp a block over it to press the veneer flat while the glue sets.

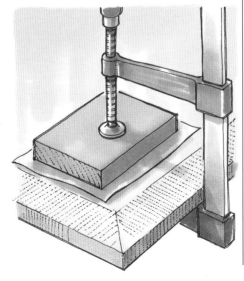

Patching a damaged edge

The edges of surface veneer, edge bandings or cross-banded lippings are susceptible to damage, and often need patching. Whatever the situation, it is important that the figure of the patch is a good match; a lighter colour can be modified with wood dye. If you are matching thicker saw-cut veneer, you may have to cut your own on a circular saw. Otherwise, laminate pieces of knife-cut veneer. Make the veneer slightly thicker than the finished size, to allow for final sanding.

1 Taping the patch

Cut your selected patch-veneer slightly larger than the area of the repair. Position it with the figure matching as closely as possible, and tape it in place.

2 Cutting the patch to fit

Try to make cuts that run at an angle to the grain. Cut through the patch-veneer, using a sharp knife and straight-edge, and score the veneer beneath. When cutting curly grain, make the cuts freehand, following a curving line.

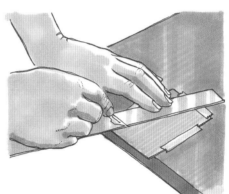

3 Cleaning the cut-out

Cut the old veneer along the scored lines, then remove remnants of broken veneer within the cut area, using a sharp chisel. Scrape the groundwork smooth with a wide chisel held vertically.

4 Gluing the patch

Apply animal glue or PVA to the ground-work and the veneer. Tape the veneer into place and press it flat with a cramp and wooden block. When set, turn the panel over and trim the overhang flush with the edge.

Patching the surface

Damage within the main surface area of the veneer, such as scorched wood, can be patched in a similar way to an edge repair. Select and cut the veneer to follow the grain. 'Boat' or diamond shapes are often used, but let the grain be your guide.

Veneer punches in a range of sizes are available from specialists, and are convenient if you need a number of similar patches. Use the punch to make an irregular cut-out in the surface and an identical patch from a matching veneer.

1 Cutting a patch

Select the patch veneer. Align the grain and tape it over the damaged area. Cut the patch to the required shape through both layers. Trim away the waste, and glue the patch in place.

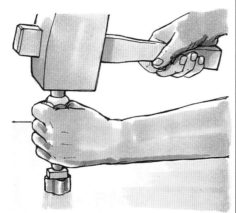

2 Using a punch

Position the appropriate-size punch over the damaged area, and strike it with a mallet. Remove the waste from the cut shape. Stamp out a patch from the matching veneer and glue it into the prepared recess.

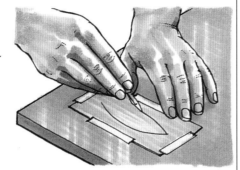

Patching groundwork

Repair scorched or damaged groundwork before replacing veneer. If the charred patch is shallow, you can scrape it clean and fill the depression with a wood filler. Insert a wooden plug into a deeper repair.

Fitting a plug

Prepare and cut the veneer patch, making it slightly larger than the damaged area of groundwork. Cut away or drill out the damaged material forming a diamond or round recess in the groundwork, and make a plug of matching wood to fit. Glue the plug into place with the grain in the same direction, and trim flush.

Removing veneer

In order to preserve the patina of old furniture, keep repairs to a minimum. However, there are times when the condition of a veneered surface dictates that the veneer has to be lifted. You may be fortunate enough to be able to reuse the stripped veneer, but if not, keep it for future repairs.

1 Applying moisture

First remove the old finish (see pages 20-1). Cover the top with a thick layer of damp cloth, and leave overnight. Remove the cloth and work over the surface with a hot iron and damp cloth pad.

2 Lifting the veneer

Ease the veneer off the groundwork with a wide wallpaper scraper, applying extra heat as required. Lay the veneer face-down and remove old glue with a warm damp rag and scraper.

3 Flattening the veneer

To stop it buckling, place the damp veneer between flat panels of chipboard lined with paper and leave to dry.

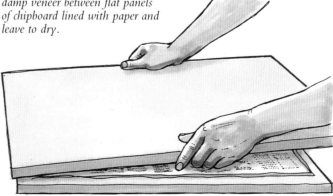

LAYING VENEER

Nowadays it is standard practice to veneer a table top on both sides, in order to prevent a single face veneer bowing the groundwork as it shrinks; this was not often done in the past. Veneer can be laid using the 'hand method' or with cauls.

The traditional hand method uses animal glue to bond the veneer, which is pressed into place, using a veneer hammer. This is worked with hand pressure, to squeeze out surplus glue and ensure a tight bond. Alternatively, use a modern heat-sensitive glue film.

Caul veneering uses flat or shaped boards, or blocks that are clamped to press the veneer into place. This method is particularly suited to laying veneer made up from pieces taped together. It also enables both sides of a panel to be veneered at the same time. Traditional animal glue can be used, as well as cold-setting resin glues, which allow more time for placing or 'laying up' the veneer.

When re-veneering a surface, try to use the original veneer, but replace it with new material if it is beyond repair.

Preparing the groundwork
It is essential that the groundwork is perfectly flat and smooth, as any undulations will show through a thin veneer and will be highlighted by a gloss finish. Large splits can be filled with a strip of wood (see page 137), while fine cracks can be treated effectively with a wood filler.

*1 Washing
off old glue*
Scrape off thick deposits of old animal glue, then scrub the groundwork with hot water, using a coarse cloth. Leave to dry.

*2 Keying
the surface*
Having made good any faults in the groundwork, key the surface with coarse abrasive paper wrapped around a sanding block. Work the block diagonally; finish by removing all traces of dust.

Hand veneering
Traditionalists prefer to use animal glues for hand veneering. For this method you need a veneer hammer, which you can buy or make from hardwood, or you can use a cross-peen hammer for small repairs. You will also need an electric iron, a sponge, a bowl of warm water, gummed tape, a sharp knife and a straightedge. However, it is a lot simpler to lay veneer with glue film.

Using heat-sensitive glue film
Heat-sensitive, paper-backed glue film is clean and non-staining. The sheet is easily cut to size and shape with scissors. Use an electric iron to soften the glue, and a veneer hammer or wide wooden seam-roller to press down the veneer.

1 Laying the film
Cut the sheet to size and lay it on the groundwork, with the backing paper uppermost. Set the iron at medium heat, and run it over the surface to induce the glue to grip.

*2 Peeling
the backing*
When the glue has cooled, peel off the backing paper. Now lay the prepared veneer in place over the glue-lined surface of the groundwork.

3 Ironing veneer
Cover the veneer with the backing paper, to protect it. With the iron set to medium heat, slowly work over the surface to melt the glue, pressing down the veneer as you go. Do not overheat the glue, and do not stretch the veneer by reworking it too much.

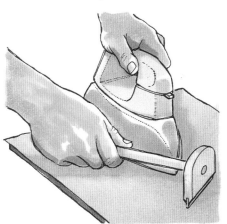

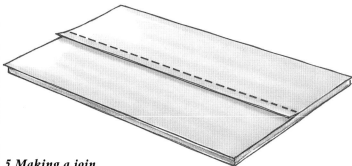

Laying veneer with animal glue

Animal glue is available in bead form and needs to be prepared in a double-jacketed glue pot, or improvise using a clean food-can in a small saucepan. Quarter-fill the glue pot with glue beads, cover them with hot water and leave to soak. Half-fill the saucepan with water and heat the glue to not more than 49°C (120°F), stirring to a smooth, free-flowing consistency.

1 Sizing the work

If you are veneering new groundwork, seal the wood with thinned glue after keying the surface. Lightly sand the board when dry. Old groundwork that has been stripped of its veneer does not need this treatment.

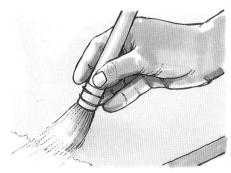

2 Laying the veneer

Brush a thin, even coat of full-strength glue onto the ground-work and veneer, and leave it until tacky. Place the veneer into position, and press it flat with your hand. Dampen the surface with a hot, well-wrung sponge.

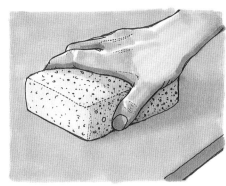

3 Pressing the veneer

Set the iron to a moderate heat, and work it over the dampened surface to melt the glue. If the iron is too hot, this causes the glue to degrade and leads to shrinkage problems with the veneer.

4 Using the veneer hammer

Follow immediately with the veneer hammer, working along the grain with a zigzag action. Work from the centre of the veneer towards the ends, squeezing out surplus glue and air. If the glue chills, dampen and heat the veneer as you work.

5 Making a join

Should you need to join leaves of veneer together to cover a panel, arrange them so the join is symmetrical. For example, lay two pieces, with the figure opened like the leaves of a book and the join placed down the middle of the panel. Glue them with the edges overlapping by 25mm (1in) at the centre.

6 Cutting the veneer

Lay a straightedge down the centre line, and cut through both layers of veneer with a sharp knife. It is best to make the cut in one pass.

7 Removing the waste

Peel away the top strip, then lift the edge of the over-lapping veneer and pull the lower strip clear. You may need to dampen and heat the strip to make it easier. Press the edges flat, using the hammer, and tape the joint to prevent the veneer parting as it dries.

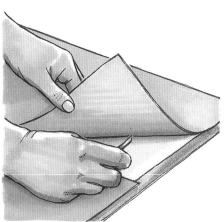

8 Trimming the edges

When dry, turn the panel over and, with the veneer face-down on a flat surface, trim away the surplus material all round with a sharp knife. Finish by sanding the edges smooth.

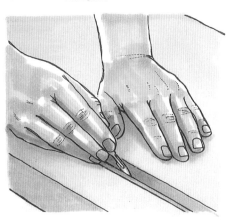

CAUL VENEERING

Taped veneers or veneers that are brittle and difficult to lay by hand are best laid between clamped cauls. Traditionalists would opt for using hot animal glue, especially as it is always possible for a restorer to reverse the work should another repair be required in the future. However, cold-setting resin glue has definite practical advantages when caul veneering large panels.

Making cauls

Make flat cauls, slightly larger than the area of the groundwork, from panels of thick blockboard or chipboard. In order to be able to clamp large cauls firmly and evenly, prepare enough pairs of stiff wooden bearers for your purpose.

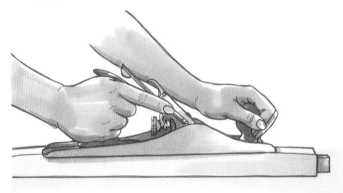

1 Planing the bearers
Plane the clamping faces of the bearers to a shallow convex curve, to provide pressure at the centre. This ensures that any surplus glue is squeezed out to the edges of the veneer, even though the clamping force is applied to the ends of the bearers.

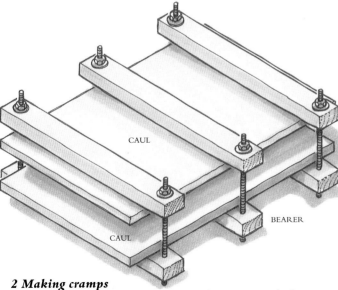

2 Making cramps
You could use conventional cramps to apply pressure to the bearers, but it may be cheaper to fit threaded rods, using nuts with large washers to provide the clamping force.

Using animal glue

It is necessary to work quickly when using animal glue, as the cauls need to be hot. You therefore need to prepare the workbench with all the equipment to hand and, if possible, recruit an assistant.

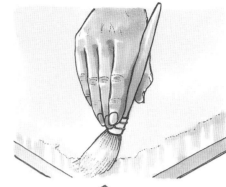

1 Applying the glue
Key and size the groundwork if required. Apply even coats of animal glue to the groundwork and veneer. Allow it to gel so that the veneer does not slip on the glue as pressure is applied.

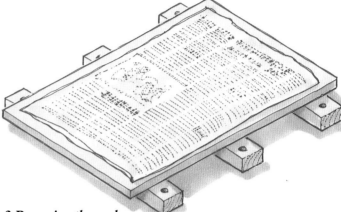

2 Preparing the cauls
Preheat the top caul on both sides in front of a heater. Meanwhile, lay the bottom caul on a row of evenly spaced bearers. Place the veneer-covered groundwork on top, and cover with sheets of newspaper.

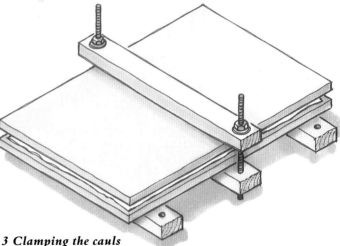

3 Clamping the cauls
Quickly place the hot caul on the veneer, then clamp the centre bearers first, applying even pressure to both ends. Apply the other bearers in a similar way. Once the glue has set, remove the bearers and trim the edges of the work. If required, lay a balancing veneer on the other side as soon as possible.

Using cold-setting glue

Once cured, cold-setting resin glues are strong and resistant to heat and moisture, and are ideal for veneering table tops. However, they are only suitable for caul veneering, as cold-setting glues require sustained pressure to make a tight bond. Since they do not have to be kept hot, there is no hurry when assembling the lay-up, and both sides of a panel can be veneered at the same time. Glue is applied to the groundwork only, but it is essential that the surface is covered evenly.

1 Preparing the veneer

If the veneer needs to be joined in order to cover the panel, lay the leaves together and plane the mating edges straight, using a long plane and a shooting board. Clamp long pieces of veneer between two straight-edged battens before planing them.

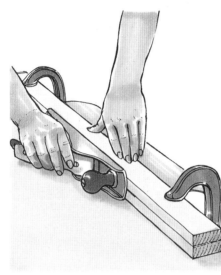

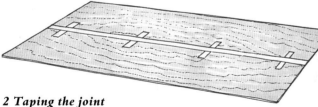

2 Taping the joint

Arrange the leaves face-up with planed edges together, then bind them with short strips of gummed tape across the joint, followed by a continuous strip along it.

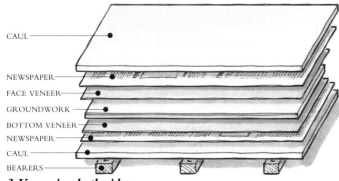

CAUL

NEWSPAPER

FACE VENEER

GROUNDWORK

BOTTOM VENEER

NEWSPAPER

CAUL

BEARERS

3 Veneering both sides.

Prepare the work area with the bottom bearers in position and one caul laid on top. Apply glue to the back of the groundwork and lay it on the bottom veneer. Glue the top surface, and place the face veneer. Position the panel between the top and bottom cauls, and clamp together with even pressure.

Preparing veneer for finishing

Newly laid veneer should be left for several days before cleaning up. Take care not to remove too much material, particularly if you use an orbital sander.

1 Removing gummed tape

First dampen and peel off any gummed paper used to tape joints or splits in the veneer. Wipe the surface with a damp cloth to remove all traces of animal glue, then allow the wood to dry thoroughly.

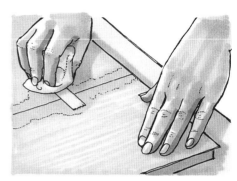

2 Using a cabinet scraper

Use a scraper to level the surface. Following the grain, hold the scraper square to the line of movement when working a single sheet of veneer, but hold it at an angle when scraping across joined veneers or bandings, and when starting at an edge.

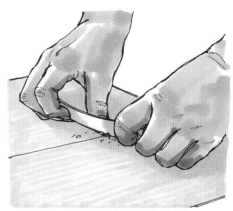

3 Sanding the surface

Sand the surface with very fine abrasive paper wrapped around a sanding block, working with the grain. If this is not possible with joined veneers and bandings, sand in one direction only. Use an orbital sanding machine on large areas. Wipe off the surface dust ready for polishing.

4 Sanding mouldings

You could use a shaped scraper to clean up veneered mouldings, but it is easier to sand them with very fine abrasive paper and a shaped sanding block.

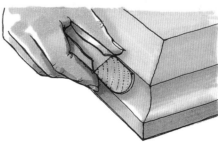

Veneering moulded shapes

Small shaped work, in the form of cornices, bases and mouldings, is sometimes made from a cheaper wood and faced with decorative cross-grain veneer (see page 152). For repairs, it is often easier to employ sand as a means of applying pressure to the veneer rather than make shaped cauls.

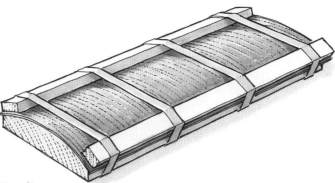

1 Making the impression
Press the workpiece into the sand to form the shape in reverse, then lift it out and brush off any grains of sand.

2 Laying the veneer
Apply resin glue to the groundwork and lay the veneer over it. Cover the veneer with newspaper, and place the assembly carefully onto the shaped sand.

3 Pressing into the sand
Press the workpiece into the mould with cramps and a block to distribute the forces.

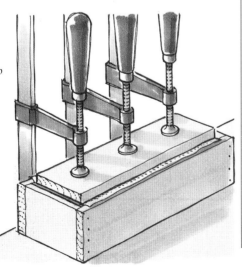

Bending cross-grain veneer
Pre-form the veneer that will run across the width of the moulding, to make it easier to handle. Dampen the veneer, place strips of wood along the edges and pull it over the shaped groundwork with elastic bands or adhesive tape. Allow the veneer to dry before applying glue and pressing it in a sandbox.

Using a sandbag
As an alternative for veneering simple shapes, make a canvas bag to cover the area of the work, and fill it with fine dry sand. Prepare the groundwork and veneer, then apply the glue. If you are using animal glue, heat the sandbag and place it over the paper-covered veneer. Clamp the assembly between cauls.

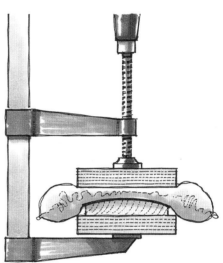

Gluing with contact adhesive
Instant-bond contact adhesive can be used to fix veneer to shaped groundwork without cauls. Apply the adhesive evenly to both surfaces. Leave the glue to become touch-dry then, working from one edge, lower and press the veneer onto the workpiece.

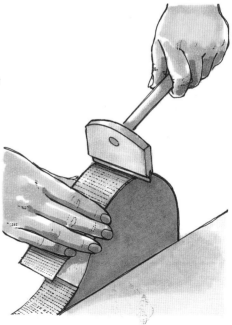

125

CROSS-BANDING

Cross-banding is a method used to create decorative borders on a panel. It is often applied to table tops and cabinet doors. Fine strips of wood known as stringing are sometimes used to define the different areas of the veneer. Decorative bandings are made from sections of coloured wood in various patterns and widths. Bandings can be incorporated with other veneers or inlaid into a solid-wood ground.

Cross-banding repairs

The cross-banded borders laid around the edges of a panel are particularly vulnerable to chipping. You can patch-repair chipped bandings, and it is possible to replace them entirely if the damage is too extensive.

1 Patching an edge

Select a matching veneer, and tape a slightly oversize patch over the damaged portion. Make two cuts square to the edge with a sharp knife, following the grain of the banding. Cut the inner edge level with the banding line. Cut through the patch, but only score the banding veneer.

2 Preparing the cut-out

Remove the trimmed patch and waste, and cut through the banding on the marked lines. Pare away the damaged veneer within the cut lines. Dampening the veneer may help.

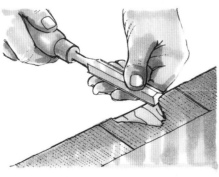

3 Gluing the patch

Apply glue to the groundwork, place the new patch and clamp it flat. Trim the outer edge, and sand ready for finishing.

Laying cross-banding

If the banding is beyond repair, dampen the veneer and carefully remove it, making sure you do not disturb the inner panel. Clean away the old glue, ready for the new banding. Select the veneer to match the original as closely as possible.

1 Cutting cross-banding

As bandings are cut across the grain, first trim the end of the leaf straight, using a straightedge and a very sharp knife. Cut successive parallel strips from the end of the veneer, making them slightly wider than the finished banding.

2 Using a cutting gauge

An alternative method is to cut strips for narrow bandings with a cutting gauge set to the required width; run the tool along the straight edge of a board.

3 Dealing with mitred ends

Apply gummed paper to the end of a strip being mitred, in order to prevent the veneer breaking away at the corner. Set a sliding bevel to the angle of the existing banding, and use it to mitre the end of the new veneer strip.

4 Gluing the banding

Dampen the pieces of banding prior to laying them. Starting at one of the mitred ends, apply glue to the groundwork and the face of the first piece. Position the veneer, and press it into place with a veneer hammer.

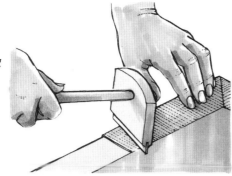

5 Joining the banding

Apply glue and lay the next strip of veneer in the same way, with the end slightly overlapping the first piece. Using a straightedge and sharp knife, cut through both strips and peel away the waste, then press the joint flat.

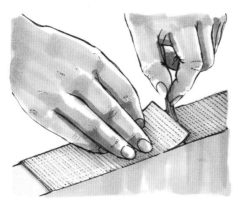

6 Finishing off

Continue in the same way until you reach the other mitred corner. Butt the last strip into the mitre before cutting its other overlapped end to make a square butt joint. Tape all the joints, and leave to dry. Trim the overhanging edge and prepare the surface ready for finishing.

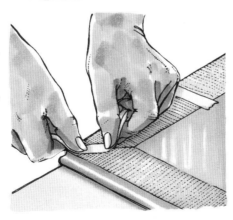

JOINING THICK VENEER

Thick veneer bandings are best cut to length with a fine saw. When making end-to-end butt joints, plane the meeting edges of each piece square on a shooting board. Try the fit and, if necessary, make adjustments as each piece is laid.

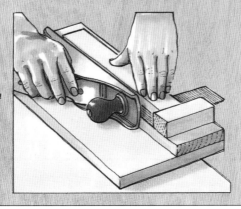

BANDINGS AND STRINGING

Decorative bandings are available as patterns made up from side-grain sections of coloured hardwoods. The strips are cut to approximately the same thickness as knife-cut veneer and are produced in various widths. They can be taped together with other veneers for caul veneering, or inlaid into a groove cut into a solid-wood top.

Strings are single strips or 'lines' of wood made in a limited range of flat and square sections. Used to outline decorative details, they are produced in 'white', a light-coloured wood, or 'black', a dyed version, to contrast with the surrounding veneer.

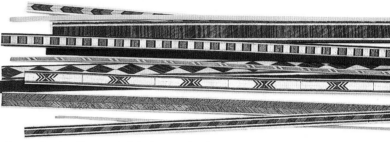

Decorative bandings and plain boxwood strings

Repairing bandings

Bandings are laid like veneer, and may need patch-repairing if the top is damaged. Try to match the design precisely, but if this is not possible, replace a full length of banding with one that is similar.

1 Cleaning the groove

Scrape the groove clear of old glue and fragments of the damaged banding, using a narrow chisel held almost vertically. If you need to clear part of the banding still in place, cut down the sides with a fine knife and chisel out the waste.

2 Fitting the banding

Match the pattern, and cut the banding to length. Mitre the end if it is required to fit a corner. Apply glue, and then press the banding into place with a cross-peen hammer.

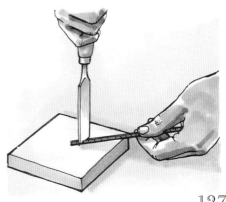

Repairing stringing

Strings may be laid in the surface of a top or at the edge. Because they are flexible, they are often set in a curve. If you find it necessary to follow a curve, wet the stringing, as this makes it easier to bend.

1 Preparing the groove

Clean out the groove to receive the new stringing. You may be able to use a narrow chisel, but a knife blade may be better if the string is very narrow.

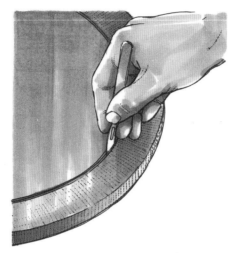

2 Fitting the string

Dry-fit the string into the groove, and mark the required length. Remove it and cut to size with a chisel. Apply glue, push the string into the groove, and press home with a small cross-peen hammer.

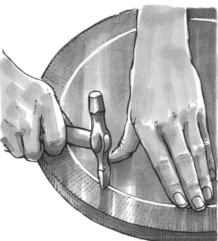

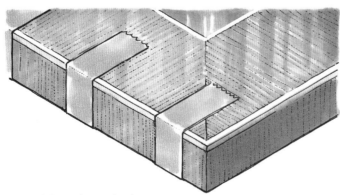

Repairing edge stringing

Clean the edge rebate with a scratch stock or chisel. Apply glue, press the stringing in place, and hold it with strips of masking tape fastened at close intervals over the edge.

MARQUETRY AND PARQUETRY

Marquetry and parquetry are decorative treatments which use coloured veneer to create ornate patterns. Marquetry designs are pictorial in style, using naturalistic and abstracted flora-and-fauna motifs. Parquetry, a form of marquetry, employs geometric shapes such as diamonds and squares. Small pieces of veneer are often missing, but unless you are fairly experienced it is best to leave all but the simplest of repairs to a professional restorer.

Ready-made marquetry motifs are still used to decorate furniture in the traditional manner. They are produced in various coloured woods, and are available in a range of shapes and sizes. They come with a paper backing ready for laying, and can be set into a veneered panel or inlaid into solid wood. These ready-made motifs can be used to replace a badly damaged original, or in some cases to cover the damaged section of a veneered top.

Ready-made veneer motifs

Replacing missing parts

Use a sharp knife and a steel rule when cutting straight edges, and use the knife freehand when cutting curved shapes.

1 Tracing the shape

Clean out the recess and tape a thin sheet of paper over it. Take a rubbing of the recess, using a soft pencil or crayon.

2 Preparing the new piece of veneer

Stick the paper pattern onto the face of the selected piece of veneer with water-soluble gum. Make sure that the grain runs in the required direction. Cover with a weighted block, and leave to dry.

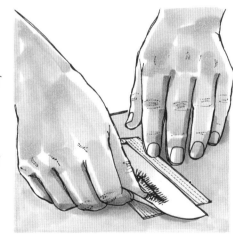

3 Fitting the veneer

Cut the part to shape, following the marked outline, and check for fit, making slight adjustments if required. Apply glue and press into place. When set, dampen the paper pattern and remove it.

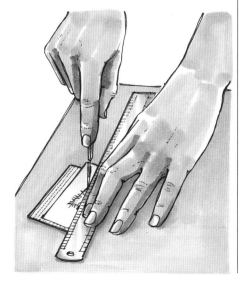

Shading veneer

Traditional inlay motifs sometimes have sections of the design shaded to give a three-dimensional effect. You can reproduce a similar effect, using heated sand.

1 Dipping a patch in hot sand

Pour fine silver sand into a flat tin can or foil dish until almost full. Place the container on a cooker hob and heat it on a low setting. Cut the required veneer a little oversize, and insert the edge into the sand. Lift out the veneer with tweezers after a few seconds, to check the colour.

2 Checking the colour

Lightly sand the charred surface, and dampen it to get an impression of the finished colour. If satisfactory, cut the patch to shape with the shading following the required direction, and glue into place.

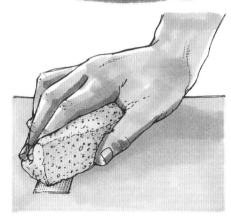

Laying a veneer motif

Select a motif suitable in design and scale, and tape it to the surface veneer, paper side up, in the required position.

Cutting through the surface veneer

If the motif is already shaped, cut round it with a sharp knife. If not, mark out the required shape and cut through the motif and the surface veneer simultaneously. In either case, remove the veneer and clean out the waste, then glue the motif into the recess. Soak off the paper cover.

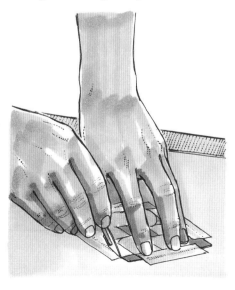

CHESTS AND CABINETS

THE MODERN ANSWER TO OUR STORAGE needs is to group a whole range of cupboards and drawers together; the same basic units serve anonymously in the kitchen, bedroom or lounge. Older items of furniture were invariably made as free-standing items, each with a specific function, hence the seemingly different categories of storage furniture – chests of drawers, wardrobes, tallboys, dressing tables, bureaux, dressers and so on.

From the humble blanket chest to an antique sideboard, they are all basically boxes (carcases) fitted with doors, lids or drawers, and the methods for repairing them apply to most items of storage furniture.

SOLID-WOOD CONSTRUCTION

The problem, as always when using panels of solid timber, is the inevitable shrinkage and expansion of wood caused by changes in humidity. Consequently, furniture was designed to allow the wood to move without it adversely affecting the structure or appearance of the piece.

Chest of drawers

The traditional chest of drawers is a perfect example of the ingenuity of cabinetmakers bent on creating a functional piece of furniture from solid wood. The side panels, and possibly the bottom panel too, are normally made by gluing several planks of wood together. They are joined at the bottom corners with lapped dovetails – a strong joint that spreads the load across the entire width of the panels. The solid-wood top may be joined in a similar manner, but more often it is screwed from below to two rails dovetailed to the side panels.

The drawers slide on runners screwed to the inside of the cabinet; each drawer is supported across its width by a rail. A thin panel of wood protects the contents from dust.

Half-width drawers are separated by a short vertical post and slide on a combined drawer runner and guide running from front to back. The back panel is held in grooves or rebates cut in the surrounding panels and pinned to the rear top rail.

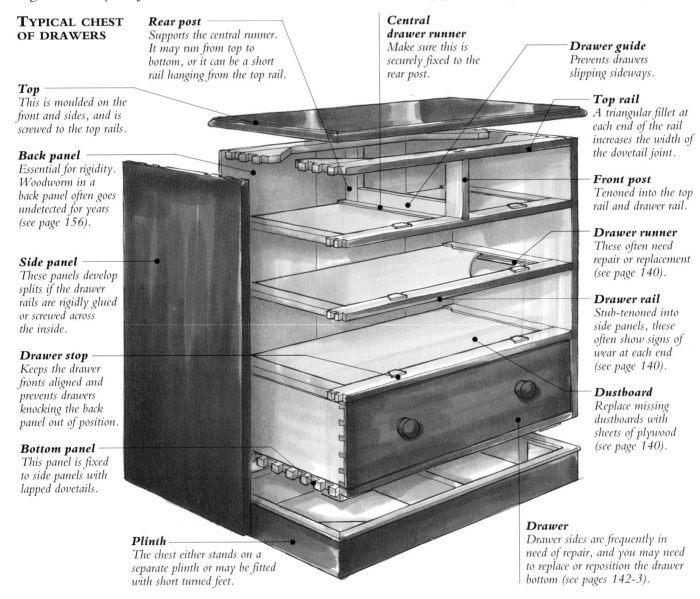

TYPICAL CHEST OF DRAWERS

Rear post
Supports the central runner. It may run from top to bottom, or it can be a short rail hanging from the top rail.

Top
This is moulded on the front and sides, and is screwed to the top rails.

Back panel
Essential for rigidity. Woodworm in a back panel often goes undetected for years (see page 156).

Side panel
These panels develop splits if the drawer rails are rigidly glued or screwed across the inside.

Drawer stop
Keeps the drawer fronts aligned and prevents drawers knocking the back panel out of position.

Bottom panel
This panel is fixed to side panels with lapped dovetails.

Plinth
The chest either stands on a separate plinth or may be fitted with short turned feet.

Central drawer runner
Make sure this is securely fixed to the rear post.

Drawer guide
Prevents drawers slipping sideways.

Top rail
A triangular fillet at each end of the rail increases the width of the dovetail joint.

Front post
Tenoned into the top rail and drawer rail.

Drawer runner
These often need repair or replacement (see page 140).

Drawer rail
Stub-tenoned into side panels, these often show signs of wear at each end (see page 140).

Dustboard
Replace missing dustboards with sheets of plywood (see page 140).

Drawer
Drawer sides are frequently in need of repair, and you may need to replace or reposition the drawer bottom (see pages 142-3).

Kitchen dresser

Kitchen dressers were originally made by individuals or small workshops, and were constructed according to local tradition. The base unit of the dresser shown has two identical half-width drawers above a pair of cupboard doors. The frame is made up from rails and door stiles glued to solid-wood side panels. The cupboard bottom is housed into the sides and the oversailing top is screwed down from below. The cupboard invariably has one fixed shelf.

To save timber, the bank of open shelves is usually constructed separately and is plugged on top of the base unit. The shelf-unit top may be dovetailed or simply nailed to the narrow side panels, and the fixed shelves are located with housing joints. A deep cornice moulding is attached with glued blocks to the top and sides. The back panel, usually made from tongued-and-grooved boards, is pinned to the back of the shelf unit.

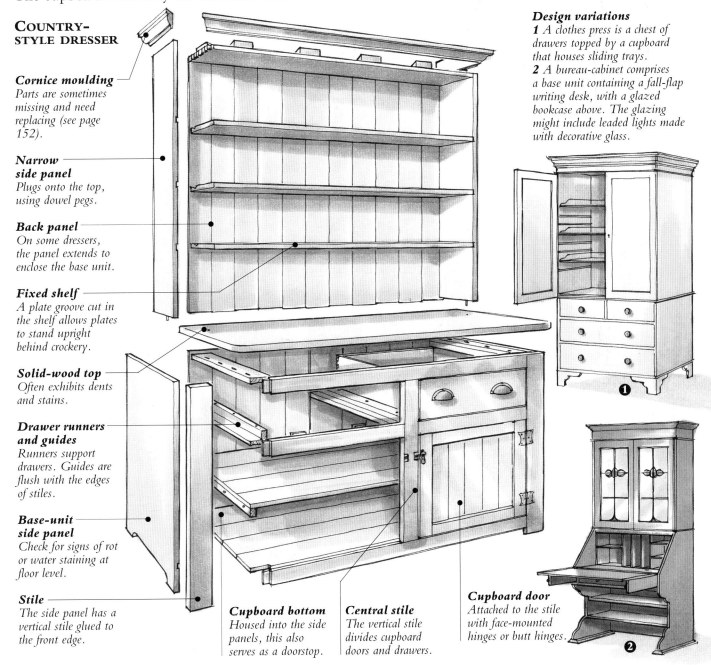

COUNTRY-STYLE DRESSER

Cornice moulding
Parts are sometimes missing and need replacing (see page 152).

Narrow side panel
Plugs onto the top, using dowel pegs.

Back panel
On some dressers, the panel extends to enclose the base unit.

Fixed shelf
A plate groove cut in the shelf allows plates to stand upright behind crockery.

Solid-wood top
Often exhibits dents and stains.

Drawer runners and guides
Runners support drawers. Guides are flush with the edges of stiles.

Base-unit side panel
Check for signs of rot or water staining at floor level.

Stile
The side panel has a vertical stile glued to the front edge.

Cupboard bottom
Housed into the side panels, this also serves as a doorstop.

Central stile
The vertical stile divides cupboard doors and drawers.

Cupboard door
Attached to the stile with face-mounted hinges or butt hinges.

Design variations
1 *A clothes press is a chest of drawers topped by a cupboard that houses sliding trays.*
2 *A bureau-cabinet comprises a base unit containing a fall-flap writing desk, with a glazed bookcase above. The glazing might include leaded lights made with decorative glass.*

❶

❷

133

FRAME-AND-PANEL CONSTRUCTION

Frame-and-panel construction was developed to allow for the movement in solid timber while reducing the weight of storage furniture. The side of a cabinet, for example, comprises a thin panel of wood held in grooves, or sometimes rebates, on the inside of a framework of rails and posts. The panel is always left free, since gluing or pinning it in place inevitably promotes splitting of the wood.

Plywood, manufactured in quantity since the turn of the century, is designed to resist the tendency to warp and crack; the ideal substitute for a solid-wood panel. It could even be glued to the outside of a cheap frame, creating the illusion of a continuous plank of good-quality timber, but at a fraction of its weight and cost.

Chiffonier

A late-Victorian chiffonier demonstrates basic frame-and-panel construction. Long horizontal rails join the side panels, creating an open framework that is clad with a divided solid-wood back panel. The bottom rests on the lower framing. The top of the chiffonier is made from inexpensive timber that is veneered and lipped all round.

This cupboard is enclosed by two doors, which feature carved, raised-and-fielded panels. Furniture of this quality is typically fitted with a brass bolt on the inside of one door and a lock on the other.

The veneered upstand, edged with applied carving, carries a narrow shelf supported by carved brackets. Screws are used to attach the upstand.

VICTORIAN CHIFFONIER

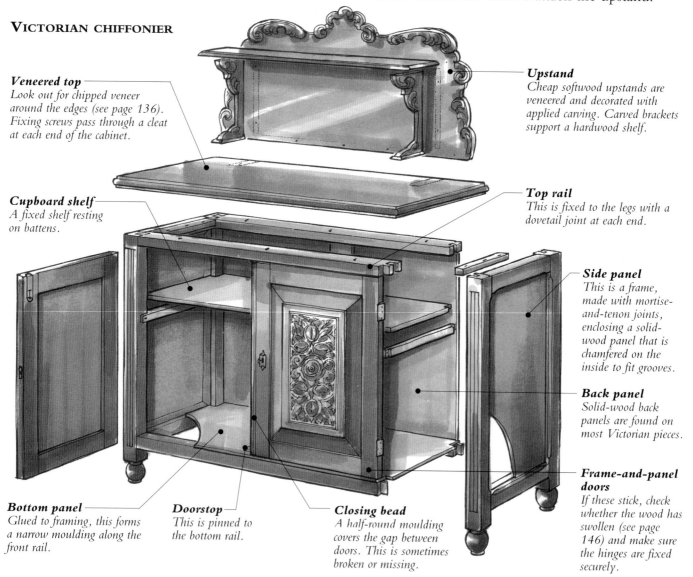

Veneered top
Look out for chipped veneer around the edges (see page 136). Fixing screws pass through a cleat at each end of the cabinet.

Cupboard shelf
A fixed shelf resting on battens.

Bottom panel
Glued to framing, this forms a narrow moulding along the front rail.

Doorstop
This is pinned to the bottom rail.

Closing bead
A half-round moulding covers the gap between doors. This is sometimes broken or missing.

Upstand
Cheap softwood upstands are veneered and decorated with applied carving. Carved brackets support a hardwood shelf.

Top rail
This is fixed to the legs with a dovetail joint at each end.

Side panel
This is a frame, made with mortise-and-tenon joints, enclosing a solid-wood panel that is chamfered on the inside to fit grooves.

Back panel
Solid-wood back panels are found on most Victorian pieces.

Frame-and-panel doors
If these stick, check whether the wood has swollen (see page 146) and make sure the hinges are fixed securely.

134

Dressing table

This type of dressing table, made in the 1930s or 1940s, is essentially a chest of drawers that is tall enough to enable a gentleman to shave while standing at the pivoting mirror. It embodies the same frame-and-panel principles described and illustrated opposite, but by this period plywood was more often used for the panels, dustboards between drawers, and back panel.

The arrangement of drawer runners and rails is very similar to that described for a solid-wood chest of drawers (see page 132), but, because of the frame-and-panel construction, each runner requires a matching drawer guide in order to prevent the drawer from sliding sideways.

Design variations
Frame-and-panel construction is suitable for practically any type of storage furniture, but particularly for large items.

1 A wardrobe is essentially a cupboard like the chiffonier, but on a larger scale. This 1930s version is constructed with veneered-plywood panels.

2 A chest is a cupboard lying on its back. This blanket chest has a solid-wood lid attached with handmade iron strap hinges.

3 Many washstands are simply marble-top tables. This version is a small frame-and-panel cabinet with a tiled upstand.

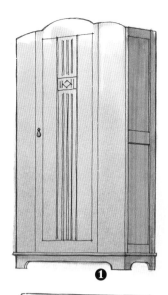
❶

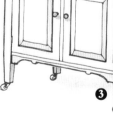
❷

GENTLEMAN'S DRESSING TABLE

Mirror
If it is very badly damaged, it might be worth having a bevelled mirror re-silvered. Your local glazier should be able to recommend a reliable company.

Mirror stand
Screwed to the dresser top, either with visible raised-head screws or with screw heads covered by wooden plugs.

Solid-wood top
The finish can often be spoiled by water stains or white rings.

Drawers
These have show-wood fronts with cheaper backs and sides. You can disguise scratches found around handles (see page 19).

Drawer runners and guides
With frame-and-panel construction, every runner requires a drawer guide.

Bracket
Brackets pinned to legs and rails are purely decorative and contribute practically nothing to the stability of the piece. If missing, they are easily replaced.

Plywood back panel
A panel screwed to the side panels and rails. Plywood is particularly susceptible to woodworm (see page 156).

Side panel
Slim framing houses a veneered-plywood panel.

Dustboard
These panels, made of plywood, are easily replaced.

REPAIRING CARCASES

The carcase, also called the cabinet, is the actual storage 'box', which may be enclosed by doors or fitted with drawers, depending on its intended purpose. Traditionally constructed carcases are very strong and rarely suffer serious structural damage in normal use, unless they are subjected to extreme changes in humidity. The exceptions to this rule are those parts of the carcase that need repairing or replacing because they have gradually been worn down by the drawers sliding back and forth, or, to a lesser extent, as a result of a relatively heavy door putting undue strain on its hinges.

Patching chipped veneers

A great many cheaper storage items were made with tops of veneered softwood. Unless they are protected by solid edge lippings, the vulnerable veneers become chipped, exposing the softwood groundwork. Repair the damage with patches of veneer (see page 119).

Dealing with stained finishes

Various solvents will etch stains into surface finishes. A sideboard, for example, may be covered with white rings left by alcohol or water smeared on the base of a glass or decanter. Similarly, many dressing tables are spoiled by spills of nail varnish or make-up. Try burnishing out such stains with a finish reviver (see page 19).

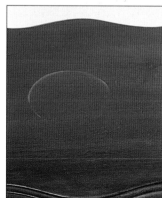

Cleaning and repairing marble

Being porous, marble stains easily and should be cleaned regularly, to prevent it absorbing dirt and grease. Wash a grimy marble top with a mild solution of ammonia or use a poultice to lift a stubborn stain (see page 113). A cracked marble top can be repaired successfully (see page 114).

Damaged tops

The top of a chest of drawers or low cupboard may share many of the problems more commonly associated with table tops. A solid-wood top, for example, is normally constructed by gluing several planks edge-to-edge and, provided the top is allowed to expand or contract without restriction, these joints remain perfectly sound. However, when a top has been fixed rigidly, there is every chance that one or more of the butt joints will come apart. Dismantling a damaged top and regluing the joints is relatively straightforward (see page 111).

1 Repairing a moulded edge

A broken edge is very disfiguring, and should be repaired if at all possible. Glue the broken piece in place immediately, binding it with self-adhesive tape until the glue has set.

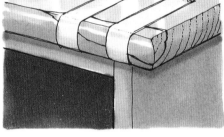

2 Remaking a damaged edge

When wood is missing, plane the damaged section flat and square, then cut a slightly oversize replacement block. Make sure the timber matches the colour and grain direction of the original wood.

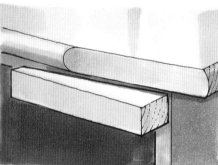

3 Gluing and clamping

Attach the glued block with a sash cramp. If repairing a missing corner, clamp scrap wood to the side of the carcase, to prevent the block sliding sideways.

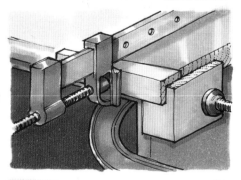

4 Shaping the repair

Once the glue has set, plane the block flush, then shape it to match the original moulding. Use rasps, files and sandpaper to shape a simple moulding, but use gouges, chisels or a moulding plane for anything complicated.

Repairing split side panels

Side panels made from solid wood, in particular, tend to reveal longitudinal splits where drawer runners have been glued across the inner face, preventing the wood shrinking naturally. When movement is restricted at both ends, the forces exerted across the grain are capable of pulling one of the panel's butt joints apart, resulting in a gap running from top to bottom. In theory, it is possible to dismantle the carcase in order to repair open butt joints, but this is an unnecessary and potentially damaging practice when it is possible to make repairs *in situ*.

1 Enlarging a narrow split
A narrow tapering split that follows the grain may be so insignificant that it is not worth repairing. If you decide to go ahead, open up the split with the point of a fine saw until it is wide enough to insert a piece of veneer.

2 Inserting veneer
Glue a narrow strip of veneer into the split. If necessary, plane or sand down a slightly thicker lath to fit a wide split. When the glue has set, plane or scrape the veneer flush and disguise the repair with coloured wood dye and polish.

1 Preparing an open joint
Make a mild-steel hook scraper to clean old glue from both edges of the open joint. If you file the hook to a slight taper, it will shape both sides of the slot, and makes a snug fit for the lath that will be inserted at the next stage.

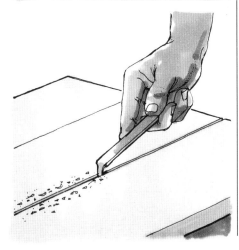

2 Shaping a lath
Cut a narrow wedge-shape lath from matching timber, and file or plane both sides until it fits the tapered slot in the side panel. Glue the lath, tap it into the slot with a hammer, and plane flush when the glue has set.

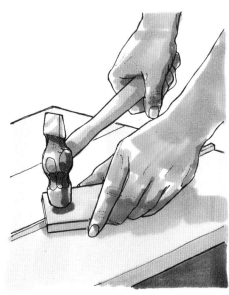

Repairing and replacing back panels

A back panel does more than prevent the contents spilling out of the back of a cupboard. Without it, the carcase has little lateral stiffness and could be rocked from side to side, thus loosening the joints, until the cupboard collapses. It obviously pays to attend to loose or missing panels urgently.

On an older cupboard, the back panel will have been made from solid wood, although it may have been replaced with plywood or hardboard at some later date. It is normally screwed or pinned into a rebate all round or fixed directly to the back edges of the carcase.

A wide panel may be made in two halves, separated by a grooved muntin, similar to those used to support drawer bottoms (see page 141).

Removing a back panel
When replacing a panel, remove the fixing screws or tap it out from inside with a hammer, using a softwood block to spread the load and prevent the panel splitting. Pull out any old nails with pincers before fitting a new panel.

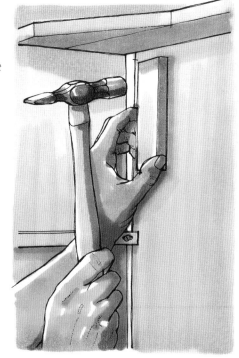

Feet and plinths

Plinths and feet are invariably scuffed and dented where they have been kicked and struck by brooms, carpet sweepers and vacuum cleaners over the years, but most of us are content to live with these minor blemishes. However, when feet have been lost or completely destroyed by woodworm or rot, you have no other choice but to make an exact replica.

Turned foot

Turned bun-shape feet are plugged into an underframe or into the bottom of the carcase. Sometimes the foot is attached by a coarse-threaded peg. Copy one of the remaining feet or turn four new ones on a lathe.

Bracket foot

This type of foot comprises two bracket-shape pieces of wood mitred at the corner. It is attached with screws and possibly glued blocks to a moulded underframe, or directly to the underside of the cabinet. Trace the outline onto a cardboard template and cut out replacement brackets, using a coping saw.

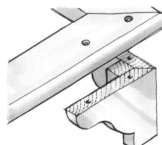

Applied bracket

A simple cut-out bracket is sometimes pinned and glued to the leg and bottom rail of a frame-and-panel cabinet. A split bracket can be repaired with glue, or you can make a replica as described above.

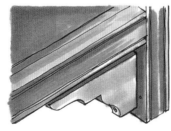

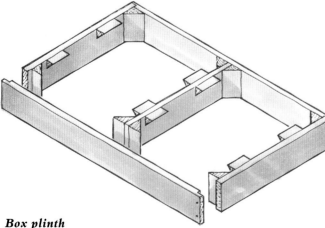

Box plinth

Plinths are usually crudely made, being held together by a number of glued blocks. To replace a badly damaged component, dislodge the blocks by driving a chisel behind them.

Drawer runners and rails

Whenever a drawer sticks or jams, take a close look at its supporting rails and runners. One can almost guarantee that these elements will be worn to some extent, due to persistent rubbing by the bottom edges of the drawers. In particular, softwood runners may be scored by deep grooves that extend right across the transverse drawer rails. The extent of the damage will determine whether you can repair the original components, or whether it would be better to replace them altogether.

How rails and runners are fitted

The way drawer runners and rails are fitted will determine your approach to repairing and replacing them. The examples shown below show typical methods of construction.

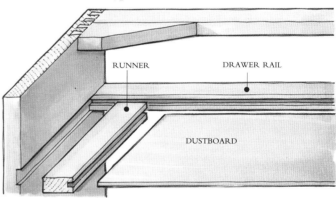

Solid-wood construction

The transverse drawer rail is tenoned into a solid-wood side panel, and is grooved on the inside to take the dustboard. Each drawer runner is located in a shallow housing cut across the side panel; a small tenon on the front of the runner fits into the dustboard groove in the rail. There is a similar groove on the inside of the runner. Sliding the dustboard in from the back of the cabinet holds the runner firmly in its housing.

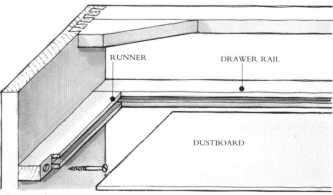

Screwed runner

Runners should never be glued across the side panel, but they are often fixed with a single screw near the back. A screw slot in the runner allows for movement across the side panel. Although they are sometimes housed into the side panel as described above, screw-fixed runners can be attached to a plain panel.

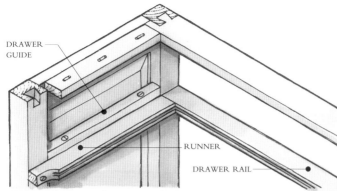

DRAWER GUIDE

RUNNER

DRAWER RAIL

Frame-and-panel construction

Similar screw-fixed runners are to be found in a frame-and-panel carcase. However, since the side frame is unlikely to shrink across its width, a screw slot is unnecessary. An additional batten, the drawer guide, is screwed to the runner to keep the drawer running straight.

Double runner

A wide runner is used to support two narrow drawers in the middle. A single guide batten screwed to the runner keeps the drawers apart. A central runner may be supported at the back by a vertical post (see page 132), or held in place by nails through the back panel on cheaper cabinets.

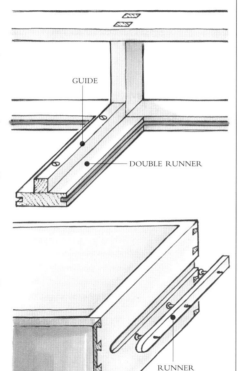

GUIDE

DOUBLE RUNNER

Side-run drawers

Instead of being supported from below, some drawers are side-run – slots in the drawer sides are located over the runners. Although this is often thought to be a relatively modern method of construction, side-run drawers were used as long ago as the seventeenth century.

RUNNER

Side-run trays

As a variant, a runner fixed to the drawer sometimes runs in a housing cut across the side panel. This system is used to support shallow trays behind the doors of a clothes press (see page 133).

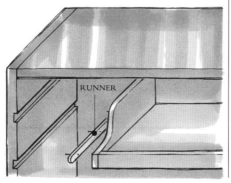

RUNNER

Fitting drawer stops

Without drawer stops, there is nothing to prevent a drawer slamming into the back panel, eventually splitting the wood or even dislodging the panel. Drawer stops also serve to keep all the drawers aligned neatly with the face of the cabinet.

1 Marking the drawer stop

Set a marking gauge to the thickness of the drawer front. Allow for any mouldings that project beyond the cabinet face, and mark the front edge of the stop on the rail. Fit a single stop centrally for a short drawer, and one about 75mm (3in) from each end of a wide rail.

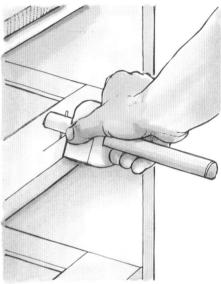

2 Gluing the stop

Make a new stop from 6mm (¼in) plywood, and glue it to the rail. Squeeze out excess glue by rubbing the stop from side to side, finally aligning the front edge of the stop with the marked line.

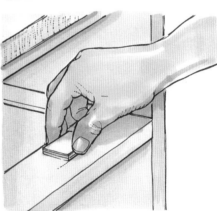

3 Securing with panel pins

Carefully insert the drawer to check that it fits perfectly, then fix the stop with two panel pins. Wipe off traces of glue with a damp cloth.

139

Replacing drawer runners

Wormed, split or exceptionally worn runners should be removed and used as patterns for making new ones. Even if the original runners were made from softwood, it is a good idea to use hardwood for the replacements.

Swapping runners

Provided the wood is sound, try swapping the drawer runners at opposite sides of the cabinet. Remove the back panel and fixing screws, then tap a chisel under the end of each runner to dislodge it. Turn the runners over and re-fit them with the worn side face down. Make sure the dustboard grooves align.

Repairing side-run trays

Sliding trays with worn runners will fall upon each other until the whole set drops to the bottom of the cabinet. Either pin new runners to the trays, or increase the running surfaces by pinning and gluing a moulded hardwood batten just below each housing in the side panels.

Repairing drawer rails

Having removed runners for repair, take the opportunity to insert a patch of matching wood at each end of the drawer rail.

1 Marking out the recess

Mark out the depth of the recess by scribing a line on the front edge of the rail, just below the notch worn in the wood. Then mark a line across the rail to represent the edge of the recess, which should taper slightly from front to back. The cut itself should be at an angle of about 60 degrees to form a dovetail.

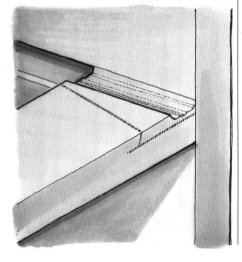

2 Cutting the recess

Saw across the rail, following the marked line, then pare out the waste with a bevel-edge chisel to form a neat dovetailed recess. Refit the drawer runner.

3 Fitting the patch

Glue and insert a slightly oversize patch, giving it a tap with a hammer to make a snug fit. Clamp it in place until the glue sets, then plane and pare the patch flush with the drawer rail.

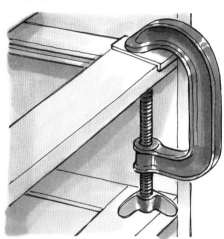

Replacing dustboards

Dustboards that hold drawer runners in their housings are obviously essential items (see page 138), but in many cases a chest will perform perfectly well without them. However, fine wood dust from wearing runners trickles into the drawer below, and it pays to replace dustboards, if only to keep the contents clean. Additionally, dustboards are in some cases security measures, as they prevent anyone from gaining access to a locked drawer by removing the one above.

Inserting new boards

Cut new dustboards from plywood and, having removed the back panel, slide them from behind into the grooves in the rails and runners.

REPAIRING DRAWERS

A typical drawer found in most old cabinets will be constructed from solid wood throughout and made with dovetail joints at each corner. Country furniture and cheap chests in general, were fitted with softwood drawers, whereas hardwood would have been used for better-quality work. The drawer front was nearly always cut from wood with an attractive figure, or at least faced with a superior–quality hardwood veneer. The drawer bottom was slid from the rear into narrow grooves cut on the inside of the drawer – or into slip mouldings glued to the front and sides – and was pinned or screwed to the underside of the drawer back. Glue was never used to secure drawer bottoms.

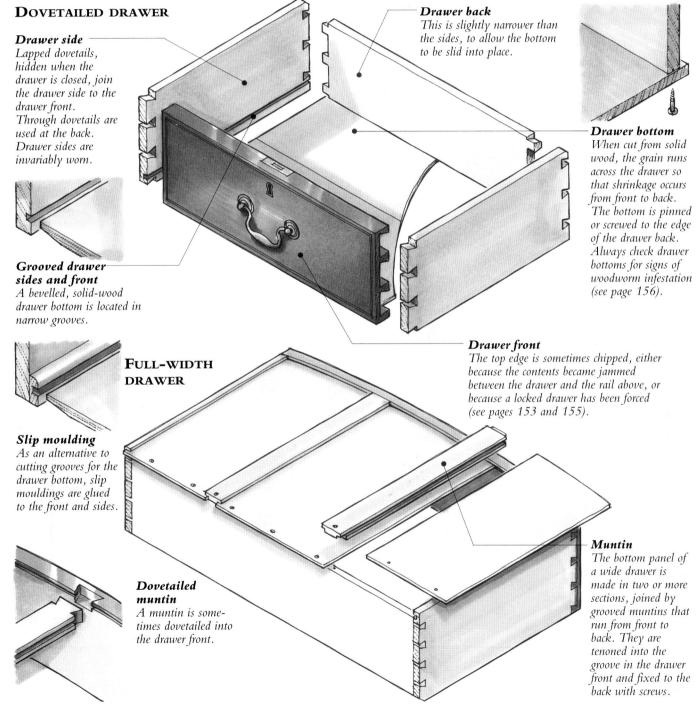

DOVETAILED DRAWER

Drawer side
Lapped dovetails, hidden when the drawer is closed, join the drawer side to the drawer front. Through dovetails are used at the back. Drawer sides are invariably worn.

Grooved drawer sides and front
A bevelled, solid-wood drawer bottom is located in narrow grooves.

Slip moulding
As an alternative to cutting grooves for the drawer bottom, slip mouldings are glued to the front and sides.

Dovetailed muntin
A muntin is some-times dovetailed into the drawer front.

FULL-WIDTH DRAWER

Drawer back
This is slightly narrower than the sides, to allow the bottom to be slid into place.

Drawer bottom
When cut from solid wood, the grain runs across the drawer so that shrinkage occurs from front to back. The bottom is pinned or screwed to the edge of the drawer back. Always check drawer bottoms for signs of woodworm infestation (see page 156).

Drawer front
The top edge is sometimes chipped, either because the contents became jammed between the drawer and the rail above, or because a locked drawer has been forced (see pages 153 and 155).

Muntin
The bottom panel of a wide drawer is made in two or more sections, joined by grooved muntins that run from front to back. They are tenoned into the groove in the drawer front and fixed to the back with screws.

141

Curing a sticking drawer

Badly worn runners and missing drawer guides will cause a drawer to jam, and the only way to cure this is to make the necessary repairs. On the other hand, a little maintenance may be all that is required to restore smooth running.

1 Waxing running surfaces

Remove the drawer and look for shiny patches where the drawer is rubbing. Before attempting further repairs, rub a white candle across these areas and also along the bottom edges of the drawer. Wax the drawer runners and guides at the same time.

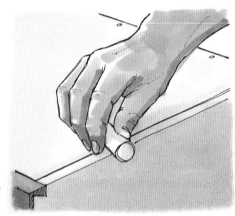

2 Skimming with a plane

If waxing does not cure the problem, skim the rubbed patches with a very finely set smoothing plane. Take care not to remove too much wood, or the drawer will be slack and may jam even more.

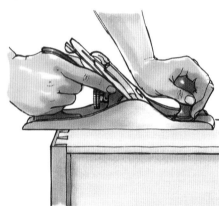

Remaking drawer sides

In most cases, the main reason why an old drawer sticks or runs poorly is that the bottom edges are badly worn. Weight concentrates friction toward the back of a drawer, the wear getting progressively worse towards the back corners. This is sometimes evident with the drawers closed, when the drawer fronts are seen to slope backwards.

1 Planing the edges

Plane a square edge, sloping towards the back corner on each side of the drawer.

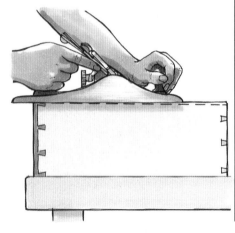

2 Rebuilding the edges

Glue a strip of wood on each planed edge, flush with the inner face of the drawer side. When the glue has set, plane each strip flush with the outside face.

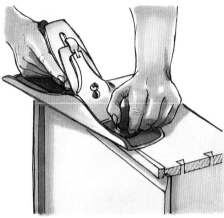

3 Marking the width

Set a marking gauge to the width of the drawer sides. Score a line along each strip, parallel to the top edge of the drawer side. Plane down to this line on both sides of the drawer.

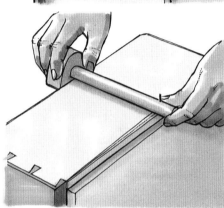

Refitting drawer bottoms

Since a drawer bottom is only fixed along its back edge, any appreciable shrinkage tends to pull it out of the groove or moulding along the drawer front. Being unsupported, the bottom then bows under the weight of the contents and gets trapped behind the drawer rail.

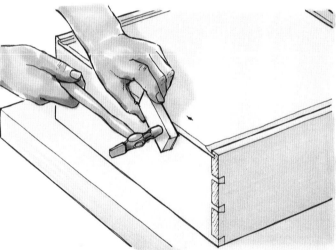

Repositioning the bottom panel

Remove the fixings holding the bottom panel to the drawer back. Drive the pins right through the panel with a nail punch if necessary. Tap the panel forward into the groove, using a softwood block and hammer, then refix to the drawer back.

Repairing a split panel

As it is such a slim panel, a drawer bottom will split readily if it is glued or pinned into any of the grooves. Provided the split edges are still clean, it should be possible to make an invisible repair by regluing the panel.

If the two parts of a split panel are warped, wet them and place a heavy weight on top until they are flat enough to be glued together.

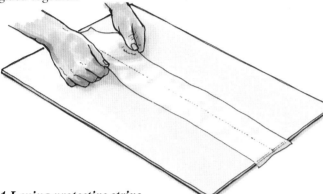

1 Laying protective strips
Glue and join the split edges, wipe off surplus glue, then cover the split on each side with a strip of polythene.

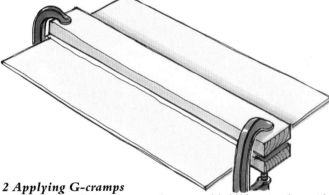

2 Applying G-cramps
Sandwich the split between stout battens and hold them in place with a pair of G-cramps, placing one at each end.

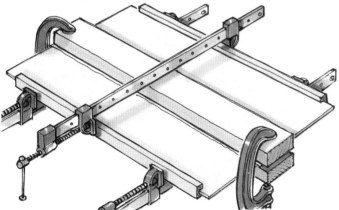

3 Closing the split
Before you fully tighten the G-cramps, slip grooved battens over the long edges of the panel and close up the split, using sash cramps. Make sure the bottom panel is not bowed, then leave the glue to set.

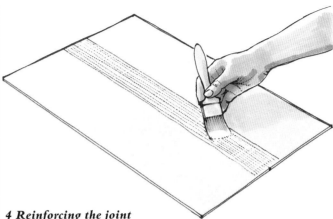

4 Reinforcing the joint
If you are unable to make a perfect joint, reinforce the repair with a strip of canvas glued to the underside of the drawer bottom.

Replacing drawer bottoms

If a drawer bottom is beyond repair, make a replacement from plywood or medium–density fibreboard (MDF).

1 Making the bottom panel
Choose a board that fits the grooves cut in the drawer – should it be necessary, plane a very shallow bevel along the edges on the underside of a slightly thicker board.

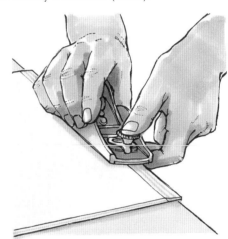

2 Fitting the bottom panel
Slide the panel into place, and then secure it to the drawer back with small counter-sunk screws.

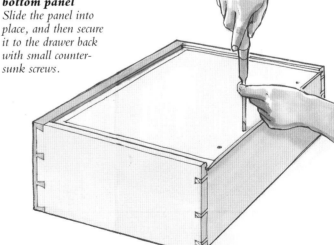

REPAIRING DOORS

The way cupboard doors were made mirrors the general methods of carcase construction. Frame-and-panel doors, for example, resemble a carcase end panel, with an outer frame infilled with a thin board cut from solid wood. Wide doors are often divided by muntins and sometimes horizontal rails, to prevent a large door panel shrinking.

Although flush doors have been made since the introduction of veneering, they are more often associated with twentieth-century furniture. Originally, the veneer was laid over solid-wood boards glued edge-to-edge, but the availability of stable man-made boards subsequently led to the greater use of flush doors.

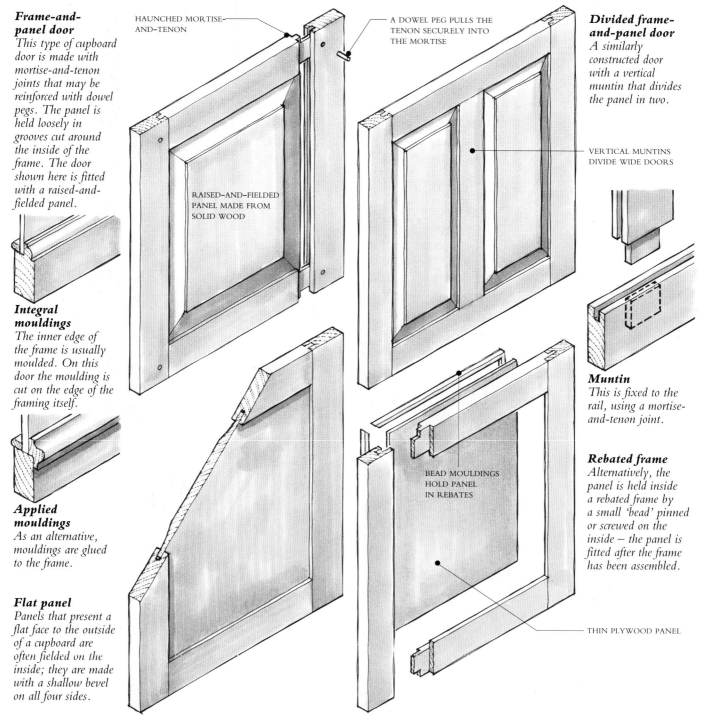

Frame-and-panel door
This type of cupboard door is made with mortise-and-tenon joints that may be reinforced with dowel pegs. The panel is held loosely in grooves cut around the inside of the frame. The door shown here is fitted with a raised-and-fielded panel.

HAUNCHED MORTISE-AND-TENON

A DOWEL PEG PULLS THE TENON SECURELY INTO THE MORTISE

Divided frame-and-panel door
A similarly constructed door with a vertical muntin that divides the panel in two.

RAISED-AND-FIELDED PANEL MADE FROM SOLID WOOD

VERTICAL MUNTINS DIVIDE WIDE DOORS

Integral mouldings
The inner edge of the frame is usually moulded. On this door the moulding is cut on the edge of the framing itself.

Muntin
This is fixed to the rail, using a mortise-and-tenon joint.

Applied mouldings
As an alternative, mouldings are glued to the frame.

BEAD MOULDINGS HOLD PANEL IN REBATES

Rebated frame
Alternatively, the panel is held inside a rebated frame by a small 'bead' pinned or screwed on the inside – the panel is fitted after the frame has been assembled.

Flat panel
Panels that present a flat face to the outside of a cupboard are often fielded on the inside; they are made with a shallow bevel on all four sides.

THIN PLYWOOD PANEL

144

Solid-wood flush door

Softwood boards, glued edge-to-edge, are veneered on both sides. The grain direction is reversed deliberately on alternate boards, to counter any tendency for the door to warp. However, solid-wood lippings, applied to hide the end grain, are often apparent beneath the veneer if the door shrinks across its width.

SOLID-WOOD LIPPING GLUED ACROSS TOP AND BOTTOM

BOARDS GLUED EDGE-TO-EDGE

THICK VENEER ON BOTH SIDES OF DOOR

Battened door

A simple flush door made from boards joined with tongue-and-groove joints. Cross-battens are screwed across the inside, to hold the boards together and keep the door flat.

TONGUE-AND-GROOVE BOARDS

CROSS-BATTENS SLOTTED FOR WOODSCREWS

Man-made board

Plywood and other man-made boards are ideal for making flush doors. The veneer around the edge of the door is vulnerable (see page 119).

NARROW LIPPINGS PROTECT EDGES OF MAN-MADE BOARD

PLYWOOD PANEL

VENEER COVERS PANEL AND LIPPINGS

Sticking doors

Cupboard doors stick for a variety of reasons. Perhaps the furniture has been stored in damp conditions so that the wood has swollen; in this case, drying it out naturally in a warm environment is all that is needed to cure the problem. It could also be that the furniture is not standing level, and the door is jammed in a twisted carcase. Try lifting one corner of the cabinet to see if it improves the situation – if this appears to work, slip a packing piece under the raised foot. More importantly, ensure the door is not hanging from a loose hinge.

Tightening loose screws

Lift the door by the closing or lock stile, and inspect the hinges for any sign of movement. You may find that hinge screws have worked loose and that tightening them with a screwdriver is enough to prevent the door sticking. However, if the screws have pulled out of the wood, you will have to plug the holes so that the screw threads grip.

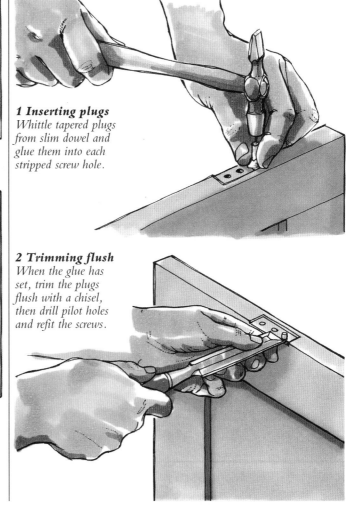

1 Inserting plugs
Whittle tapered plugs from slim dowel and glue them into each stripped screw hole.

2 Trimming flush
When the glue has set, trim the plugs flush with a chisel, then drill pilot holes and refit the screws.

Repairing split wood

On examining the carcase or door stile, you may discover that the wood has split along the line of the screw holes, making it impossible to tighten the screws.

Gluing the split

Take the door off its hinges and work glue into the split with the blade of a knife. Use a G-cramp to close the split, removing excess glue with a damp cloth. When the glue has set, remove the G-cramp and refit the hinge.

Patching a broken stile or side panel

When a piece of wood has broken away from the door edge or carcase side panel, insert a patch to provide a strong fixing point for the hinge.

1 Marking out

Mark out a dove-tailed housing for the patch, retaining as much of the original hinge recess as possible.

2 Rebuilding the corner

Rebuild the missing corner with a glued patch. When the glue has set, plane the patch flush on both sides and recut the hinge recess. Replace any mouldings (see pages 152-3).

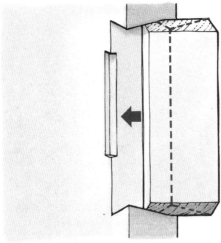

Correcting swollen doors

If there seems no obvious reason why the door is sticking, the best option is to skim it very lightly with a finely set plane.

1 Checking for binding

Look for signs of scuffing or shiny patches along the door edges and on the carcase, to find just where the door is 'binding'. If you are still not sure, slip a piece of notepaper between the door and carcase until you can feel where they touch.

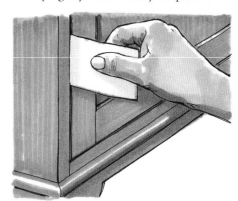

2 Skimming with a plane

Clamp the door in a bench vice and skim only those patches that show signs of abrasion. If the door is veneered on the edge, you will have to remove wood from the hinge stile. This is a relatively tricky operation that may involve refitting the hinge leaves.

Split door panels

It is important that a solid-wood panel is free to move. If it is inadvertently glued or pinned into place, the wood may split; and should the panel shrink, a butt joint may pull apart.

With a rebated frame, you can unscrew or prise off the beads and reglue the panel as described for a drawer bottom (see page 143). If the panel is held in grooves, you can insert a strip of veneer or a narrow batten into the split (see page 137). However, it may also be possible to pull the two halves of the panel together without having to dismantle the frame.

Closing a split with cramps

Before inserting glue, clamp G-cramps to both halves of the panel at the top and bottom of the door. Protect the wood with softwood blocks. Use sash cramps to pull the G-cramps toward each other, gradually closing the gap in the panel. If this works, glue the split and repeat the procedure.

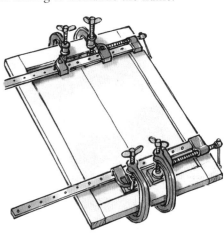

Doors that won't close

To keep forcing a door shut when it insists on springing open will eventually do harm, either ripping out screws or even splitting wood around the hinges. Check the hinges first to see whether one or more screws have worked loose – the protruding heads may be preventing the door closing properly. Alternatively, over-large screws may have been substituted and need replacing.

Replacing oversize screws

Replacing loose screws with slightly larger ones avoids having to plug the stripped holes in the wood. Unfortunately, the oversize screw heads no longer fit the countersunk holes in the leaf and prevent the hinge closing properly.

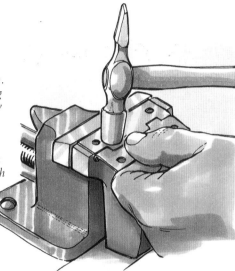

Flattening the hinge leaf
Remove the hinge and plug the screw holes with tapered plugs (see page 145). Continuously forcing the door to close may have bent the hinge leaf, in which case hammer it flat on a metal vice before you replace the hinge with the correct screws.

Refitting a deep-set hinge

Insert packing behind the hinge leaf until it lies flush with the surrounding wood.

Inserting packing
Cut a strip of card or veneer to fit the hinge recess and, using the hinge leaf as a template, punch holes through the packing for the screws. Fit the middle screw only to check that the door operates satisfactorily, then screw the leaf securely in its recess.

Somewhat more difficult to ascertain is whether the leaves of one or both hinges have been set too deeply into the wood. Check by closely scrutinizing the hinge knuckles as you close the door – if you can see either hinge flexing out of its recess, it should be packed out to allow it to close smoothly without putting strain on the screws, and thereby the surrounding wood.

Curing warped doors

No amount of tinkering with the hinges is going to encourage a warped door to stay closed and, to be realistic, there is not a great deal you can do to resolve the situation, except to rely on a lock or strong catch. You could try soaking the concave surface of a flush door, in the hope that it can be clamped flat, but the chances of long-term success are slim. It may be possible to correct a warped frame-and-panel door, but this is only worth attempting if the frame bows inward so that repairs can be made to the back of the door.

Before you begin, check that the work is feasible by looking along the stiles and rails to see how many are actually bowed, and by how much. If you discover that the distortion is confined to the one corner, for example, you may decide to tackle the job yourself; if it is worse than that, it might be wiser to pay an expert to do the work.

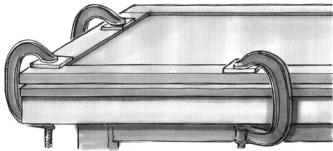

1 Clamping the work
Using G-cramps, clamp the door face-down on the corner of your workbench. Make sure the bench is absolutely flat by covering the top surface with a sheet of plywood or blockboard.

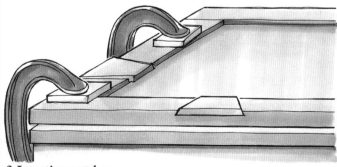

2 Inserting patches
Mark out a tapered and dovetailed recess across the stile (and possibly the adjoining rail), in order to relieve the stresses in the timber. Tap a glued patch of matching hardwood into each recess. Do not release the cramps until the glue has set, then plane the patches flush on all sides.

Glazed doors

Whatever their social status, past generations tended to accumulate all manner of glass and china ornaments, proudly displaying their collections in glazed cabinets. Display cabinets were made in huge quantities, from exquisitely made examples that have since become collectors' items in their own right, to cheap mass-produced furniture for the aspiring middle classes.

The nature of display cabinets, with their tracery of fine wooden glazing bars, makes them highly vulnerable. Even the slightest accident can result in one or more broken glass panes and, unless you are extremely lucky, at least minor damage to the delicate woodwork.

Similarly constructed glazed doors were fitted to bureau-cabinets and bookcases. However, since their prime function was to protect the contents from dust, large transparent panes were not essential, and the doors were often made with decorative leaded lights, using coloured and textured glass.

Door construction

The outer frame of a glazed door may be constructed from solid hardwood or, at the cheaper end of the market, from softwood faced with cross-banded veneers. The glazing bars invariably comprise two parts: a decorative moulding glued onto the edge of a flat strip.

In the majority of cases, the glazing bars describe simple geometric patterns. Where they cross, the flat strips are joined with halving joints; at other intersections glazing bars are butted together, using mitres. Particularly delicate joints are reinforced with glued linen. The ends of the flat wooden strips locate in small notches cut into the main door frame.

Glass panes are held in the rebates with fine pins and putty, or with delicate wooden beading. Curved glass may be used in better-quality bow-fronted cabinets, but most bowed doors are glazed with small flat panes.

GLAZED DOOR FROM A DISPLAY CABINET

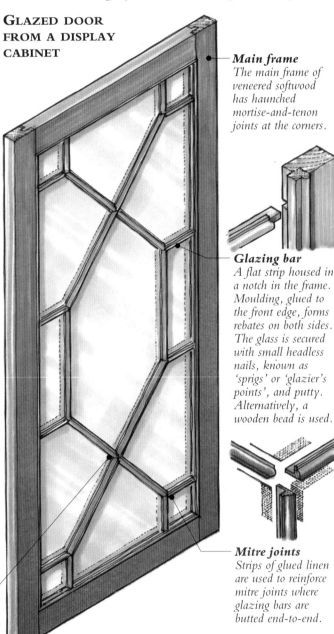

Halving joint
A halving joint is used where the flat strips cross.

Main frame
The main frame of veneered softwood has haunched mortise-and-tenon joints at the corners.

Glazing bar
A flat strip housed in a notch in the frame. Moulding, glued to the front edge, forms rebates on both sides. The glass is secured with small headless nails, known as 'sprigs' or 'glazier's points', and putty. Alternatively, a wooden bead is used.

Mitre joints
Strips of glued linen are used to reinforce mitre joints where glazing bars are butted end-to-end.

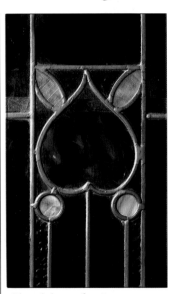

Glazed doors often incorporate decorative motifs

Lead cames
The relatively small panes of glass surrounded by H-section 'cames' of lead are known as leaded lights. The joints between cames are soldered.

Types of glass

Most display cabinets are glazed with 2mm (¹⁄₁₆in) transparent glass – the type used when framing pictures. A panel of leaded lights is often a combination of clear, coloured, and sometimes textured glass. You may have to obtain matching glass from specialist stained-glass suppliers listed in craft magazines.

Removing broken glass

Take the door off its hinges and lay it on a bench. Wearing strong gloves and goggles, remove any beads holding the broken glass in place, or gently rock the remaining shards back and forth to loosen old putty.

Clearing the rebates

Chop out the last remnants of glass and putty, using an old chisel. If the putty is so hard that there is a risk of damage to the flimsy glazing bars, first try using a heated soldering iron to soften it. Remove sprigs with pliers.

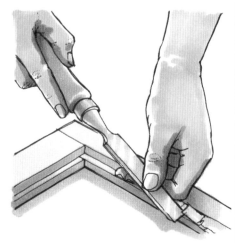

Solid-oak display cabinet from the 1930s

Cutting glass

Make a cardboard template that fits between the glazing bars, allowing a slight tolerance to ensure the glass will slip into place easily. It pays to have complicated shapes cut by a glazier, but you can cut simple straight-sided panes yourself.

1 Cleaning the glass

Lay a blanket over your bench and place the glass flat on top. Wipe the surface, using methylated spirit to remove any fingerprints and traces of grease.

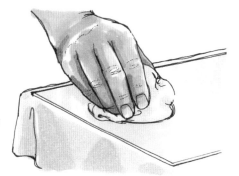

2 Scoring the glass

Using the template as a guide, place a wooden straightedge along the line of the cut. Holding a glass cutter between your index and middle fingers, dip the tip of the tool in light oil, then score the glass from edge to edge with one continuous stroke towards you.

3 Propagating the cut

Slide the glass until it overhangs the bench. Propagate the cut by tapping the cutter on the underside of the glass, directly beneath the scored line.

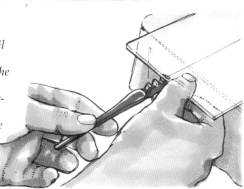

4 Snapping the glass

Placing a thumb on each side of the scored line, snap the glass in two with a twist of your wrists.

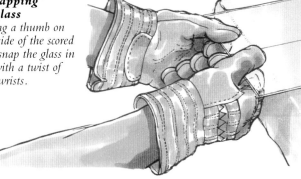

Inserting a new pane

Secure a new pane with beading, or prepare a ball of linseed-oil putty by kneading it to a soft, even consistency. You can adjust the colour of the putty by mixing in black grate polish or touches of artists' oil paint.

Fitting the glass

Lay the new pane in the rebates, then tap sprigs into the wood, using the side of your chisel. Press putty into the rebates to cover the sprigs, then shape it with a putty knife to form shallow bevels. Dip the blade in water from time to time, smooth the putty and form neat corners. Clean any smears from the glass with meths.

Repairing glazing bars

Whenever you have to replace broken glass, it pays to inspect the glazing bars for signs of damage. The woodwork may have been sufficiently resilient to absorb the blow to the glass, but by gently flexing the bars you may reveal splits that are not immediately apparent.

Gluing and reinforcing a split glazing bar

Open the split slightly by applying gentle pressure to the front of the glazing bar, and brush some glue into it. Clamp the split closed, using a small G-cramp, or bind the bar with adhesive tape. Reinforce the repair by gluing a small strip of linen on each side of the bar.

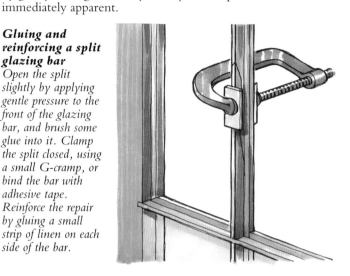

Repairing damaged leaded lights

A severely damaged leaded panel can be rebuilt completely, but recreating sections with new cames is beyond the capability of the inexperienced amateur restorer. Get a quote from professional stained-glass artists working in your area. However, provided the shapes are not too intricate, you may wish to replace one or two pieces of broken glass yourself.

Remove the fixing screws, or prise off the beads that hold the leaded panel in the door frame. Lift the panel carefully out of its rebates and, holding it vertically to avoid bending the lead, carry it to your workbench and lay it face-down. Wearing protective gloves and goggles, remove any remaining shards by picking them out of the cames with a penknife.

1 Cutting the corners

Using a sharp craft knife, slice the lead at each corner to open up the soldered joint.

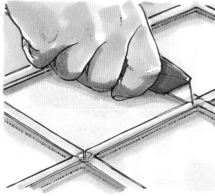

2 Opening the cames

Tape the jaws of a small pair of pliers, and use them to open the cames by bending back the flanges. Take care not to crease the lead, or it might prove impossible to flatten the flanges again.

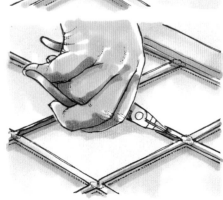

3 Inserting the new glass

Trap the new piece of glass in the cames by rubbing the flanges flat with a pointed strip of wood. It should be possible to make neat joints without having to resolder them.

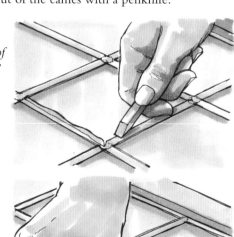

4 Adding putty

Colour a small ball of linseed-oil putty by mixing it with some black fire-grate polish. Use your thumbs to pack putty into the cames all round the new pane of glass, on both sides of the door. Remove excess putty with the strip of wood, then brush across the cames with a shoe brush to consolidate.

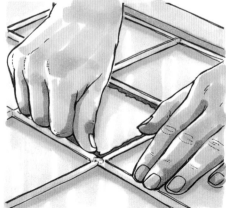

Types of glass

Most display cabinets are glazed with 2mm (1/16in) transparent glass – the type used when framing pictures. A panel of leaded lights is often a combination of clear, coloured, and sometimes textured glass. You may have to obtain matching glass from specialist stained-glass suppliers listed in craft magazines.

Removing broken glass

Take the door off its hinges and lay it on a bench. Wearing strong gloves and goggles, remove any beads holding the broken glass in place, or gently rock the remaining shards back and forth to loosen old putty.

Clearing the rebates

Chop out the last remnants of glass and putty, using an old chisel. If the putty is so hard that there is a risk of damage to the flimsy glazing bars, first try using a heated soldering iron to soften it. Remove sprigs with pliers.

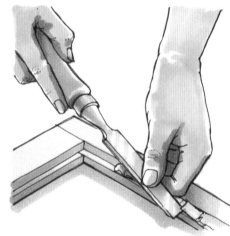

Solid-oak display cabinet from the 1930s

Cutting glass

Make a cardboard template that fits between the glazing bars, allowing a slight tolerance to ensure the glass will slip into place easily. It pays to have complicated shapes cut by a glazier, but you can cut simple straight-sided panes yourself.

1 Cleaning the glass

Lay a blanket over your bench and place the glass flat on top. Wipe the surface, using methylated spirit to remove any fingerprints and traces of grease.

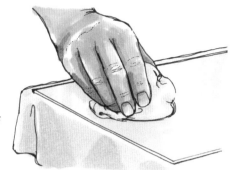

2 Scoring the glass

Using the template as a guide, place a wooden straightedge along the line of the cut. Holding a glass cutter between your index and middle fingers, dip the tip of the tool in light oil, then score the glass from edge to edge with one continuous stroke towards you.

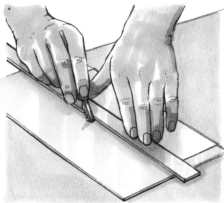

3 Propagating the cut

Slide the glass until it overhangs the bench. Propagate the cut by tapping the cutter on the underside of the glass, directly beneath the scored line.

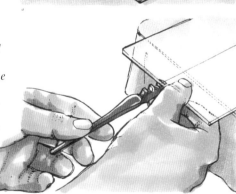

4 Snapping the glass

Placing a thumb on each side of the scored line, snap the glass in two with a twist of your wrists.

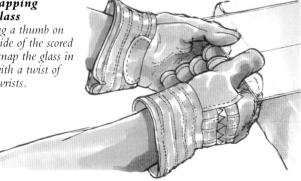

Inserting a new pane

Secure a new pane with beading, or prepare a ball of linseed-oil putty by kneading it to a soft, even consistency. You can adjust the colour of the putty by mixing in black grate polish or touches of artists' oil paint.

Fitting the glass

Lay the new pane in the rebates, then tap sprigs into the wood, using the side of your chisel. Press putty into the rebates to cover the sprigs, then shape it with a putty knife to form shallow bevels. Dip the blade in water from time to time, smooth the putty and form neat corners. Clean any smears from the glass with meths.

Repairing damaged leaded lights

A severely damaged leaded panel can be rebuilt completely, but recreating sections with new cames is beyond the capability of the inexperienced amateur restorer. Get a quote from professional stained-glass artists working in your area. However, provided the shapes are not too intricate, you may wish to replace one or two pieces of broken glass yourself.

1 Cutting the corners

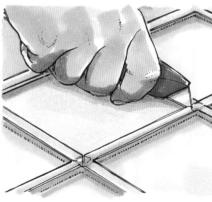

Using a sharp craft knife, slice the lead at each corner to open up the soldered joint.

2 Opening the cames

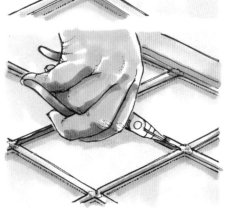

Tape the jaws of a small pair of pliers, and use them to open the cames by bending back the flanges. Take care not to crease the lead, or it might prove impossible to flatten the flanges again.

Repairing glazing bars

Whenever you have to replace broken glass, it pays to inspect the glazing bars for signs of damage. The woodwork may have been sufficiently resilient to absorb the blow to the glass, but by gently flexing the bars you may reveal splits that are not immediately apparent.

Gluing and reinforcing a split glazing bar

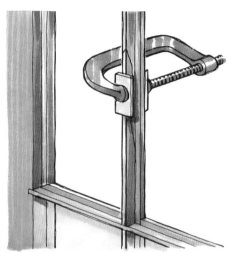

Open the split slightly by applying gentle pressure to the front of the glazing bar, and brush some glue into it. Clamp the split closed, using a small G-cramp, or bind the bar with adhesive tape. Reinforce the repair by gluing a small strip of linen on each side of the bar.

Remove the fixing screws, or prise off the beads that hold the leaded panel in the door frame. Lift the panel carefully out of its rebates and, holding it vertically to avoid bending the lead, carry it to your workbench and lay it face-down. Wearing protective gloves and goggles, remove any remaining shards by picking them out of the cames with a penknife.

3 Inserting the new glass

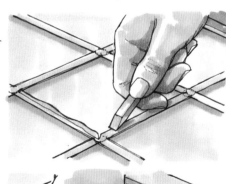

Trap the new piece of glass in the cames by rubbing the flanges flat with a pointed strip of wood. It should be possible to make neat joints without having to resolder them.

4 Adding putty

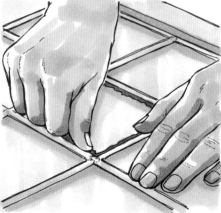

Colour a small ball of linseed-oil putty by mixing it with some black fire-grate polish. Use your thumbs to pack putty into the cames all round the new pane of glass, on both sides of the door. Remove excess putty with the strip of wood, then brush across the cames with a shoe brush to consolidate.

REPAIRING AND RESTORING MOULDINGS

Mouldings are one of the main features that distinguish old furniture from modern mass-produced products. It would appear that to leave an edge or corner unworked was unacceptable to cabinetmakers of the past; they were accustomed to applying some form of decoration to improve visual proportions, not only to the better-quality pieces, but also to furniture that must have been considered at the time to be run-of-the-mill merchandise. However, there were also more practical reasons.

Mouldings were frequently used to disguise the effects of movement on the appearance of doors, drawers and panels. Linear mouldings, for example, could be used to cover any gaps that might result from shrinkage, or at least serve to draw one's attention away from them. The practice was so widespread that, except for when working on the very simplest and plainest of country furniture, sooner or later you will find it necessary to restore broken or missing mouldings.

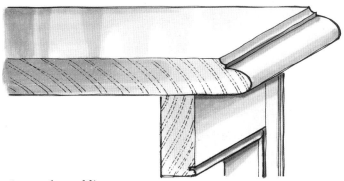

Antique moulding planes and a home-made scratch stock

Types of moulding

Although tradition would have suggested where mouldings should be used and approximately what form they should take, each furniture maker would decide just how to apply a particular moulding. Depending on the scale and location, mouldings were either made as an integral part of a component, or were made separately and applied later.

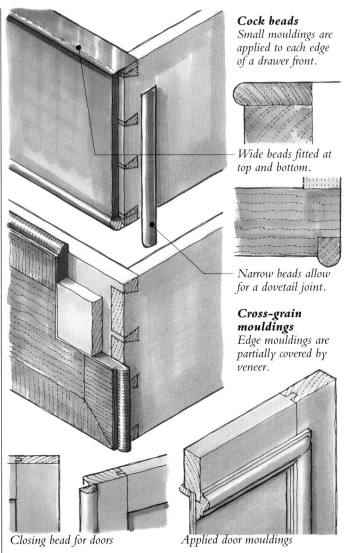

Cock beads
Small mouldings are applied to each edge of a drawer front.

— Wide beads fitted at top and bottom.

— Narrow beads allow for a dovetail joint.

Cross-grain mouldings
Edge mouldings are partially covered by veneer.

Closing bead for doors   *Applied door mouldings*

Integral mouldings
Moulding planes were once essential tools in every workshop. Some were reserved for creating specific mouldings only, for example along the edge of a serving top. Others, such as 'rounds' and 'hollows', were used in combination to create practically any simple moulding.

Very small mouldings were often formed by scraping along the edge of a component, using a scratch stock, a crude home-made tool incorporating a piece of steel filed to the required shape. As well as being versatile and extremely cheap to make, a scratch stock could be used on curved workpieces as easily as straight ones. Consequently, simple scratch mouldings were applied to all manner of components, from curved chair legs and back rests to drawer fronts and doors.

Applied mouldings
The technique of applying at least partly prefabricated mouldings offered certain advantages to the cabinetmaker. As with veneers, applied mouldings made economical use of expensive hardwoods, and since mouldings are made from separate pieces of wood there was no restriction on grain direction, thus opening the way for attractive cross-grain mouldings.

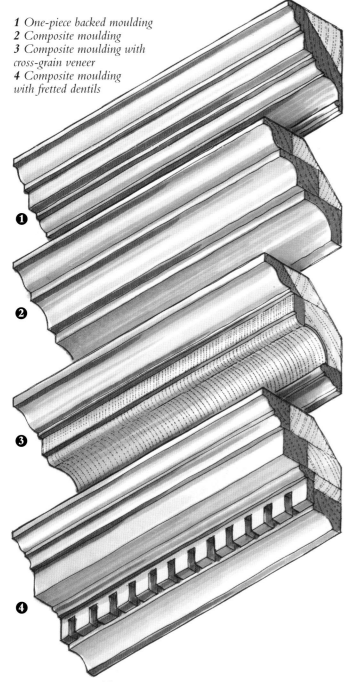

1 *One-piece backed moulding*
2 *Composite moulding*
3 *Composite moulding with cross-grain veneer*
4 *Composite moulding with fretted dentils*

Composite mouldings

Some mouldings – cornice mouldings, for example – were often too large and intricate to be made in one piece; it is easy to appreciate the physical effort required to plane wide mouldings in one operation. It is theoretically possible to make such a moulding from a single piece of wood, working it section by section with different moulding planes. However, it is easier to construct intricate mouldings from a number of different, separately moulded pieces of wood. The common practice was to glue hardwood sections onto a softwood base which was often partly veneered, especially when cross-banding was required. With a composite moulding, it was also possible to incorporate fretwork as additional decoration.

Replacing small integral mouldings

Most modern cabinetmakers employ power routers when cutting new mouldings, but it is not always possible to match a standard cutter to an already existing profile. However, provided the shape is not unduly complex, you can use a home-made scratch stock to reproduce any small moulding on a replacement rail, for example, or to integrate a patch in a moulded edge.

1 Making a scratch stock

Make the cutter from an old hacksaw blade, shaping it roughly on a grindstone, then filing the reverse shape of the actual moulding on the cutting edge. Clamp the finished cutter between two shaped pieces of plywood screwed together to form the stock.

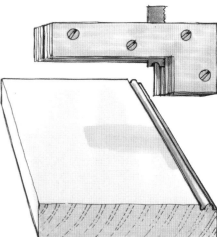

2 Shaping the work first

Before you use the scratch stock, remove as much waste as possible from the workpiece with a plane or chisel.

3 Using the scratch stock

With the fence held firmly against the work, lean the scratch stock away from you at a slight angle and push the tool in the same direction. Gradually scrape away the wood until the stock comes to rest against the work, preventing the cutter from biting any deeper into the work.

Reproducing applied mouldings

The cock beads applied to drawer fronts are typical of the sort of applied mouldings you might need to repair or reproduce from time to time. The moulding along the top edge, for example, can become crushed or broken if the drawer is slammed shut while some of the contents are hanging out. The short length of cock bead applied to each side can also become detached and lost.

If possible, repair a broken moulding with a glued patch that can be shaped in place. However, if you need to reproduce a new length of moulding, don't attempt to work a very slim section of wood. It is far easier to cut the moulding on the edge of a larger piece of timber and saw it off when the shaping is finished.

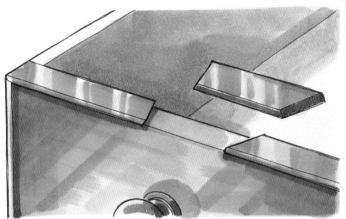

Patching a broken cock bead
Cut out the damaged section of moulding to leave a dovetailed notch which is wider towards the inside of the drawer. Glue and insert a slightly oversize tapered patch, clamping it in the notch until the adhesive has set. Finally, plane the patch flush and shape the moulding with a scratch stock and sandpaper.

Replacing a detached moulding
When a drawer front shrinks across its width, the mitred cock beads at the top and bottom tend to bow the very slim side mouldings. Remove the side mouldings and trim them at each end until they fit snugly again, then reglue and tape them in place until the adhesive sets. If a moulding is missing, reproduce a new length as described above.

Making cross-grain mouldings
To replace missing cross-grain cock beads, first glue a very slim band of cross-grain show wood to a strip of hardwood, with the grain running lengthways. Having worked the shape with a bead plane, or possibly a scratch stock, saw the finished moulding off the edge of the strip.

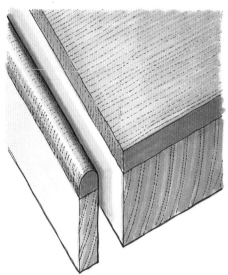

Carved mouldings

Even when a great deal of furniture was made by hand, wood-carving was still considered to be a specialist trade. When carved work was required, it was usual for a cabinetmaker to prepare the work and to then hand it over to a woodcarver for completion. Considering the intricacies of woodcarving and the number of specialized tools required, it makes sense to follow the same procedures when reproducing missing or damaged carving on a piece of furniture.

Make sure the piece of wood you use is large enough to encompass the size of the carved motif you require. However, that does not necessarily mean that the whole component has to be cut from a single piece of wood. Very often a separate piece of wood, perhaps already carved roughly to shape, is glued onto the body of the work, then finally shaped with chisels and gouges.

Repairing damaged carving
It is not too difficult to recreate a small piece of carving that has broken off. Plane the damaged section flat and rub-joint a glued piece of wood onto it by applying glue to both surfaces and then rubbing them together to squeeze glue and air out of the joint as you align the pieces. When the glue has set firmly, shape the patch to blend in with the surrounding work. A beginner might find it easier to shape the wood with a file before resorting to chisels and gouges.

CABINET HARDWARE

To an experienced eye, the wrong handles can ruin the appearance of a cabinet and may even reduce its value. Specialists can date a set of handles precisely, but you don't need expert knowledge to detect holes where handles of another style were once fitted. There is every chance that these holes will have been plugged and even covered with veneer, but only a perfectionist will have bothered to disguise traces of the work on the inside of a drawer. Alternatively, you may be able to discern slight indentations in the old finish, indicating the previous position of a shaped back plate.

Having identified clues to the type and position of the original handles, you still have to decide whether authentic restoration is advisable. It is debatable whether there is any point in fitting new turned knobs, for example, if it results in unsightly patches on each drawer front: it may be preferable to live with the present set of handles, even though they may not be entirely authentic. On the other hand, you might be able to cover a plugged hole with the back plate of a metal cabinet handle. In the end, only you, as the owner and restorer, can make the final decisions.

Tightening loose handles
Secure loose metal handles before their fixing bolts begin to enlarge the holes through the drawer front or door. Tighten the nuts on the inside of the cabinet, and consider fitting washers if the nuts appear to be crushing the wood.

1 Gluing a loose knob
A turned wooden knob is normally made with an integral screw that is inserted in a coarse-threaded hole in the drawer front. If the thread has worn, try gluing the knob in place, perhaps winding thin twine around the already glued screw, to increase its girth.

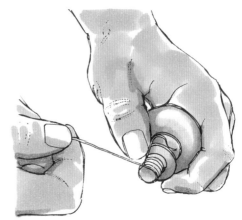

2 Inserting a glued wedge
Alternatively, saw a slot in the screw and then, with the knob held firmly against the drawer front, spread the screw in its hole by tapping a glued wedge into the slot. Plane the wedge flush once the glue has set.

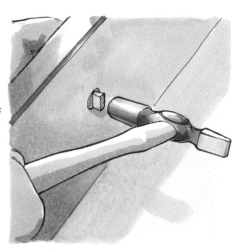

1 Swan-neck cabinet handle
2 Yellow-glass cupboard knob
3 Teardrop handle and escutcheon
4 Drop handle on fretted back plate
5 Pressed-metal plate handle
6 Cast-iron drawer pull
7 Ring pull
8 Drop handle on solid back plate
9 Flush handle
10 Ring pull and pressed escutcheon
11 Cabinet lock with drive-in brass escutcheons
12 Turn button

Replacing missing handles
Even though there is a large range of excellent reproductions, you are unlikely to find a perfect match for a single metal handle. It is probably best to replace the whole set. However, it is fairly easy to copy a wooden knob on a lathe.

Cabinet locks

A number of drawers and cupboard doors are secured with small brass cabinet locks. Because turning the key is often the only way to open a door, cupboard locks are usually intact and in good working order. Drawer locks, however, are invariably missing entirely, or the keys have been lost long ago. This rarely constitutes a problem unless the drawer happens to be locked.

Opening a locked drawer
Before resorting to drastic measures, make sure that it is not merely the contents of a drawer that is preventing it from being opened. Insert a plastic ruler or the blade of a table knife above the drawer front, using it to hold down any object that is jammed behind the drawer rail.

If the drawer appears to be empty, try removing the drawer above to gain access to the screws that hold the lock in place. Remove the back of the cabinet if you need to slide a dustboard out of the way.

If the top drawer is locked, take off the back panel and attempt to remove the drawer bottom (see page 141).

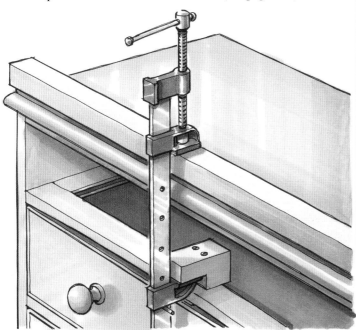

Bending the drawer rail
It may be possible to release the lock bolt by bending a long drawer rail. Screw an L-shape block to the rail above the locked drawer and, using a sash cramp hooked over the top of the cabinet, slowly pull the rail upward. Take great care not to put too much strain on the rail, or you may split the wood or break the joints at each end.

Hiring a locksmith
As a last resort, some restorers cut a notch out of the front of the drawer rail to free the lock, and then patch it afterwards. But rather than spoil a nice piece of furniture, it would pay to hire a locksmith to pick the lock and to supply you with a replacement key.

Repairing a broken drawer rail
It is not unusual to find a splintered drawer rail, as a result of someone having levered a locked drawer. Remove all the splintered wood by cutting a tapered notch in the underside of the drawer rail, as described for patching a broken cock bead (see page 153), then glue a piece of matching hardwood into the rail.

1 Marking a mortise
If you intend to reinstate the lock, mark the position of the mortise for the lock bolt. Either transfer the measurements from the lock, or paint nail varnish onto the tip of the bolt and then operate the lock, to press the bolt against the drawer rail.

2 Cutting the mortise
Clean the lock with acetone before the nail varnish sets, then use a cranked chisel to cut a shallow mortise in the underside of the rail, using the imprint left by the varnish as a guide to its position.

Replacing a missing escutcheon
Brass escutcheons were used to line keyholes in drawer fronts and doors. Authentically shaped drive-in escutcheons are made in a variety of sizes to replace any that have been misplaced. This type of escutcheon is designed with a slight taper to make a tight fit in the keyhole.

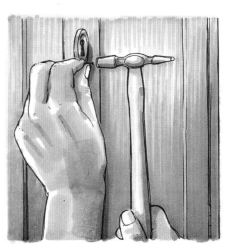

Fitting a face-mounted escutcheon
Crudely cut keyholes were often masked with small decorative escutcheon plates. You can buy period-style reproductions for pinning to the drawer front or door stile.

ERADICATING WOODWORM

To many people, an outbreak of woodworm spells disaster and suggests to them that the infested furniture is fit for nothing but the bonfire. This is far from the truth, provided that the infestation is discovered at a relatively early stage and is dealt with quickly. The aim of treatment is to get rid of the present incumbents and to discourage future attack.

Flight holes signify attack

Telltale signs

The common furniture beetle, better known as woodworm, lays its eggs on unfinished timber, especially in cracks, open joints and other crevices where they can remain undisturbed until the larvae hatch. The burrowing larvae do the damage, as they create a network of inter-connecting tunnels inside the wood. Eventually, the adult beetles emerge, leaving the flight holes that we recognize as woodworm damage.

Where to look

If you detect holes in the polished surfaces of a chest or cabinet, you can be sure there is more activity elsewhere. Take out the drawers and examine the sides and especially the bottom. Use a strong torch to check the inside of any cabinet and, if possible, move it away from the wall so that you can scrutinize the back panel – for some reason, woodworm larvae are partial to the glue

used in the manufacturing process for plywood.

Check out other items of furniture in a similar way. Turn tables over so that you can examine the unpolished surfaces of tops and rails, and look for signs of woodworm at the base of table legs. Don't be surprised to discover when you strip off old upholstery, that a chair frame is riddled with woodworm.

Can it be saved?

A few flight holes do not necessarily signal the demise of your furniture. As long as the wood is structurally sound you still have time to deal with the problem – in any case, the woodworm may no longer be active.

The insides of fresh flight holes are always clean and pale in colour – old ones have usually darkened. More importantly, look for deposits of very fine wood dust in the vicinity. This is frass, left by the furniture beetle chewing its way out of the wood, and any evidence of it is a sure sign of recent activity.

Testing for serious infestation

The extent of the damage can only be ascertained by probing the areas of obvious infestation. Take a penknife and press the tip of the blade into the wood. Badly wormed wood will offer very little resistance to the blade, and may even crumble under the pressure. Weakened wooden components must be replaced, but timber that is basically sound can be treated with chemicals.

Treating woodworm

Unless the present owner of the furniture can guarantee that it has been treated for woodworm in the recent past, take precautionary measures before even bringing it into the house.

Chemicals for exterminating woodworm are available from any DIY outlet. You can buy the fluid in cans fitted with pointed nozzles for injecting the chemical into the flight holes, and there are aerosol cans designed for the same purpose.

1 Injecting the flight holes
Fit the pointed nozzle onto the can and squirt fluid into a flight hole about every 50mm (2in). Wear goggles to protect your eyes against fluid emerging under pressure from an adjacent hole. Wipe excess fluid from polished surfaces.

2 Brushing onto bare wood
Pour some fluid into a shallow dish and brush it liberally onto all unfinished surfaces. Leave the work to dry out overnight, then treat it again with fluid.

3 Filling flight holes
Use an appropriately coloured wax stick to fill flight holes in a polished surface (see page 22).

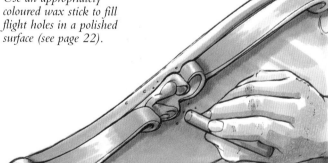

Preventative measures

When repairing furniture, take the opportunity to protect vulnerable timber from woodworm attack by painting it with eradicating fluid. Once the fluid is dry, you can apply any finish to treated timber. Insecticidal furniture polish, available from specialist suppliers, helps maintain permanent protection of finished surfaces.

INDEX